VICTORIAN BEST-SELLER

CHARLOTTE M. YONGE AT TWENTY
George Richmond, R.A.
By courtesy of the National Portrait Gallery

Victorian Best-seller

The World of Charlotte M. Yonge

by
Margaret Mare
and
Alicia C. Percival

KENNIKAT PRESS
Port Washington, N. Y./London

VICTORIAN BEST-SELLER

First published in 1947
Reissued in 1970 by Kennikat Press
Library of Congress Catalog Card No: 70-103202
SBN 8046-0839-3

Manufactured by Taylor Publishing Company   Dallas, Texas

PREFACE

In his penetrating analysis of the people of this island, *The English Way*, Pierre Maillaud gives it as his opinion that the faculty of making much of little things and the tendency to seek for some form of escapism in this mechanized world are more marked in England than elsewhere. In them, however, he sees not weakness, but strength, and those of us who have recourse to the world of Charlotte M. Yonge would surely agree with him.

Escapist literature is enervating when it leads one into wishful thinking about problems which must be faced. On the other hand, certain ageless books, marked by an understanding of the constant elements in human nature but concerned with problems no longer urgent, can be as healthy as dreamless sleep after a day of heavy toil. It is perhaps indicative of the effect of Charlotte Yonge's work that one of the authors of this book was enabled by typing a large part of it to withdraw her attention from the bombs raining down on London during the Battle of Britain.

Miss Yonge set out to be a didactic writer, with the motto *Pro Ecclesia Dei*—which to her meant the Anglican Church of Pusey, Keble, and (in his earlier days) of Newman. Fortunately, her characters usually got beyond their creator's conscious control, and, impelled by some inner necessity, developed as they would. So little, in the best of her books, does Miss Yonge obtrude religious dogma that the casual reader hardly realizes with any precision what views her people do hold. On comparing notes about our own first acquaintance with such tales as *Countess Kate*, *The Daisy Chain*, and *The Pillars of the House* we discovered that each of us had imagined the type of piety practised therein to be similar to that of her own upbringing. One of us, indeed, had spent the larger part of her schooldays in an Anglican convent school, where she devoured one tale after another, often in the original serial form from bound volumes of *The Monthly Packet*, appropriately housed beside a genuine Victorian backboard. The other, however, was brought up among persons of Broad, rather than High Anglican, churchmanship, and read Miss Yonge's stories at home, but was no less fond of them.

We wish to express our thanks to all the members of the Yonge family who generously put original manuscripts and photographs at our disposal; to the many kind friends who passed on to us memories and traditions of Miss Yonge; to the Reverend Mother of the Society of the Holy and Undivided Trinity, who gave access to works so hard to procure as *Last Heartsease Leaves*; to Miss E. M. Carus-Wilson, who gave us an expert opinion on the value of Miss Yonge's historical writings; and to Miss D. M. Stuart, whose help and encouragement were invaluable. We are also indebted to Messrs Macmillan and Co., Ltd., for permission to make use of copyright material.

M. M.
A. C. P.

CONTENTS

BOOK ONE
CHARLOTTE'S CHILDHOOD

BOOK TWO
THE VICTORIAN SOCIAL SCENE

BOOK THREE
FAMILY CHRONICLER

BOOK FOUR
VICTORIAN FAMILY LIFE

BOOK FIVE
"SMALL BEER"

BOOK SIX
VICTORIAN RETROSPECT

BOOK SEVEN
MISS YONGE: HER WORKS AND VIEWS

ILLUSTRATIONS

BOOK ONE
CHARLOTTE'S CHILDHOOD

CHAPTER I

THE YELLOW CHARIOT ARRIVES

ON a late autumn day in the year 1822 a yellow chariot passed through the long, straggling village of Otterbourne, which lies some four miles out of Winchester on the Portsmouth road. It contained Mr William Crawley Yonge, late of the 52nd Regiment, and his bride, Fanny. They were bound for the house of her mother, Mrs Bargus, which was henceforth to be their home. In appearance the bridal pair presented a great contrast—he a handsome-featured man of nearly six foot, with an upright, military bearing and dark, keen eyes, and she, a delicate little blue-eyed creature with soft brown hair, aquiline nose, pretty mouth, and tiny hands and feet. If we can trust the picture taken from traditions of those early days and reproduced by their daughter, Charlotte Mary Yonge, some seventy years later in *The Carbonels*, we may imagine Mr Yonge as "a gentleman in blue coat and nankeen trowsers," and Mrs Yonge in "a white tambour-worked gown" with narrow skirts—narrow, that is, when compared with those of the end of the century—full sleeves, silk mantle, poke bonnet, her hair in great shining rolls under the bonnet cap, and her neat little feet, in crossed sandalled shoes and white stockings, showing beneath her gown. The chariot stopped in front of the solid late Georgian house in which, a year later, Charlotte Mary was to be born.

Miss Yonge can very truly be considered a Victorian author, for her life corresponds in time almost exactly to that of Queen Victoria herself. She was fourteen years of age when, in 1837, the young queen came to the throne, and she died in March 1901, two months after her. In her work one can trace several of the most significant trends of Victorian life. To the end of her days she was writing without, in the eyes of her own public, growing stale. Her first biographer, Christabel Coleridge, wrote of her stories of village life:

> Some of them are village idylls of a perfect kind. The types most true and vivid and the whole range of village life—from the old unlettered peasant in his smock frock to his smart and intelligent young grandson in fashionable tweeds . . . trace the development of the Victorian age, let us note, without the smallest grudge towards it or that melancholy harking back to the smock frock with which we are too familiar.

This applies to other ranges of society and other traditions; her attitude towards girls' education, for example, altered similarly. Miss Yonge was deeply rooted in her period, yet—a rare gift— she could watch things move without too great regret.

Her own life was uneventful; it does not call for study except in so far as our knowledge of her surroundings helps us to check the remarkable fidelity to them in much that she wrote. Yet, because all that is freshest and most vivid in her books springs from her own experience and reflects her own age, the life and antecedents of this Victorian family chronicler are worth a glance. As with a greater predecessor, it may be that the very limitations of her experience forced her to find in the material at hand the lights and shadows, the delicately contrasting shades of colour, that enrich her books; it is only when she goes outside her own sphere that she overpaints. Broadly speaking, it may be said that in the way of adventure *things* did not happen to Miss Yonge, but *people* happened, and it is people, together with those details which build up the characters of people, that she excels in portraying.

Except for periods of time passed at the houses of relations and friends, for occasional visits to London and the Universities, and for one brief stay abroad, the whole of Charlotte Yonge's life was passed in the village to which the yellow chariot brought her parents at the opening of their married life. On their arrival poor William's heart must have sunk. During his honeymoon journey he had been the supreme authority to his little wife, but now he was to live as the guest of a rival power, his bustling, managing mother-in-law. Remarkable indeed must have been the love for his Fanny which induced the promising young officer of twenty-seven, with all the glories of service in the Peninsula and at Waterloo behind him, to give up every hope of further honours, and settle down into a humdrum existence for her sake. The very fact, too, that his retirement into civilian life was to be in Hampshire rather than in his native Devon was a further hardship.

The Yonge family had taken root in Devon as far back as the time of James I, when its founder had migrated there from Norfolk. His grandson, James Yonge, consolidated the position of the family by acquiring through marriage the estate of Puslinch, on the Yealm. James, like his father and grandfather, was a physician of some note. He was also a man of parts, for he edited the works of Charles I, with the earliest defence of the royal authorship of the *Eikon Basilike* (a fact which his descendant Charlotte noted with sympathetic pride), and while practising at Plymouth he discovered some improvement in trephining. This gentleman provides one of the few vivid patches in the otherwise sober history of the Yonge family. He embalmed the King of Portugal and Sir Cloudesley Shovel; he was taken prisoner by the Moors and became a galley slave. When he finally settled down as a country squire, he bought the living of Newton Ferrers for his eldest son, and for the next hundred and fifty years squarsons reigned over Puslinch, while the family practice in Plymouth became the heritage of some younger son.

Charlotte Yonge's grandfather bore his mother's family name of Duke, and was Vicar of Cornwood. Duke Yonge had settled at Cornwood so as to be near his elder brother, James, the Vicar of Newton Ferrers and Squire of Puslinch. These two brothers had, in their Oxford days, entered into a friendship with Thomas Bargus, son of a naval officer, and his visit to Puslinch was commemorated by the acquisition of triple copies of a set of watercolours portraying the lovely scenery of the Yealm estuary. This friendship was to become a close connexion by numerous marriages among the children of all three.

Duke Yonge himself married Catharina Crawley, a lady of a good Gloucestershire family, who was an excellent mother and mistress of the house, though her children stood in wholesome awe of her, and never thought of addressing her otherwise than as 'Ma'am' to the end of her long life. Her portrait shows her as a handsome, stately lady with bright cheeks, dark eyes, and arched eyebrows, and dressed in a most becoming gold-sprigged muslin gown and turban. Her husband was certainly no typical eighteenth-century parson. Despite the slackness of the times, he was a keen clergyman, without being given to any "Methodistic excesses," and he filled Cornwood Church by his excellent preaching—so much so, indeed, that he was forced to put up two galleries. As well as being an active magistrate he was the first to provide a manual of prayers to be used in prisons. He was also true to the family medical tradition, and doctored the whole village gratis; and their verdict on him was, "Old Mr Yonge up to Cornwood, he was a real gentleman, and cared no more for the rich than the poor." Clergy such as Duke Yonge kept well tended their patch of the Anglican vineyard, ready for the fresh grafts of the Oxford Movement.

William Yonge, Charlotte's father, born in 1795, was the seventh of the nine children of Duke and Catharina. The family grew up at Cornwood, which Charlotte later described as

> a very beautiful place on the borders of Dartmoor. The Vicarage stood on the side of a steep hill with a precipitous bank covered with brushwood and ferns descending to the Yealm. Higher up the stream is a lovely ravine, full of wood and rock, the river dashing through, and beyond lies the wild moor. It was a place of out-of-door freedom, and of power of sport most delightful, and bound the hearts of the lads who grew up there with the charm of mountaineers.[1]

Together with the nine Cornwood children grew up the six children of James Yonge of Puslinch, for they had lost their father early, and had been left to their uncle's guardianship. Those were adventurous times, and the children were near enough to Plymouth for "Boney" to be a lurking fear. They knew that Mr Yonge had in readiness a store of guineas in case the invasion really did take place and the women and children had to be sent into the heart of the moors.

All the cousinhood began their education at the school kept at Ottery St Mary by Mr George Coleridge, a connexion of the Yonge family and of the poet. (The two branches of cousins were known at school as the "Puss" Yonges—that is, of Puslinch—and the "Cat" Yonges, or children of Catharina.) Here

[1] Christabel Coleridge, *Charlotte Mary Yonge*, pp. 12–13 (Macmillan, 1903).

they suffered the rigours of a most ferocious discipline, but it apparently did no harm to William Yonge and his brother James, for they took such good places when they got to Eton that they had little need to exert themselves. At sixteen William left Eton, and after studying mathematics and military drawing with an engineer he was gazetted to the 52nd Regiment, at that time commanded by Colonel Colborne, a stepson of Mr Bargus and a man of heroic mould, bound to inspire a young subaltern with enthusiasm. The newly arrived officer found his regiment in the thick of the siege of San Sebastian, where he showed a youthful disregard of danger by crossing a bridge under fire without bending his head below the parapet, until the older officers showed him how misplaced was this intrepidity. By the time Lieutenant Yonge had progressed by way of Nive, Nivelles, Orthes, and Toulouse to Waterloo he had learnt the wisdom of the old campaigner, for we hear of him after the battle hunting for something to replace the officers' stolen luggage, and triumphantly producing a saddle-bag containing two women's coarse shifts. This was all the change of linen they had on the march to Paris, though they did their best to smarten their appearance by all getting into a pond and passing on the single razor among them.

The occupation of Paris was a momentous time for William, who spent many a long hour studying Napoleon's ill-gotten collections in the Louvre, and was commissioned to buy prints for his family at home. In this he showed great discrimination and some independent judgment, for among his purchases was an excellent copy of Dürer's *The Knight, Death, and the Devil*, which could hardly have been much in fashion in 1815. This engraving was to make a deep impression in later years on his daughter.

In the meantime the ties between the Bargus and the Yonge families had been growing closer year by year. We left Mr Bargus as a young man just down from Oxford visiting his friends in their Devonshire home. On his ordination the Reverend Thomas Bargus became tutor to Lord Warwick's sons, and in 1788 he married Mrs Colborne, a beautiful widow of Irish family, with whom he also acquired two stepchildren, Cordelia (Delia) and John Colborne, later Lord Seaton. His first wife having died in 1791, leaving her husband with little Alethea Henrietta, then two years old, Mr Bargus married again the next year, his second wife being Miss Mary Kingsman, the daughter of the Rector of

Botley, in Hampshire. In January 1795 they had a daughter, Frances Mary, the future wife of William Yonge, who was born in this same year.

In 1799 Mr Bargus moved with his composite family to Barkway, a few miles out of Cambridge, where Lord Selsey had presented him to the living. He seems, like his friend Duke Yonge, to have taken his duties as parish priest seriously, and he kept up such pious habits as giving a Bible to every child that could say its Catechism. He was, moreover, typical of his century in being scientifically minded, for he was much interested in botany and in making experiments in electricity. His epitaph, which he himself chose from *The Spectator*, certainly smacks of his period: "What he was will be known at the last day."

The Bargus household was further complicated by the addition of Maria Kingsman, a niece of Mrs Bargus, and of "Aunt Betsey," half-sister of Mr Bargus and a thorough Mrs Malaprop. Even some forty years after the Barkway days her nieces delighted their children by recalling such sayings as, "I believe he took me for a Statute of Venus," a threat to a dog to "whip his little posterity," and a statement that she had been "to explode the country." Little Fanny was not entirely happy among all the conflicting elements of her environment. Her mother had married late, and was a lively, bustling lady, ready to pet and care for her delicate little daughter, but not the right kind of person to understand the nervous, sensitive temperament of the child. Perhaps her father was more sympathetic, for we hear of her trotting by his side to Newsells, Lord Selsey's house, to take the newspaper telling of Trafalgar. The library at Newsells was a place of enchantment to Fanny, and Lord Selsey gave the run of his books to this exemplary child who, as he said, could be trusted "never to eat bread and butter over them."

At this time the connexion between the Yonge and Bargus families was kept up by frequent visits to Barkway of the younger Duke and Charles, two of the Cornwood Yonges, who had now come up to Cambridge. It was Delia Colborne, Fanny's grown-up stepsister, who started the family habit of falling in love with Yonges, though it was not until 1806 that Duke, lately presented to the living of Antony, in Cornwall, was able to marry her. Fanny, meanwhile, had been sent to a fashionable school in Bedford Square, where she was to be made into an accomplished young lady. This educational establishment appears to have been on a par with that of the Misses Pinkerton. The unfortunate Fanny once lost a place for pausing to consider whether Henry III was a good or a bad king, and was never able to rise above the mark 'mediocre,' though, according to John Colborne, his little stepsister was really particularly intelligent—a fact never suspected by the modest little thing herself. Her sojourn in Bloomsbury among silly, chattering girls was, indeed, such a time of penance to a child accustomed to the conversation of grown-up people that she could neither eat, sleep, nor play, and was hardly capable of dragging her bonnet upstairs after being paraded round the square with the other young ladies for the regulation walk. It may be that her dislike of this period was passed on to her daughter, who seldom has a good word to say for girls' boarding schools. Fanny could only cheer herself by surreptitious peeps at her little watch and calculations on the passage of her time of bondage, and by heartening glances at the house on the other side of the square where lived some friendly relations.

But a change was soon to come. In 1808 her father died of a fit of apoplexy during a magistrates' meeting, and soon afterwards Mrs Bargus, Maria Kingsman, and Alethea settled in Sloane Street in a house overlooking Bray Park, so called because the asses that supplied infants and invalids with their milk grazed there. It was not long before Fanny was restored to her family and allowed to settle into a life very pleasant to one of her quiet and intelligent tastes. Her mother indulged her with lessons from the best masters, in French, Italian, and drawing— this art consisting of nothing but copying pictures, in which Fanny so excelled that often her drawing could not be distinguished from her master's. The connexion with the Yonge family was kept up, when Alethea Bargus became the wife of John Yonge, the Squire of Puslinch, now old enough to be ordained and presented to the living of Newton Ferrers. In the same year (1813) John Colborne married Elizabeth Yonge, sister of John Yonge, and known as "the beauty of Devon."

Fanny Bargus must have been more aware of the wars than most of the young ladies of the time, if Jane Austen's picture of them is a true one. When she was the only daughter left at home, she became the proud recipient of Colonel Colborne's letters from the Front, and she tells of her excitement and joy when in 1814

B

she saw the Regent go in state to St Paul's to give thanks for the peace, and, by contrast, of the anxiety caused by Napoleon's escape from Elba a year later.

Perhaps Fanny's thoughts went out to another officer on the plains of Waterloo, more humble than the gallant General Sir John Colborne, for Lieutenant William Yonge was there too, doing his part in covering the 52nd with glory. It is certain that when Lady Colborne offered to take Fanny Bargus to share in the peace festivities of Paris, her mother sternly forbade any such dissipation. Mrs Bargus may already have begun to connect her dislike of her daughter's "marrying into a marching regiment" with the handsome person of William Yonge. We know that the couple were attached to each other for five years before their engagement was sanctioned. Mr Yonge of Cornwood was strongly opposed to the idea of his son's giving up the Army to satisfy the scruples of Mrs Bargus. He did his best to direct the young man's thoughts into other channels by sending him to conduct a consumptive cousin to take the 'cow-house' cure, then in fashion, at Hyères. (The cousin, cough and all, survived to be an old man of seventy.) This "Paradise of orange-trees and big blue violets" made a deep impression on William Yonge, and many years after he was able to make it live for his daughter, who uses Hyères as the setting for a scene in *Hopes and Fears*.

Mrs Bargus also did her utmost to distract Fanny's attention, by taking her for a lengthy tour in Scotland, where the girl grew even more enthusiastic over Scott than she had been before. (William too, over in France, was indulging in Scott, writing out in his pocket-book "Huntsman, rest" from *The Lady of the Lake*.) But even Scotland did not succeed in driving the image of William from Fanny's heart, and her mother next tried leaving Sloane Street and buying a small house and field in Otterbourne. All these attempts, however, were of no avail, and at last William persuaded his father to consent to his selling out, and prepared to face existence tied to his mother-in-law's apron-strings. On October 25, 1822, the constancy of the lovers was rewarded, and this brings us back to the young couple just returned from their honeymoon and alighting from their chariot on the doorstep of Otterbourne House.

The family situation was bound to demand tact from all three members, and particularly from Mr Yonge, who had not even a study where he might escape from his womenfolk. There was but little land attached to the house, so that he had not the resource of farming on anything but a very small scale, and was reduced to carpentry and working in the garden. During the first years of his marriage, before he had created for himself the multifarious occupations of his later days, time must have hung heavy on his hands. Fanny also had unlimited time for books, drawing, and her William, since Mrs Bargus, an active and formidable old lady, would suffer no interference in house or poultry yard. In this state of affairs a pious and serious-minded couple like Mr and Mrs Yonge were bound sooner or later to turn their thoughts to the deserving poor. Mr Yonge's first move was to write for advice to his brother James, who had succeeded to the family practice at Plymouth; to study Buchan's *Domestic Medicine* and the Pharmacopœia; and to set up as amateur physician to the village, which in those hard times had scant attention from any regular practitioner, and was left to the mercies of those learned in herbs and simples.

Having begun on the bodies of the poor of Otterbourne, the Yonges turned naturally to their souls, which were most inefficiently cared for by the casual attentions of a curate. They began to see visions of Sunday schools—on the Hannah More pattern. But for the moment the needs of the poor were thrust into the background, for on August 11, 1823, Fanny gave birth to a daughter, Charlotte Mary Yonge.

Charlotte was named after her father's favourite sister, who was one godmother, the other being Mrs Vernon Harcourt, Lord Selsey's daughter, whose husband was son to the Archbishop of York. At six weeks old Charlotte became a traveller and set out with her mother for Devonshire, whither her father had been summoned for old Duke Yonge's last illness. After his death William Yonge returned with his family to Otterbourne, the first place of which Charlotte had any conscious recollection.

In the 'twenties of the last century even the kindest of parents had no idea of giving up large rooms with southern aspects to their babies, and poor Charlotte was lodged in a sort of passage room, its window darkened by trees, where her nurse slept in a press-bed, and where the maids used to work. This encroachment on her domains was especially hateful to the child—in particular when one of the maids would insist on repeating Jane Taylor's tragic poem on the "Melancholy Adventures of Poor Puss," for the amusement of seeing Charlotte roll about on the floor in the agony caused by this sad tale. Mercifully, Mr and Mrs Yonge, having conscientiously waded through the two large tomes of the Edgeworth's *Practical Education*, had found there that children should not be left more than was necessary to the inferior society of domestics, but should early be taught manners fit for the parental table. So Charlotte was saved from an exclusively nursery upbringing in her unsatisfactory quarters. From her earliest years she ate with the family, and the only meal taken in the nursery was her Spartan supper of bread and milk, when even "nice crustisses," as the maid called them in congratulatory tones, were a treat. One day a would-be kind housemaid had concealed some butter on the under-side of the bread, but virtuous little Charlotte, like the true heroine of a moral tale, repudiated such forbidden luxuries and ran off to tell Mamma. Fortunately Charlotte did not always live on this elevated plane, but was apt to be noisy, disobedient, careless, and quick-tempered. She was even prone to "a certain provoking levity," as on the occasion when she was put in the corner and began squeaking out, "Begone, dull care!" to show that *she* didn't care what they did to her.

Except for the dungeon-like nursery, Charlotte's environment was a happy one. Mrs Bargus had bought three small fields behind the house and thrown them into one park-like space, surrounded by hedgerows and trees, with a path skirting the whole and making a good walk for rainy days. At the end was a wooded hollow called Dell Copse, which was covered in spring with sheets of wild daffodils. One of Charlotte's earliest memories was of rushing out in a little checked tippet with a frill under the chin and disporting herself among the daffodils, for which she retained all her life an appreciation that was quite Wordsworthian.

Charlotte also knew the country child's joy of keeping pets. Brisk little Mrs Bargus was a great keeper of poultry, and Charlotte enjoyed trotting after Grandmamma, who clattered about the yard in her pattens looking for eggs. When she grew old enough, she was set up with her own particular hens, in which she traded for pocket money. All the activities of Mrs Bargus were such as would be interesting to small girls. The nimble

feet of the old lady were for ever trotting from the store-cupboard
in the attics down to the kitchen, or out into the garden, where
she would cut a fine cabbage and pop it in at some cottage window,
with a few cheery words that made her more popular in the
village than her daughter and son-in-law with all their pains-
taking charity.

Another of Charlotte's early recollections was of churchgoing.
In those days Otterbourne was a mere dependency of Hursley
Church, and was served but indifferently by a curate on alternate
Sunday mornings and evenings. The sound of his horses' hoofs
on the main road, before he turned into the Church Lane, would
be the signal for ringing the bell for service, so that its time was
no very regular affair, and was well described to Mr Yonge by
the clerk as "At half-past ten or eleven, sir, or else at no time at
all." Proceeding down the lane at one side of Otterbourne House,
the Yonge family came to the little old church by the river, with
its picturesque boarded tower covered with ivy, and made their
way through the untidy churchyard, full of mullein spikes and
burdock leaves, with staring little boys astride on the sunken
lichen-grown tombstones. Then there was the step-ladder to be
negotiated, an ascent so perilous on rainy days that Mrs Yonge
was asked, "Law, ma'am, how do you manage with your nice
white tails on a wet Sunday?" before they finally emerged in
their own particular gallery.

Once there, Charlotte had plenty to occupy her from her post
of vantage on two hassocks. Down below there was an interesting variety of people to be seen: labourers in wonderfully embroidered smocks, farmers in velveteen, old ladies in red cloaks
and enormous black satin bonnets. But best of all were the
children on their benches in the aisle or on the chancel steps,
especially when they behaved ill and had to be cuffed into order
by Master Oxford, the clerk. He was a dear old man, very lame
from rheumatism, with a "beautiful meek face," and was always
a great favourite with Charlotte. She used to watch him as he
stumped along the nave and up into the gallery while the Thanksgiving was being said, just in time to say "Amen" and to get
among the singers and give out the psalm. For a little girl Tate
and Brady, sung with right good will to a flute and bassoon
accompaniment, was certainly by far the best part of the service,
and Charlotte used to watch intently as John Green, the leading

bass of the choir, cocked his black eyebrows and trolled forth the most effective parts of those classic compositions. Even after years of Mr Keble and the Oxford Movement Charlotte entertained a sentimental feeling for Tate and Brady that *Hymns Ancient and Modern* could not quite succeed in arousing.

When there was nothing of particular interest going on in church, Charlotte could always have recourse to the great Royal Arms over the chancel arch, where there was a unicorn with a splendid twisted horn and lions with tongues hanging out of their mouths rather like pug dogs. It was not long before she could read, and then there was plenty to do as she progressed from picking out the capitals in her prayer-book to reading the texts and Commandments painted on the walls.

Charlotte was early set on the path of learning, and began lessons with her mother when she was only three. Mrs Yonge had a natural talent for teaching, and carried out the precepts of the Edgeworths with great success on her little daughter. Charlotte's early education has often been blamed for the excessive shyness which hampered her all through her life, but if this is so, the reason for it lies not in the Edgeworth system, but in her parents' application of it. On reading *Practical Education* one is struck with the good sense of most of the views set forth and the modernity of some of them. Such, for instance, is the recommendation to get to the root of a child's fears—good advice, apparently neglected in Charlotte's case. Judicious praise is to be given, since

> in proportion as any one's confidence in himself increases, his anxiety for the applause of others diminishes; people are very seldom vain of any accomplishments in which they obviously excel, but they frequently continue to be vain of those which are doubtful.

But, on the other hand,

> the smallest quantity of stimulus that can produce the exertion we desire should be used.

This last recommendation was carried to excess by Mr and Mrs Yonge. Although it was generally agreed that Charlotte was both brilliantly clever and very pretty, with her wavy chestnut curls and large hazel eyes, the child herself was sometimes troubled by doubts, which she dared not utter to any grown-up person, whether she might not be deficient and really "so very ugly." This question worried her so much that one day she ventured on asking her mamma whether she were pretty, but all the satisfaction she got was the evasive answer that all young animals, even little pigs, were pretty. All the same, Charlotte did not, even in her early days, enjoy compliments, and she made every one laugh by answering, on the model of Miss Edgeworth's "Frank," to some one who admired her curls, "You flatter me."

In the main, however, Mrs Yonge showed herself eminently successful in her dealings with Charlotte, and their relationship was at all times a very happy one. Mother and daughter were of the same temperament, and, though Mrs Yonge's fragile health made her incapable of much physical exertion, she was always mentally active, enthusiastic, and full of playfulness. This made her a delightful teacher, and Charlotte looked back with pleasure on the mornings she spent shut up with her mother. If we compare her fate with that of the heroines of her books, who were liable to have their studies interrupted by the household cares which called away the mother or elder sister who acted as governess, we realize how fortunate Charlotte was to have a grandmother who took all housekeeping concerns on herself. Little Charlotte progressed speedily along the ways made easy for small girls by Mrs Barbauld and Mrs Trimmer, until at the age of four she made a wonderful discovery—she could read a book alone. Grandmamma was reading the newspaper to Mamma—a very dull proceeding—so Charlotte had knelt down to look at the pictures in a large book of *Robinson Crusoe* which lay spread out on a chair. As she got to the place where they were shipwrecked, it suddenly dawned on her that she could read it herself. Henceforth the greatest of all a lonely child's resources was to be hers.

Mrs Yonge, a conscientious mother, kept careful notes of her daughter's progress. The following extracts from these are reproduced in Charlotte's *Autobiography* with her comments:

Jan. 7, 1828. Charlotte began Fabulous Histories (*i.e.*, Mrs Trimmer's *Robin, Dicky, Flapsy, and Pecksy*. I loved them, though the book is one of the former generation—pale type, long s's, "ct" joined together. I have it still.).

July 5. Charlotte said, "Mamma, how do the men that write the newspaper know of all the things that occur?" (*N.B.* I had a passion for fine words.)

Sept. 26. Asked C. why Miss Blunder was laughed at for saying that if she went to France it should be by land. She answered, "Why, Mamma, she couldn't make a 'waal of waater.' "

[Charlotte was much laughed at for her drawling *a*'s, which she had learnt from a funny old curate, who was supposed to say his vowels like Titus Oates in *Peveril of the Peak.*]

March 20. It is noted that C. has done since the 1st of August, 1016 lessons; 537 very well, 442 well, 37 badly. Reading, spelling, poetry, one hour every day; geography, arithmetic, grammar, twice a week; history and catechism, once.

No mean record this, for a child not yet five!

Charlotte found all this learning no burden, and she always looked back on her childhood as being a very happy one. Her great delight was that of most lonely little girls—her dolls. She had about sixteen of them—large wooden, small wax, and tiny Dutch. This happy family used to do lessons set out in rows on the nursery chairs as soon as Charlotte had finished hers, but they came downstairs only by special invitation. Charlotte's favourite child was Miss Eliza, a big wooden doll, given her as a prize for hemming her first handkerchief. (This handkerchief was adorned with a picture of the trial of Queen Caroline, who was depicted in a hat and feathers, weeping profusely.) Dear though Miss Eliza was, Charlotte had a great longing for a large wax doll and for a doll's china tea-service, but Mamma and Papa talked seriously to her about the cost of these luxuries, and reminded her that it was wrong to spend money on toys when so many people were in need of food and clothes.

When Charlotte was not busy tending her dolls, she often spent her time making up stories about a family of ten boys and eleven girls who lived in an arbour in the garden. These children were the embryos of her book families, such as the Mohuns, Mays, and Underwoods. In spite of being at moments lost to reality in her own imaginary world, Charlotte enjoyed also all normal kinds of play. She would run boisterously about the house or the garden to let off her animal spirits, and certainly did not strike people as being an unduly repressed child. By day, indeed, she was merry enough, but at night she had to pay the penalty for excessive imagination. As soon as darkness closed in, or, worse still, darkness tempered by the weird shadows which the rushlight cast on the wall, she became a prey to wolves that lurked under the bed, or sinister figures, ready to smother her, like the Little Princes in the Tower, or to blow her up with gunpowder. But the worst terror of all was that of the Last Judgment. Charlotte imagined that this could not happen so long as some one was watching for the coming of the Lord—thus interpreting the text, "Watch lest He cometh." So she did her best to keep awake by pulling the hairs out of her mattress. With the morning light all these fears became no more than fantastic dreams of darkness, but as sure as another night came round, there would be the same dread terrors lying in wait for poor Charlotte, until sleep brought her release from their power.

The religious teaching of Charlotte's parents, however, was on the whole sensible enough, for she describes them as being "of the old reticent school, reverent and practical, so as to dread the drawing out of feeling and expression, for fear of unreality." As a matter of course they submitted Charlotte to the rigours of the grim Victorian Sunday, but the commiseration poured out by modern writers on those who suffered from this institution would be quite wasted on Charlotte. It did not trouble her at all that Sunday reading was exclusively moral, and she enjoyed the evening spent in the repetition of hymns and the Catechism, and looking at the pictures in the Dutch Bible history.

But the greatest delight of all was the Sunday school. Like all tactful reformers, Mr and Mrs Yonge believed in starting on the children, and as soon as might be after their arrival they had set up a Sunday class in a room in the village. There the children were instructed according to the principles of Mrs Trimmer and Miss Hannah More, of whom Mrs Yonge was a great admirer. The cultural background of the Yonge's scholars was negligible. It was supplied by a dame, more picturesque than efficient, who sat enthroned in the chimney corner in black silk Quaker-shaped bonnet, blue gown with buff kerchief folded across it, complete with rod, spectacles, and spelling-book. Mrs Yonge realized that a change must be made, and was delighted when in 1826 she was presented by her mother with a strip of waste land and funds to build a school on it. Mr Yonge, who had leanings towards architecture, set zealously to work to plan a one-storied building with mud walls and brick floor, consisting of a schoolroom and a bedroom and kitchen for the mistress. Here they installed a former servant of the Heathcotes of Hursley Park, whose main qualifications for the post were nice manners and an aptitude for plain sewing. At the modest fee of a penny a week (writing and arithmetic were extras, and cost threepence) they collected some thirty children. Most of the neighbouring parents did not hold with education, or said the children were busy minding the baby or "keeping a few birds" (bird-scaring). But in a little while the male portion of the school got beyond the disciplinary powers of the mistress, and Mr Yonge had them transported to a school built for them near the churchyard and put under the care of Master Oxford.

Mrs Yonge and Charlotte were concerned only with the girls. They both had a natural talent for teaching, and Charlotte tells how Mrs Yonge's lessons were remembered fifty years afterwards, and had even "been referred to on death-beds." Charlotte's talents, however, had hardly come to maturity when, having already passed the top class in religious knowledge, she was set to teach at the age of seven. Favouritism was her first difficulty. It was quite impossible to keep from slyly prompting the most attractive little girl to bring her to the top of the class; and then, adding a lie unto a fault, Charlotte actually maintained that the child had reached this position by fair means alone. This sin weighed heavy for some time on the small teacher's conscience, till, with a finger on a pane of glass in the schoolroom window, she had wept it all out to Mamma and had been forgiven.

Charlotte had the best of all antidotes to these precocious activities in the yearly visit to Puslinch, where she was plunged into the society of a large and merry family of cousins. It was a most exciting moment when the lengthy preparations were begun for the visit of the family to Devon—excluding Mrs Bargus. The Yonges' sulphur-yellow chariot had to be packed with all things necessary for a protracted round of visits, a purpose for which such vehicles seemed expressly constructed, if we can believe Miss Yonge's remembrances of them in *Chantry House*:

> The capacities of a chariot were considerable. Within there was a good-sized seat for the principal occupants, and outside, a dickey behind, and a driving-box before, though sometimes there was only one of these, and that transferable. The boxes were calculated to hold family luggage on a six months' tour . . . there was the

imperial, a grand roomy receptacle, which was placed at the top of the carriage, and would not always go upstairs in small houses; the cap-box, which fitted into a curved place in front of the windows, and could not stand alone, but had a frame to support it; two long narrow boxes with the like infirmity of standing, which fitted in below; square ones under each seat, and a drop box fastened on behind. There were pockets beneath each window, and, curious relic in name and nature of the time when every gentleman carried his weapon, there was the sword case, an excrescence behind the back of the best seat, accessible by lifting a cushion, where weapons used to be carried, but where in our peaceful times travellers bestowed their luncheon and their books.

By the time the post-horses were harnessed and they were off Charlotte was wrought up to such a pitch of excitement that a feeling of carriage-sickness was apt to mar the perfect felicity of the expedition. In fact, the very sight of the blue lining, yellow blinds, and blue and yellow lace of the interior of the chariot was enough to arouse the unpleasant sensation. This was, however, the only drawback, and everything else on the journey was a delight. Sometimes a coach would come thundering past with the guard cheerfully tootling his horn; or you might see a pony-carriage or donkey-cart, and this time it was your turn to win the race. Then there were entertaining glimpses of a great variety of people at the turnpike gate or at the inns, where the horses were changed and a fresh lot harnessed by another spruce postboy in corduroy breeches and blue or yellow jacket. If these delights began to pall, Papa was always ready to amuse you by reading a story or playing a lovely game that he had invented himself. You each had to look out of a window and see who could first count up to a hundred animals on his or her side of the chariot, unless you had the luck to catch sight of a cat looking out of a window, which won you the game straight away.

Among the joys of travelling were the picnic meals. At mid-day the sword-case would be opened and hard-boiled eggs, biscuits, and what Charlotte called "spotted meat" produced. The day ended with a "mutton chop" tea, and then bed. After two days on the road came the first thrilling sight of a tor which once moved Mr Yonge, after his long banishment among the downs of Hampshire, to quote Lucia's words in *I Promessi Sposi*: "I see my mountains." Every mile increased Charlotte's excitement,

and when finally the summit of the last hill was reached and the
twinkling lights in the windows of the large square house in the
valley could be seen, she would give vent to a shriek of ecstasy.
When the tall front door had opened to admit her into the flagged
hall full of a merry, welcoming throng of children, her felicity
was complete.

Charlotte's elders were Alethea, who was eight years older and
seemed almost grown up, James, Mary, and Jane; her contemporary was Duke; and below her came Anne, Edmund, Charles,
and Frances, who was a tiny, newly arrived baby when Charlotte
went to stay at Puslinch in 1829. Although Anne was two years
younger, she was Charlotte's favourite cousin. Among a high-
spirited family Anne was particularly naughty, and the stories
of her sins were legion. Perhaps her worst misdemeanour was the
occasion when she was sent to lie down in her mamma's room at
the same time that some raspberry jam had been brought in
there to be put away; later on Miss Anne was found sitting up on
the bed "all over jam," right up to the elbows, and with the rest
spread out over the table and the counterpane. Anne's curiosity
over the taste of things was quite insatiable, and she had even
been caught serenely smiling and licking her lips after eating
the poultice off her Uncle William's blister. Charlotte did her
best to restrain Anne in these excesses, telling her severely that
it was stealing when she saw her taking Aunt Marianne's sugar
while paying a visit to that lady. Another time they were taken
to lunch with Admiral Mudge, and when they were afterwards
left alone with his son, Zachary, the teasing fellow tried to get
them to drink some wine that he had in vain first offered to the
dogs. Of course, Anne's spirit of enterprise got the better of her,
and she drank some and made herself sick. Charlotte, having
abstained, felt heroically good.

Contact with these lively and mischievous beings quickly went
to Charlotte's head. Almost as soon as she had arrived she was
seen with Uncle Yonge's bands on, preaching to her cousins with
a locker as her pulpit. Each of the mothers imagined the other
to have given permission, and, though shocked at such irrever-
ence, did not like to begin scolding, so Charlotte got off scot-free.
Retribution soon followed, however, when, getting wilder and
wilder, the children ended by breaking a window. Luckily they
had many quieter pastimes also. Keeping shops in the recesses

of the study and playing at houses were great diversions. The best game was on a wet Sunday, when all the children were left alone in the house together and allowed to play in the dining-room. The recessed windows made lovely houses, and one could shut the shutters for night and open them when it was supposed to be day and time to distribute the provisions. Occasionally their games became quite poetical, and Charlotte and Anne once knelt in the patches of moonlight which poured in through the great windows and gathered it into their bosoms.

From Puslinch Charlotte was taken on by her parents to Plymouth, which was also full of delightful relations. Old Mrs Duke Yonge lived with her daughter, Anne, at Mount Pleasant. She was called by Charlotte "Grandmamma with a stick"; having broken her thigh tripping over a footstool, the active old lady had refused to stay in bed until it had mended, and was thus left very lame for the rest of her life and used to walk with a gold-headed stick. It was this grandmother who took Charlotte to evening service with her in a sedan chair—an experience that seemed very romantic when viewed from the latter years of the nineteenth century. They used to go on Sundays to St Andrew's Chapel, a wonderful building shaped like a parallelogram, where the pews were so high that they came up to grown-up people's necks, so it was not surprising that poor six-year-old Charlotte once nearly fainted from suffocation.

The next stage of the round of family visits was to Duke Yonge's parsonage at Antony, in Cornwall. Crossing the Tamar by the Torpoint ferry was the most interesting part of all Charlotte's journeyings. There was a big ferry-boat for the horses, and in this Grandmamma was transported bodily in her carriage, but Mamma was afraid of the horses, so she and Charlotte went in another boat. It was an exciting moment when the *San Josef*, one of the Trafalgar prizes, loomed out high above them through the dusk of a late autumn evening. Charlotte enjoyed the high waves also, and when some foolish lady cried out, "We shall all be upset!" she answered gleefully, "Oh, then we shall catch a fish!" As soon as they were out of the boat, Charlotte was sent on with the maids to walk and get warm, while her mother and father waited for the carriage, and when they overtook her, she made every one laugh by saying, "I'm as wet as a shag!"

The cousins at Antony were less companionable than those of

Puslinch and Plymouth. All except Arthur, who was a fearful tease, were much older than she, and the dark, handsome Alethea dragged her round until she made her feel "like the ploughman whom the giant's daughter stole for her toy," as she afterwards confessed. (Mamma once explained 'forgiveness' to Charlotte as the feeling she ought to have about Alethea's teasing!) Arthur was singularly gifted at making anyone's flesh creep. Dark cupboards and closed doors all assumed a mysterious significance under his interpretations, and he thoroughly frightened Charlotte by telling her that the cracks in the old plaster meant that the house was going to fall. Her worst fright was when Arthur deluded her into referring to William IV as "King Bill." He then informed her that this was high treason, and that he was going to write to have a guillotine sent down to behead her; all of which she believed implicitly. Antony would have been a place of complete torment had there not been a few alleviations. The nursery was papered all over with pictures out of children's books, and Arthur's nurse had some purple-and-gold plates which were the prettiest Charlotte had ever seen. Then, about a mile and a half off, there was a lovely beach of white sand where one could pick up all kinds of beautiful shells. When Charlotte was an old lady, a windy night would still make her dream of the roll and dash of its waves and the delight of those sands. And, as if to make up for the teasing of their children, "Uncle and Aunt Duke" were very kind, merry, engaging people, who lived such an easygoing, scrambling life that they were said to be found dining at any hour from eleven to eight o'clock. Duke was a contrast to his precise military brother William.

The William Yonges' series of visits somewhat resembled the figure of that name in the Lancers, and after Antony, to Charlotte's joy, they found themselves back again at Puslinch. This visit was, however, cut very short, for Aunt Yonge developed measles, and Charlotte and her mother were hurried off to Yealmpton, to the house of deaf old Mrs Yonge of Puslinch, Uncle Yonge's mother. Charlotte called her "Grandmamma with the trumpet," and imagined that she had three grandmothers. Having kept the quarantine there, while the Puslinch children were having measles in rotation, they were free to pack into the yellow chariot again and return to Otterbourne.

CHAPTER II

PATERNAL EDUCATION

ON the morning of January 13, 1830, Charlotte lay in her crib in the dark, wondering why Nurse was so late in coming to get her up. This irregularity was the beginning of a strange and momentous day. After breakfast Charlotte was not given a chance of saying good-morning to Mamma, but was hurried off for a walk in the snow with Papa over the downs to Twyford. Here she first made the acquaintance of Anna Maria and Conway Shipley, who had lately come to live there, and who were about her own age. It was very nice to have friends so near home, though, unfortunately, Anna Maria and Conway called all "pretending games"—which were her favourites—"falsehood." The snowy walk and the new friends, however, were quite put in the shade by the wonderful piece of news that awaited Charlotte on her return to Otterbourne. She was taken to Mamma, whom she found in bed, and shown a tiny baby. This was the new brother, for whom Charlotte had always longed. Of course, she set to work immediately to choose names for him, and, being well versed in classical lore, finally pitched on Alexander Xenophon. When the christening day came round, however, the baby was merely called Julian Bargus.

Baby Julian took up a great deal of Mrs Yonge's time, so part of Charlotte's education was now handed over to her father, and he began to teach her to write. Mr Yonge adopted the original method of setting her to write huge S's in chalk on a slate without resting finger, wrist, or arm on the table. This arduous discipline resulted in the beautiful flowing hand that was to stand the future authoress in good stead; but in her early struggles to wield the refractory chalk Charlotte recked nothing of any such recompense in store. At the least sign of inattention or inaccuracy Mr Yonge was apt to grow very hot and loud, and poor Charlotte to be reduced to tears. Charlotte herself refused to see in this sternness anything but "righteous anger" at her faults, and refers to his "patience and perseverance," the first virtue, however, being hardly apparent to other people. She felt herself to be amply compensated by his rare approval of her efforts, and, like all nervous, excitable, children, was soon up again in the heights of merriment after his wrath had plunged her into the depths of despair. Mr Yonge's dark eyes were just as apt to "beam with tenderness" on his little daughter as to flash with anger—alternations of which a psychologist would in these days gravely disapprove.

Charlotte's father showed his devotion, however, when in the summer of 1830 he nursed her through an attack of measles, having greater confidence in his native ability for medicine than in the apothecaries of Winchester. Charlotte liked having Papa sleeping on the nursery floor, always alert to give her a drink or smooth her pillow. Her convalescence was a delightful time, for Mr Yonge read her that entrancing book *The Pilgrim's Progress*, and Grandmamma bought her the latest thing in dolls, a huge creature with leathern body and *papier-mâché* head. "Anna" was a particularly opportune gift, because dear "Miss Eliza," the largest and favourite wooden doll of Charlotte's fifteen children, had been considered a dangerous companion for the baby and given away to a little girl in the village. (Some sixteen years later Charlotte came across the youngest of this little girl's eleven brothers and sisters "hugging the stump of Miss Eliza, without a rag upon her, paintless, hairless, eyeless, noseless, the last wreck of doll-anity, but still caressed.") Charlotte would lie in bed with her arm round Anna, while her mother sat by her making clothes for this paragon.

Her visit to Puslinch in this year was a very merry one. The journey was even more entertaining than usual. Mason, the nurse, and the baby travelled inside the chariot, so Charlotte was freed from the qualms of carriage-sickness by being perched on the box with Papa, who beguiled the way with the tale of Bel and the Dragon and of his old magpie, which he had cured of sucking eggs by giving him one filled with mustard. When it came to Mason's turn to sit with Charlotte, they indulged in the more frivolous pastime of "Button," a game in which you tried how long you could keep your mouth pursed up, while the other player did her best to make you laugh.

At Puslinch itself licence reigned, as Aunt Yonge was this year lying ill in her room and the children were left to the

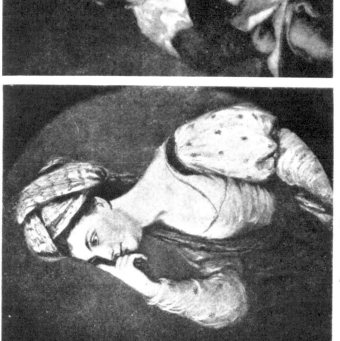

CATHARINA YONGE
From a portrait

FRANCES MARY AND JULIAN BARGUS YONGE
From a portrait

Reproduced, by courtesy of Messrs Macmillan and Co., Ltd., from "Charlotte Mary Yonge," by Christabel Coleridge

PUSLINCH

By courtesy of John Yonge, Esq.

33

inadequate supervision of a daily governess. Charlotte was somewhat relieved, for she was rather afraid of stern Aunt Yonge and
resented her reproofs. Excitement soon threw Charlotte off her
balance and made her unduly shrill-voiced. There was even a
certain game called "Cats and Mice" that the children were forbidden to play when she was there, as it roused her to such a
pitch. This vividness of feeling was displayed in a quieter manner
in her intense friendship with Anne—a friendship she calls "the
great love of our lives." The two little girls were only restrained
from walking about all the time with arms round each other's
waists by being coldly told by their mothers that 'pawing' was
silly. They shared all their pleasures, from the ecstasy of picking
bluebells together in a wood sloping down to the sea, to the more
sober joy of indulging in long words, for which they both had a
passion.

The Puslinch visits continued to be Charlotte's yearly treat
until the summer when she turned thirteen, when there came a
gap of several years. This visit of 1836 was to her the landmark
set at the end of childhood, which was curtailed for the Victorian
young lady by the increasing proprieties of life. Charlotte herself
was forbidden any such unmaidenly action as writing to her boy
cousins after she had turned thirteen, and by the middle 'teens
it was considered hoydenish to take the wet day's exercise of a
game of ball or battledore in anything but female company.

Thus Charlotte and Anne, making hay while the sun of childish
liberty still shone, had their culminating riot on Duke's thirteenth
birthday, when they were put into wild spirits by Uncle Yonge's
writing an answer in doggerel verse to their request to get up
early and finish Duke's present. On their walk into Yealmpton,
they ended by plunging ankle-deep into the black mud of the
estuary in search of winkles, which brought on them torrents of
wrath from the nurses:

HARVEY, *the Puslinch nurse*. Now, Miss Anne, you don't care,
and there's Miss Charlotte sorry, she's crying.
MASON. Now, Miss Charlotte, don't be crying. It's all pretence.
I'd rather you were like Miss Anne, who doesn't pretend to care.

Luckily the amusement of the two Mrs Yonges at these scold-
ings, which were really an attempt on the nurses' part to cover
up the gossiping that had made them oblivious to their charges'

C

escapades, averted punishment. So the children had their feast, Charlotte, as the visitor, being honoured with the one winkle they had taken, and a great effort of politeness it was to accept the slimy creature from the end of a pin.

But the days of childish abandon were numbered. There were still merry romps with Julian and games at "Shops" or "Doctors," where Dr C. and Dr J. would gravely take turns at prescribing magnesia and rhubarb made of chalk and brick-dust, but each year tightened up the discipline of life. A schoolroom had been added to Otterbourne House, and here Charlotte repaired for an hour's arithmetic with Mr Yonge before breakfast. The accuracy he demanded did not come naturally to her, and no one could bear to hear him thundering at her and to see her frequently in tears under his instructions. The poor child had been called at six, or soon after, and one wonders whether there would have been less weeping if she had not confronted her mathematics on an empty stomach. Mr Yonge did, however, make some amends for his ferocity, for at the end of the first winter he rewarded her diligence with a watch, to her intense delight and surprise. Eventually either he must have become less savage or Charlotte more accurate, for she went on with her lessons with him until she was well over twenty, when she had come to the end of "such Greek, Euclid, and Algebra as had furnished forth the Etonian and soldier of sixteen." Charlotte's Latin lessons began when Julian was turned five and thought old enough to share them with her. In these lessons poor Julian had the worst of it, for it was not easy to keep pace with a clever sister six years older, even if she did help him to prepare the work set by their father —a task which no doubt pleased the didactically minded young lady, already an experienced teacher of Sunday schools.

Breakfast put an end to Mr Yonge's rule in the schoolroom. It was followed by a welcome scamper in the garden and the feeding of the hens, cats, and other pets. Then came the serener atmosphere of Mrs Yonge's lessons. After the exacerbating effect of mathematics and Latin it was indeed soothing to be put to copy drawings and learn the skill at needlework required of all nicely brought up young ladies, while her mother read some history book aloud. In after-years Charlotte regretted the antiquated methods of her drawing lessons, for she inherited a love of art that craved a fuller expression than mere copying.

Mrs Yonge may have been old-fashioned as a drawing mistress, but as a teacher of history she was both sound and inspiring. No doubt Charlotte's wonderful memory and quickening imagination played their part in training her historical sense, but Mrs Yonge must be given her share of credit for the achievement. She insisted on Charlotte's reading twenty pages of some such work as Goldsmith's *Rome* before she was allowed her daily chapter of the Waverley Novels, thus giving her a well-balanced mental diet and useful habits of self-discipline.

During her morning hours in the schoolroom Charlotte also prepared her work for Monsieur de Normanville, whose lessons were added to the curriculum when she was about twelve. Here again Charlotte was fortunate, for not every girl had the chance of learning French from a genuine old *émigré* with powdered hair and old-fashioned courtesy, one who was, moreover, an excellent teacher. He did not insist on intricate proses and boring grammatical exercises, but allowed Charlotte to translate some of her favourite English stories, such as *The Faithful Little Girl*, and, perceiving that he had here no ordinary pupil, he let her make up French stories about the Melville girls, some of the inhabitants of her imaginary world. Charlotte evidently enjoyed learning foreign languages, for she later added Spanish and Italian to her repertory. In the latter tongue she grew so proficient that she was able to translate the whole of *I Promessi Sposi*, one of her favourite novels, into English for the benefit of Mr Yonge, who knew no Italian—a tremendous task for a girl only just out of the schoolroom.

Charlotte's other visiting master was not so successful as Monsieur de Normanville. A lugubrious gentleman from Southampton was engaged to teach her dancing; but, as he thought going to balls "contrary to his profession," and counteracted the effects of his frivolous instructions by distributing tracts to his pupils, he seems hardly to have entered into the spirit of the subject. Charlotte, though well made, was clumsy in her movements, partly from nerves and partly from the self-consciousness that grew on her during her 'teens. It is not surprising that she hated her dancing lessons and never was much addicted to balls. Probably cousinly banter taught her more graces than did her gloomy dancing-master. It was wholesome to be teased for her fashion of getting over stiles, and one of her boy cousins actually

succeeded in breaking her of a queer contortion of the lip that
she indulged in when laughing by telling her in all good nature
that she reminded him of Charles the Bold in *Quentin Durward*,
who had a "diabolical grimace." Charlotte clearly fell short of the
standard of perfection for 'accomplished' young ladies of the days
of Queen Victoria's girlhood. As well as a very moderate success
in deportment she showed a painful lack of any musical ability.

Lessons were officially over by lunch-time, but Charlotte
managed to suck a good deal of information from the rest of the
day's avocations. According to modern notions, the afternoon's
exercise was the worst-managed part of the programme. Mrs
Yonge's elegant ill-health made long walks an impossibility, so
Charlotte was reduced to accompanying Julian and nurse, or
taking a constitutional by herself along the path round the home
field, except when she enjoyed the rare treat of walking with
Papa. Even cottage-visiting was allowed only under strict supervision, for the Yonges feared that the small-talk of the village
might be detrimental to their carefully guarded miss. In this
way there grew up a barrier between Charlotte and the village
folk which she was only able to surmount when teaching them,
and, try as she would, she could never manage to unbend in her
ordinary intercourse with them. The most enjoyable kind of
walk was one on which she could botanize, for Charlotte had inherited from her grandfather Bargus a taste for this scientific
pursuit, and by her 'teens she had laid the foundation of the *hortus
siccus* to be found among the possessions of most early Victorian
girls.

An even greater passion was that for conchology. It began with
the mere childish delight of hunting for shells on the muddy
beach of the Yealm estuary at Puslinch, where, being yet innocent
of the use of acid, the children would spend hours on hands and
knees in the vain endeavour to polish their shells on the library
carpet. Soon Charlotte was recognized as a genuine collector.
Great was every one's amusement when Uncle Duke, spending a
day at Southampton while on a visit to Otterbourne, brought
back an argus cowrie as a present to his little niece, and Aunt
Duke triumphantly returned from an expedition to Winchester
with an exactly similar shell. Unlike some youthful collections,
Charlotte's did not pass away, but grew till it was found worthy
to be bequeathed to Winchester College.

Arranging her collections was but one of Charlotte's pursuits during the long evenings after the half-past-five or six-o'clock dinner to which she was early promoted. There were games of chess or backgammon, and, most regular of occupations, needlework, to the accompaniment of a club book read out loud by Mr Yonge. The circulating libraries of the time were little better than they had been in the days of Miss Lydia Languish, and the gentry of a neighbourhood would club together to acquire all the outstanding literature of the time, which they discussed and selected amid much pleasant gossip at meetings held at the house of a member of the circle. These readings and the discussions arising out of them were among the most important formative influences on Charlotte's development. It was thus that she heard such books as Lockhart's *Life of Scott*, which added fuel to the fire of her undying enthusiasm for the novelist.

Many people who lived either before, or at least in the early days of, railways led what seem to us extraordinarily restricted lives. Compared with her own Ethel May, for instance, who by the time she was eighteen had never been beyond the next town, Charlotte Yonge was a travelled young lady. In 1833 the Yonge family set off in the phaeton for London. They began by a round of visits, including one to West Dean, in Sussex, Lord Selsey's place, which, with its long passages and hosts of empty rooms, each provided with one copper tea-kettle, greatly impressed Charlotte, and appears years after as Belforest in *Magnum Bonum*. The culminating point of the tour was London, where the Yonges stayed with Mr Serjeant Coleridge (afterwards Sir John Taylor Coleridge). Charlotte went through a course of sightseeing, which included the Museum, the Zoological Gardens, the Panorama of the Siege of Antwerp at the Coliseum, and the impressive sight of the Serjeant in wig and gown at Westminster Hall. The visit was made doubly delightful by the friendship that she struck up with Mary and Alethea Coleridge.

In the next year Charlotte went to Oxford for a great occasion. Her father's sister had married Dr Jones, the Rector of Exeter College, who this year was Vice-Chancellor, and the Duke of Wellington was to be installed as Chancellor. Charlotte was nearly eleven, and had already digested many of the solid histories that were read out loud in the schoolroom. With this background she was well fitted to appreciate Oxford, and from the moment when the Yonges' carriage swept into the High the visit was one vision of delight. Cloisters, gardens, chapels, Christ Church meadows, cathedral services, all led up to the supreme experience of the Encænia. The shouting undergraduates, the massed colours of the ladies' gallery, the scarlet doctors, the Duke of Cumberland's fine uniform, and finally the Duke himself in robes of black and gold, made an unforgettable impression. And when young Lord Maidstone, delivering the Newdigate from his rostrum, pointed dramatically at the Duke, with the words, "We have one hero, and that one is here," the tense emotion of the crowd overflowed in wild applause. Charlotte was fortunate enough to see the central figure of this resplendent pageant in a lighter moment also. When the Duke of Wellington came to Exeter College to visit the Vice-Chancellor, Charlotte and Julian were brought into the drawing-room to gaze at their father's great hero, and Mrs Yonge boldly stepped forward, saying, "Will your Grace shake hands with a soldier's little boy?" The great man kissed Julian and shook hands with Charlotte.

Even at Otterbourne House Charlotte could peep through the gates out to the main London–Portsmouth road and indulge in daydreams about the far-off destinations of the fifteen coaches that whirled past daily with tootling horn and flourishing whip —Mail, Independent, Telegraph, Red Rover, Hirondelle, all London bound; then the Oxford Coach, which brought visions of grey towers and visits to Aunt Charlotte. During the Winchester Assizes Mr Coleridge, now made a judge, would often stay at Otterbourne with his family. The Yonges were thus brought into stimulating intercourse with legal circles, and Charlotte was sometimes taken to see the trials. These, and the Judge's elucidations of them, were all stored away in her memory for future use, and were to furnish the material for many an excellent scene in the novels. The Judge was one of those truly great men who can unbend delightfully with children, and would put in his wise or humorous comment in discussions between Charlotte and his daughters on such subjects as whether Napoleon was courageous and whether St Louis was "henpecked by his mother," as May Coleridge put it.

Another pair of London young ladies who came on visits to Otterbourne were Mary and Julia Davys, the daughters of an

old school friend of Mrs Yonge's and of Dr Davys, Dean of
Chester and Preceptor of Princess Victoria. They were some
years older than Charlotte, but allowed her to share in their
botanizing, drawing, and reading, and, best of all, introduced her
to paper games, which never failed all through her life to wake
her ready wit and enjoyment. In 1837 Mary Davys had an
appointment in the Palace, and the glimpses of the life of royalty
which she passed on to her friends became more authentic and
vivid. The most amusing anecdote was of a midnight feast held
by the ladies-in-waiting. The young Queen somehow got wind
of this, so that the next morning she demurely asked, "And pray,
Miss Davys, how does Miss Cavendish look in her nightcap?"
Charlotte, who always took a romantic view of royalty, greatly
appreciated genuine accounts of the sayings and doings of the
young Queen.

The Yonges did not depend only on the visits of friends for
rumours of the affairs of the world, as they were particularly
fortunate in their immediate circle. Sir William Heathcote of
Hursley Park was a friend of Judge Coleridge's, and, besides
being a useful Member of Parliament, was an ideal enlightened
country squire. His visits to Mr Yonge had their material uses
also, for, as Member of Parliament, he generously franked the
family correspondence, and, with postage to Devon costing
elevenpence, this was no mean advantage. Charlotte generally
had to be satisfied with an exchange of letters with her dear
Anne through the boys at Winchester, but at the least rumour
of Sir William's approach she would sit down to pour out page
after page.

The year 1835 saw the establishment in Winchester of Dr
Moberly, the new Headmaster of the College, with his wife and
baby, Alice, the first member of a family with whom Charlotte
Yonge was to keep up a kind of elder-sisterly relationship all her
life. When her mother first took her to call, Charlotte was enraptured with the beauty of Mrs Moberly, and wrote that she
was "just like a Madonna in a picture." The object of this
admiration, however, merely noticed that the little girl had a
very shrill voice.

It was the year before this that there arrived in Otterbourne
the Reverend William Bigg-Wither, a shy and rather *gauche*
young Fellow of New College. He came for six weeks and stayed

there thirty-seven years. This young man, with views and zeal hot from the Oxford of Newman and Keble, set to work to stir up his parishioners, and eleven-year-old Charlotte, like others, felt the change bracing after the discourses of the sluggish old curate. Hardly a day passed without Mr Bigg-Wither's dropping in for a talk on parish matters, until he came to be viewed as a settled institution.

Having seen Church and State thus well represented on the Yonge's visiting list, and Charlotte herself well advanced from childhood into 'young-ladyhood,' we should perhaps study a little the background against which was to be set the life of this Victorian author and the influences which were to be the most formative in her character. The two elements in the English social structure being the State and the Church, we will make use of this division, though in the reverse order to Charlotte herself, who would undoubtedly have clung to the time-honoured phrase, "For Church and State."

BOOK TWO

THE VICTORIAN SOCIAL SCENE

CHAPTER III

THE RICH

In the days of Miss Yonge's youth those engaged in trade were still barred out by a high fence from the select enclosure inside which members of the aristocracy and professions were privileged to move, and it was only the magic key of a substantial fortune that unlocked the jealously guarded gates. Miss Yonge saw the inhabitants of Manchester and Birmingham only through the chinks of the fence, but among the beings of her own world she went her quiet way, taking careful note of their habits and ways of speech. This world had its own smaller divisions, and of these Charlotte Yonge undoubtedly saw in the most exact focus the clergy and squirarchy, the circles in which the Yonge family itself moved.

Though content with her own station, Charlotte, especially in her young days, was not proof against the allurements of high-sounding titles, and probably sympathized with the aspirations, expressed by one of her characters, to marry the younger son of a marquis for his pretty title. For marquises she certainly had a penchant, three of her favourite aristocratic families being those of the Marquises of Liddesdale, Rotherwood, and de la Poer. Though she constantly refers to such things as the aristocratic features and pallor of the de la Poer brothers, Miss Yonge does not succeed in making high society live for us as does Trollope in the novels centring round Plantagenet Palliser and Lady Glencora, later Duke and Duchess of Omnium. These are living and real human beings, and yet we are conscious that they breathe a more rarefied air than lesser mortals. Miss Yonge's aristocrats too have individuality, but she shows them to us rather in the capacity of squire to their country estates than as denizens of the larger world of politics and London Society. It is significant that we see the much-loved Cousin Rotherwood through the eyes of the Mohuns, whose social position resembles that of the Yonges themselves. The author very wisely does not venture into regions so elevated that they are known to her only from hearsay. The Mohun sisters have a feeling that Rotherwood's Marchioness, although full of politeness "from the teeth outwards" to her husband's cousins, comes from a different sphere. The fact that her Christian name is Victoria would perhaps lead us to infer that this sphere was one in which moved those intimate with royalty. We never see her, however, other than as she appeared to the Mohuns and Merrifields.

It is clear that Miss Yonge would tolerate only such aristocrats as lived up to the maxim *noblesse oblige*. A typical Victorian, she is scornful of those nobles who retain the eighteenth-century attitude of accepting the right to gratify their personal whims without the corresponding obligation of service to the community.

The arch-exponent of the eighteenth-century view is the wicked Mrs Nesbit in *Heartsease*, whose sole object in life has been to marry her niece to a title (though, surprisingly enough, she herself was content with a newly created "trumpery Irish" barony), and to mould her and her pliable husband, Lord Martindale, into the urbane pattern fashionable in the Age of Reason. With her West Indian hoards she provided the magnificent setting necessary to her endeavour, using her own talent for witty talk and Lady Martindale's beauty and accomplishments to gain admission into the most exclusive circles. The horizon of the Martindale family in its heyday was not bounded by the coasts of Britain. Mrs Nesbit, when talking to Theodora of the past, speaks as if they did not travel as tourists, but had the *entrée* of aristocratic houses in Continental capitals. (It was so as not to be balked of the performance of a "celebrated improvisatrice" at the house of a certain Prince K. at Vienna that Mrs Nesbit had purposely withheld from Lady Martindale until the next day the news of the death of one of her babies.) All this has a distinct flavour of the eighteenth century, when aristocrats in all European countries felt themselves to be members of the same international order. Mrs Nesbit's animosity is perhaps greatest against her great-nephew John, who exaggerated such nineteenth-century tendencies as extreme religiosity and a desire for self-abnegation in the service of others. When Mrs Nesbit and the mansion that typified her power over the Martindales had both been destroyed by a great conflagration, the atmosphere she had striven to produce vanished overnight. Lord Martindale became the honest country squire for which nature had intended him, and Lady Martindale, who, when repressed by her aunt had carried with her an atmosphere of formality wherever she went, blossomed out into quite a foolishly fond grandmother, and took to parishing instead of accomplishments.

In the case of Lord St Erme, in the same book, we can watch him growing in Miss Yonge's favour in proportion as he wakes up to his responsibilities. He too began life with the pre-Revolutionary *grand seigneur's* conception of what life owed to a man of noble blood. Being a poet of carefully cherished susceptibilities, he regarded his estate on the fringe of the Lake District as an Ultima Thule of barbarism, merely useful as the milch-cow which should sustain him in his elegant way of life among Continental *cognoscenti*. When Violet Martindale tried to make him see the fineness of the Lakeland scenery he could only remark, "To me, a fine landscape without associations has no soul. It is like an unintellectual beauty." If the Renaissance produced the Italianate Englishman, and a cultured man of the eighteenth century tended to acquire French polish, Germany was the land to which those steeped in the sentimental culture of the mid-nineteenth century were wafted "auf Flügeln des Gesanges." When he first comes on the scene, Lord St Erme reminded the Philistine Arthur Martindale of a German music-master: "Keeps his hair parted in the middle, hanging down in long lank rats' tails, meant to curl, moustache ditto, open collar turned down, black ribbon tie." Even the more cosmopolitan John thought it "too much to study the picturesque in one's own person in England." For St Erme Theodora is a "hoch beseeltes Mädchen," who inspires his "Heldensängergeist," and his idea of a proposal is through the medium of romantic German verse.

Miss Yonge evidently conceded to the aristocracy the right to be patrons of art only so long as their means were sufficient not to allow church- or school-building to suffer at the expense of a well-stocked gallery. She therefore makes Lord St Erme sell all his acquisitions, with the exception of the Ghirlandaio Madonna so much admired by Violet, as soon as he realizes that the money spent on them should have been used to improve the spiritual and mental state of his tenantry. That Charlotte fully appreciated St Erme's sacrifice is shown by her assumption that the stately homes of England could not be complete without "a preserve of statues," as Arthur expressed it, when amused at Violet's naïve surprise on recognizing *The Dying Gladiator*. "Just like the one at Wrangerton!" Again, when Countess Kate expressed a desire to see real statues, Lord Ernest could promise her an abundance in the gallery at Repworth, his father's country estate, which was a fine place for playing in on wet days. An aristocrat was in Miss Yonge's eyes a more discerning judge of art than one of the newly rich. It was a business magnate from the North who nibbled at Edgar Underwood's terrible pre-Raphaelite daub, though even he drew back from the purchase, while Lady Liddesdale and Lord de Vigny were the patrons of the more tasteful Geraldine.

Church-building or 'improving,' that constantly recurring motive in Miss Yonge's novels, was not the prerogative of any class, but it was no doubt a reflection of the Victorian distribution of wealth that it was for the most part members of aristocratic families who had means at their disposal to carry out really grandiose schemes. Lord Herbert Somerville's fortune was sufficient during his lifetime to build district churches and pay several curates in his neglected parish, and after his death to build and endow a convent, which later was able to extend its activities to founding daughter houses even as far afield as Australia. Where the small squire, such as Felix Underwood, was able by dint of self-denial to create a model country parish, the big land-owning nobleman could set up as the benefactor of a large town. Lord Rotherwood owned a considerable part of the seaside town of Rockquay, and, though he did not live on his estate there, felt it his duty to spend a large sum of money in building a second church for the expanding population. Nor was he forgetful of his civic duties, for, several years afterwards, we hear of his endowing a park as a thank-offering for his escape from serious injury when he had an accident caused by falling rocks.

In the nature of things, mention is sometimes made of a peer's attendance at the House of Lords. Miss Yonge very wisely, however, did not venture where her feminine stock-in-trade would have been inadequate, and we get from her no accounts of what went on inside either House, such as flowed so vividly from Trollope's pen. Lord Ormersfield is the most fully drawn of all her political figures, but even in his case there is no indication what office he has held: he might have been anything from Foreign Secretary to Chancellor of the Exchequer, from all we learn from his conversation. We are merely told that he had been marked as a rising young politician in the days when he sat in the Lower House, and had subsequently attained to office. The nearest approach to anything political is the occasion when Fitzjocelyn, fired by some talk of his father's about the police, wrote a paper on historical parallels to Peel's innovation, then still fairly recent. It is, however, possible to infer from Miss Yonge's attitude to Lord Ormersfield that she did not care for the professional politician. She contrasts with some asperity his uneasy geniality towards the lower classes, cultivated for electioneering purposes, with his son's spontaneity, which came from a genuine interest in their concerns and made him really beloved. If fate took a man into the House of Lords, he would undoubtedly best gain Miss Yonge's approval by devoting himself to the furtherance of philanthropic legislation. She is obviously in complete sympathy with the Martindales, when they are pleased to read a speech Lord St Erme has made condemning the conditions under which children worked in the mines. This is the first hint of the eloquent expression of political idealism which, fifteen years later, was so to fire the imagination of Helen Martindale as to dispose her at eighteen to fall in love with Lord St Erme, then more than forty years old (*Last Heartsease Leaves*).

Although Miss Yonge was chiefly preoccupied with the rural activities of the aristocracy, she implies enough about their wider interests to show that, on the whole, her impression of the species was a favourable one. This would hardly strike her contemporary English readers, but, as we shall see, she had a large Continental public. To them the fusion of classes and accessibility of the upper ten thousand, which had developed slowly as the British social structure matured, would appear in striking contrast to the state of affairs prevalent in most countries on the Continent. In many European novels of Miss Yonge's period the educated *bourgeoisie* appear to regard scorn of the aristocracy almost as a law of nature, and are constantly giving vent to their spleen in words such as these:

> A nobleman is only polite and nice to a man of the middle classes as long as he is alone with him; if several persons of noble family are present they flow together like quicksilver. . . . I know the aristocrats and hate the aristocrats.[1]

One wonders whether a thoughtful foreigner, nurtured on such literature, would be able to see how much healthier was a society in which noblemen combined with the middle classes in carrying out the many public duties they felt to be incumbent on them.

The class designated as the 'squirarchy' covered many gradations, ranging from the large landowner, whose interests and habits were almost identical with those of the aristocracy, down to the small squire, such as Captain Merrifield, who was hard put to it to clothe and educate his brood of children in a manner befitting their station. The county families which spent the season in London and whose menfolk were frequently Members of Parliament were generally on the same side of a dividing line as the aristocracy, while the sober country squires who remained year in, year out, on their estates formed the lower division. Many of the London-going families appear to have some connexion by marriage, near or remote, with the aristocracy, which brought them within the pale of London society, in those days still so restricted. The smaller Parliament of early Victorian times, again, tended to lessen the gap between the man of title and the commoner, since it was apparently almost inevitable that the eldest son of a peer should serve an apprenticeship in the Lower House, before he stepped into his father's shoes in the Upper. Even the delicate John Martindale had had his years in Parliament, and Lord Fitzjocelyn never questioned the desirability of leaving for several months in the year the agricultural and philanthropic schemes that lay nearest his heart and devoting his energies to what he once termed a "treadmill."

---

[1] Spielhagen, *Problematische Naturen* (1874): "Der Adelige ist nur höflich und liebenswürdig gegen den Bürgerlichen, so lange er mit ihm allein ist; sind mehrere Adelige bei einander, so fliessen sie zusammen wie Quecksilber. . . . Ich kenne die Adeligen und hasse die Adeligen."

Miss Yonge's Members of Parliament are either men of idealistic outlook, like Lord St Erme or Louis Fitzjocelyn, or solid back benchers, of types varying from George Rivers to Raymond Poynsett. Dutiful to her father's precepts, she viewed allegiance to the Tory party as only second in importance to membership of the Church of England. There is in her novels no full-length portrait of a Radical politician. Such beings are only mentioned as dragons to be fought by true-blue knights in the electioneering fray. Even a dolt like George Rivers (of *The Daisy Chain*) was better in her eyes than a man who was capable of voting for "godless education," the one political question she ever touched on with any warmth. Not that she entirely approved of George's candidature, for it was part and parcel of Flora's unworthy social ambitions. Her share in his political career, from the moment when, hardly recovered from her confinement, she is more animated over the composition of his electioneering speech than in showing off her baby, up to the time when her London mornings are filled with studying "all the debates till George finds out what he has heard in the House," is represented, just as much as her social activities, as causing the neglect of her baby that led to its death. George's continuance in Parliament, as a puppet dancing to the wires pulled by Flora off-stage, is, indeed, part of the heavy punishment meted out to Flora by Miss Yonge. Ethel and Flora argue the matter out, when the latter is repenting of her previous way of life:

> "I don't think his [Dr May's] interest would bring in any sound man but his son-in-law; and George himself seems to like parliamentary life better than anything else."
> "Yes," said Flora hesitatingly; for she knew it was true—he liked to think himself important, and it gave him something to think of, and regular occupation—not too active or onerous; but she could not tell Ethel what she herself felt; that all she could do for him could not prevent him from being held cheap by the men among whom she had placed him.
> "Then," said Ethel, as she heard her affirmative, "I don't think it for his dignity to put him into Parliament to please you, and then to take him out to please you."

This motive of bringing in a "sound man" is almost the only one instanced by Miss Yonge as a reason for standing for Parliament. In *The Three Brides*, indeed, politics was more or less a profession for which Raymond Charnock Poynsett's mother had trained him from his earliest youth, making him read "history, volumes upon volumes." On his death his right-minded county neighbours hasten to secure the candidature of the sailor brother, Captain Charnock, so as to keep out some undesirable man. He talks the matter over with his young wife, whose Evangelical views give her a great dislike of gay society:

> "I've only till to-morrow to decide whether I am to be Member for Wil'sbro'."
>
> "Is that a duty?"
>
> "Not so much a duty as to bind me if it were altogether repugnant to you. I was not brought up for it, and may be a mere stopgap, but it is every man's duty to come to the front when he is called for, and do his utmost for his country in Parliament, I suppose, as much as in action. . . . But remember," he added, "there is much that can't be shirked. I don't mean currying popularity, but if one is in that position there's no shutting oneself up. It becomes a duty to keep society going, and give it the sort of tone that a nice woman can do."

Miss Yonge herself was inclined to share the puritanical Anne's dislike of London society, though not on the same grounds. She never questions that the social round was a necessary part of English life, but her favourite characters delight in sitting loose to it. Meta Rivers was obviously doing the right thing when she returned to her father at the Grange instead of remaining in London for the drawing-room, even though she had enjoyed the more serious diversions, such as concerts and plays. No really admirable heroine is allowed to become the belle of a London season, as if Miss Yonge feared that a certain amount of the scheming or flirtation, so repugnant to her taste, would be needed to achieve such a position. Marian Arundel, in *The Two Guardians*, behaves as haughtily as a marble statue to the friends of her worldly relations, the Lyddells, though she has enough snobbery in her to enjoy the more élite circles to which she is introduced by her cousin Selina, Lady Marchmont. The snobbish vulgarity of the Lyddells is delightfully brought out when they insist on Marian's showing to all their visitors one of the keepsakes, fashionable in the eighteen-forties, entitled *The Wreath of Beauty* and resplendent in blue watered silk binding, richly embossed, in which is to be found a simpering engrav-

CHARLOTTE M. YONGE IN THE GARDEN AT PUSLINCH

By courtesy of John Yonge, Esq.

ENCÆNIA AT OXFORD, 1834

The commemoration of the Duke of Wellington's Installation as Chancellor of the University.

See p. 58

ing of Selina, accompanied by sentimental verses. The perfect Violet (*Heartsease*), again, whose beauty was supposed to be so transcendent, cares only to adorn herself for the approval of her husband, and serves to throw into relief the flirtatious ways of Theodora, who favours a different lover every evening. In *Hopes and Fears* the doings of Lucilla Sandbrook are such that the chastening of many years of governessing are needed before she can emerge with a clean bill of spiritual health.

Although London was a necessary feature in the annual programme of the aristocracy and higher squirarchy, Miss Yonge was always happiest when she could send them back to the satisfying round of the country duties and gaieties she knew so well. The chief preoccupation of the country gentleman, be he nobleman, squire, or even clergyman, was agriculture. Charlotte had her memories of the never-failing topic of conversation between her father and his neighbours to draw on, when she depicted Lord Martindale's alacrity in going off with Lord St Erme to show him "the best shop to go to for agricultural implements," since "country gentlemen are happier in agricultural implement shops than anywhere else."

> Speed the plough! Farming is a happy sedative for English noblemen of the nineteenth century, thought Theodora as she heard them discussing subsoil and rocks and thought of the poet turned high farmer and forgetting even love and embarrassment.

She was quite pleased, however, to find that St Erme had still enough of the poet in him to be unwilling to "blow up the rocks and deface nature." The scenes in which Charlotte Yonge describes the trivial incidents in the life of her country squires are among the most vivid in her novels. We gain an impression of a hardy race, early to bed and early to rise, out and about regardless of wind and weather. Their outlook is often restricted, though there is generally some member of the family who has adopted one of the learned professions, and thus keeps them to some extent in touch with cultural developments, while they all have the solid foundation to a good classical education; but from this restricted outlook comes the strength of those whose judgment is not clouded by acute awareness of both sides of a question. Humfrey Charlecote, in *Hopes and Fears*, was obviously intended to embody Miss

D

Yonge's view of the ideal country squire. He is clearly the spokes-man for the landowning class as a whole, when he is preparing Honora to succeed him as owner of the Holt:

> "It may seem but a bit of earth after all, but the owner of a property has a duty to let it do its share in producing food, or maybe in not lessening the number of pleasant things here below. I mean it is as much my office to keep my trees and woods fair to look at, as it is not to let my land lie waste. . . ."
>
> "I did not suspect you of the poetical view, Humfrey," she said.
>
> "It is plain sense, I think," he said, "that to grub up a fine tree, or a pretty bit of copse without fair reason, only out of eagerness for gain, is a bit of selfishness. But mind, Honor, you must not go and be romantic. You *must* have the timber marked when the trees are injuring each other."

Nowhere is the atmosphere of life on a country estate better presented to us than in the scene in which we first meet Humfrey. It is 6.30 on a misty autumn morning, when Honora meets Humfrey and all his dogs in a garden, bright with asters, its smooth lawn silver with dew—"A sweet day for getting up the roots." When Humfrey had provided Honora with clogs to cover her London boots, they set out to survey his fields and to assess the "improvements" (sash windows instead of casements) made by one of the tenants to his farmhouse, and one is glad to find the practical Humfrey nearly as much disgusted at such defacing of a Tudor building as the sensitive Honora. Their talk alternates between remarks on farming and comments on field, wood, and flower, interrupted by a breathless historical narrative from Honora. A stubble field evokes the typical observation from Humfrey:

> Red wheat, the finest we ever had on this land . . . and the colour perfectly beautiful before harvest; it used to put me in mind of your hair. A load to the acre; a fair specimen of the effect of drainage.

(It is such remarks as the bathos of the conclusion that prevents Honora from realizing that Humfrey loves her with as romantic a devotion as the more picturesque young clergyman who has jilted her.) Nothing is too trivial to claim Humfrey's attention, and he is as ready to roar good advice into the ear of a deaf old cowman, whose "old woman" cannot cope with a refractory smoking chimney, as to deal with the higher policies of estate management.

The agricultural pursuits of the country gentleman were pleasantly varied by the county business that fell to his share. His work as a magistrate gave him an agreeable outlet for his energies and a chance of intercourse with his neighbours, so that nearly all Miss Yonge's characters who live in the country or small towns become magistrates almost as a matter of course. When Mr Kendal[1] had been roused to the demands of society by the influence of Albinia, his first move was to take his place on the Bench. The immediate incentive was his disgust at the state of unruliness in the small town in which he lived, which was condoned by a certain magistrate, a popularity-monger:

> He had set himself to attack the five public-houses and seven beer-shops in Tibb's Alley, and since his eyes had been opened, it seemed as if the disorders became more flagrant every day. At last he pounced on a misdemeanour which he took care should come before the magistrates, and he was much annoyed to find the case dismissed for want of evidence. . . . All the satisfaction Mr Kendal obtained was being told how much he was wanted on the bench. . . . The consequence was, that Mr Kendal took a magnanimous resolution, ordered a copy of Burn's *Justice*, and at the September Quarter Sessions actually rode over to Hadminster, and took the oaths.

Even though the petty and quarter sessions were an activity beyond the scope of women, Miss Yonge often succeeded in transporting her readers thither. There is the ludicrous scene in which Lord Fitzjocelyn, taken in by a specious tale, champions a young poacher against the respectable landowners of the neighbourhood. Incidentally, Miss Yonge has a certain amount of sympathy for the country squires who regard poaching as a heinous crime, being an infringement of their sporting rights. In spite of the presence of a few magistrates of such calibre as the man who had thwarted Mr Kendal, Charlotte Yonge undoubtedly regarded the right of exercising justice as one of the glories of the British constitution and as a happy factor in developing the character of the English gentleman. She recognized instinctively that the unintellectual man, redeemed by a capacity for dealing sagaciously with practical affairs, was a characteristically English product. It was this gift which Rachel Curtis[2] discovered in

[1] In *The Young Stepmother*. [2] In *The Clever Woman of the Family*.

Mr Grey (an old friend of the family usually held cheap by "the clever woman"), when she saw the clear-headed way in which he exercised his magisterial functions, and she felt deeply humiliated at being treated as a silly girl who has been taken in by a sharper

The life of the country gentleman was a full one. Besides his business as a magistrate he would find himself involved in countless boards and committees. In one of her later and little known novels, *That Stick*, Miss Yonge describes Lord Northmoor, a dull but highly conscientious peer, as so weighed down with the burdens always put upon the willing horse that he actually suffers a breakdown, only to be cured by a spell of foreign travel and baths. In most cases, however, county affairs, varied by farming and sport, made the life of the squire, though to some extent restricted, an existence of pleasant, if quiet, diversity of occupation. Perhaps we see country society, rich and poor, at its happiest at the Horticultural Show, described in *Hopes and Fears* as the great gaiety of the year:

> The day was a county holiday. The delicate orchid and the crowned pine were there, with the hairy gooseberry, the cabbage and potato, and the homely cottage-garden nosegay from many woodland hamlet. The young ladies competed in collections of dried flowers for a prize botany book; and the subscriptions were so arranged that on this festival each poorer member might, with two companions, be provided with a hearty meal; while grandees and farmers had a luncheon tent of their own, and regarded the day as a county picnic.

While the country gentleman, even if one of those less zealous for the good of the community, had his days filled with public and private business, his womenfolk were free to choose whether they would be social butterflies, housewives not looking beyond the home circle for occupation, or parish workers. The heiress was, of course, in a different category from the wife or spinster subject to male members of her family. She was permitted to leave the 'proper sphere' of woman sufficiently to oversee her estates, with the help of a bailiff. If the latter were incompetent however, his unfortunate mistress was likely to encounter difficulties. Honora Charlecote had chosen for her long absence on the Continent the moment when her old steward was almost past work, and on her return was faced with farming accounts in chaotic state. Her female intelligence was quite incapable of unravelling them, and it required the masculine mind of Humrey Randolf to reduce them to order. Countess Kate, again, had her whole time taken up with the care of her estate and poor people, until, on her marriage to Lord Ernest de la Poer, she made over part of her duties to him with a sigh of relief. She could then, even though a countess in her own right, cease being an heiress and become a mere wife and mother.

We have already seen that women of the upper classes were, at any rate during the first half of the nineteenth century, great Sunday-school teachers. Before the days of the Education Act most of them were little less keen on the secular aspects of education, though the more pious were apt to look on reading rather as the key to the Bible and the Prayer Book than as a useful accomplishment. It would be interesting to come on a record of the feelings of a schoolmistress patronized by one of the more erratic of the fine ladies indulging in this hobby. A modern educationist would shudder at a curriculum overshadowed by daily visits at the school paid by the young ladies from the big House or the Parsonage, as long as they were at home or had nothing better to do, while no sooner was their back turned than there was a complete switch-over to such work as the mistress, often only half educated herself, could manage single-handed. One wonders how much the children, so distant from the village that Theodora Martindale had undertaken to teach them at the House, remembered of her instructions when she returned to them after a season in London, followed by a long stay at Baden-Baden. Worse than irregularity, however, was the unfortunate propensity of some fine ladies to show off their pattern school to visitors. When Lucilla Sandbrook takes pride in displaying the beauty and lovely voice of Edna Murrell, the schoolmistress in her father's old parish, to Honora and the Fulmorts, she thinks nothing of upsetting the whole day's routine to make Edna and the children sing, and they do this as if accustomed to being thus made a show of. (It certainly served Lucilla right, when her brother, Owen, made a clandestine marriage with Edna.)

The other great parochial activity of the charitable lady was cottage-visiting. Miss Yonge did not, luckily, regard this merely as an opportunity for pious talk. In fact, it is her less approved characters who follow this practice, so dear to the Evangelical school of Victorian fiction. The really nice parish visitor is much

more likely to offer puddings than piety. It is a very real episode
in *Scenes and Characters* when Lilias Mohun drags her twelve
year-old brother, the only available male escort, through muddy
fields so that a poor old couple in a distant cottage shall not miss
their Christmas donation of soup, and arrives home so bedraggled
that it needs the united efforts of her sisters to make her present-
able in time for the dinner-party they are giving that evening.
Similarly one feels a hint of personal reminiscence in the em-
barrassment felt by the heroine of *Henrietta's Wish* on the first
occasion when she is left alone on a visit to a cottage and has to
talk to a deaf old man and his daughter-in-law:

> A weary waiting time she found it, shy as she was of poor people
> as of a class with whom she was utterly unacquainted, feeling bound
> to make herself agreeable but completely ignorant how to set
> about it.

She tries to recollect what a young lady in a story would say,
begins by hoping that the old man does not suffer from rheumatism, answers inquiries from the daughter-in-law about every-
one at the Hall, comments on the comfortable appearance of the
open hearth and is told that it smokes, is reduced to admiring
the elaborately worked sampler that hangs on the wall, and is
greatly relieved when her grandfather appears to take her away.
Country ladies did not always confine their charitable works to
their own parishes, but often indulged in benevolent enterprise
offering pleasant opportunities for intercourse with their neighbours. The perfect outlet for the Victorian lady, whose yearly
output of fancy-work was tremendous, was the sale of work.
These functions are constantly mentioned by Miss Yonge,
though some of her sterner philanthropists, such as Ethel May
and the Underwoods, thought that money should be freely given
in a good cause, and that such a means of raising it was mere
pandering to low motives. A sale of work was a social occasion for
all the ladies of a neighbourhood, from the poor gentlewoman
who made antimacassars up to the grand 'lady patroness.' Such
a one was a necessary adjunct to any charitable enterprise, and
was usually one of the titled, or the 'Member's lady.' One of the
few bright aspects, in the eyes of Rachel Curtis, of the worldly
marriage of Bessie to Lord Keith was that she would acquire an
imposing title to grace the list of patronesses of Rachel's pet

charity. Flora Rivers, when exultant at her husband's election to Parliament, thoroughly upsets the sensitive Miss Bracy by her offers to canvass for the admission of the latter's sisters to orphanages; the fact that she is now qualified to act the part of lady patroness obviously fills her with a delicious sense of power. By such works of charity did the Victorian lady seek to fill an existence which, unless circumstances were unusually favourable, might well have become tedious.

As we have seen, one of the most marked and salutary characteristics differentiating English nineteenth-century Society from that of most Continental countries at the same period was the fluidity of the landowning and professional classes. There could be no better example of this portent than that typical English figure 'the squarson.' The Yonge family produced squarsons, and Charlotte had no objection to the species, unless a greedy desire to add ecclesiastical to lay revenues took the place of a true vocation in urging a man to seek Holy Orders. It is this sin which poisons the existence of old Fulbert Underwood in *The Pillars of the House*. Having banished, on trumped-up excuses, his clergyman cousin who should have had the family living, Fulbert bribed his unwilling son to ordination by consenting to an unsuitable marriage with a farmer's daughter. Young Fulbert led the life of a fox-hunting parson, until cut off in his mid-thirties as the result of his dissipations. On his own deathbed the repentant father advises his heir never to drive a son into the Church.

Miss Yonge appears to accept the family living as a natural provision for a younger son with little more questioning than Miss Austen's Edmund Bertram himself. (One feels that Edmund and Fanny are not far from being one of Miss Yonge's ideal clerical couples.) She is apparently willing to admit that an honest endeavour to mould oneself to the required pattern may sometimes produce as good results in the long run as a true vocation. By the time we meet Maurice Ferrars in *The Young Stepmother* he is in every respect the model parish priest and wise guide of his family in all matters, spiritual and mundane. But:

> He had not embraced his profession entirely by choice. It had always been understood that one of the younger branches must take the family living; and as Fred had spurned study, he had been bred up to consider it as his fate, and if he had ever had other wishes, he had entirely accepted his destiny, and sincerely turned

to his vocation. The knowledge that he must be a clergyman had ruled and formed him from his youth. Yet, even up to a year or two after his Ordination, there had been a sense of sacrifice; he loved sporting, and even balls, and it had been an effort to renounce them. He had avoided coming to London because his keen enjoyment of society tended to make him discontented with his narrow sphere. . . . And now how entirely had all this passed away. . . . Without being aware of it, he had ceased to distrust a holiday. . . . And his animation and mirth were the more free, because self-regulation was so thoroughly established.

The existence of the man who held a good family living does, indeed, seem to those used to the fierce battle for lucrative work of our days most agreeable. Miss Yonge's novels abound in such clergy. They carry out their clerical duties in an ultra-conscientious manner, as we have observed, but there seems to be ample time in their life for dinner-parties, garden-parties, and any other social activities that appeal to them, though they often manage to plead stress of parish obligations if invited by people they do not care for. Their sons are educated as a matter of course at public schools, while their daughters acquire all the accomplishments suitable to their station.

Although Miss Yonge put many of her characters into a family living she esteemed even more highly the man who abjured his rights to it. We have already seen how far was Lord Herbert Somerville from taking his aristocratic birth as a right to ecclesiastical plums. In *The Three Brides* we watch the development of Herbert Bowater, who has been brought up by his father, a jovial squire, to take the family living. Herbert, though never really neglecting the small demands of his easy curacy, is too much given to cricket, Society, and very mild flirtation to leave time for his theological studies. After his consequent failure in his priest's examination and a fever that brings him to death's door he moves to a curacy in a mining district, prevailing on his father to offer the living to Herbert's correct and hard-working fellow-curate.

Prominent as the clergy are in Miss Yonge's works, she gives us no such comprehensive picture of the hierarchy as Trollope does in the Barsetshire novels. Bishops and archdeacons, other than missionary ones, are shadowy figures in the background. The only member of the cathedral clergy we learn to know intimately

s Mr Harewood, who fulfils his duties as librarian in a scholarly
and retiring manner, and seems far removed even from the
decorous social life of the Close in the medieval nook, known as
he Bailey, where he and his happy-go-lucky family have their
quarters.

Such of Miss Yonge's clergy as are not the privileged incum-
bents of family livings exist, for the most part, in comfortable
circumstances rather than affluence. If we remember that the
value of many livings has altered little in the last hundred years,
it is obvious that an income which means in these days a struggle
for existence in a large and inconvenient house with the help of
a charwoman would then have provided an adequate amount of
cheap labour, good food, and education for a family. Mr Wardour, Countess Kate's uncle, was so far from wealthy that her
adoption into his family was only made possible by the eldest
son's renunciation of a university career and entering a lawyer's
office. Yet the younger boy has a pony for his daily ride to school,
and the domestic staff is adequate enough to set Mary Wardour
free to teach her little sisters and attend to parish matters.

The only case of really dire poverty among Miss Yonge's clerical
families, described in any detail, are those of the Underwoods and
of Jem Frost (in *Dynevor Terrace*). The latter's troubles are due,
indeed, to his failure as a schoolmaster, and one is inclined to
regard him rather in that capacity than as a cleric. Isabel, Jem's
wife, is actually brought to acting nurse to the children and getting
tea for the family. The Underwoods are, however, the outstanding case of indigent clergy. When we first meet them, they are
served only by the faithful Sibby, so Mrs Underwood and her
daughters have to do many domestic tasks that did not usually
fall to the share of ladies of their period. The worldly Alda felt
very much ashamed when their rich cousin Marilda insisted on
descending into the kitchen regions to watch Wilmet doing the
family ironing. (Good, downright Marilda, who did not take
kindly to the *parvenu* gentility of her mother's circle, envied
Wilmet her practical task.) The Underwoods even suffered from
an insufficient diet, and six-year-old Robina ate chicken for the
first time in her life at the wonderful birthday feast provided by
Mr Audley for Felix. The rigid economy practised by them did
not admit of buying fruit or the hire of a bath-chair for the lame
Geraldine, except on rare occasions. Almost the only indulgence

permitted to her was bread and butter and tea for breakfast, instead of the stirabout wolfed down by the hale and hearty members of the family. Miss Yonge draws a very wholesome moral for a snobbish age from the vicissitudes of the Underwoods. She is constantly pointing out that there is nothing degrading in their poverty, and allows none of them but Alda to have any false shame about it. The latter is intensely mortified by the spiteful remarks of Lady Price, their vicar's wife, and her daughter; but Miss Yonge makes it quite clear how odious and common the latter are, while Mrs Underwood, in spite of her faded dresses, still keeps the tone of the county society in which she was bred. Mr Underwood, moreover, never allows his cares to crowd out the intellectual interests which raise the tone of his children's minds.

There is not one of Miss Yonge's large families which has not its clergyman member, and they prove almost as fruitful a recruiting ground for the Services. With Mr Yonge and his Army reminiscences always at hand, it is inevitable that the Army should attract the largest number of young officers, but the Navy claimed one of Charlotte's best-loved characters, Harry May, in *The Daisy Chain*. *Chantry House* provides us with a retrospect, taking us back to the Navy of the days just following the Napoleonic wars. At this time, when the Navy was being drastically reduced from a war to a peace footing, it was naturally far from easy to obtain a commission. The fact that Clarence Winslow (named, of course, after William IV) was passed into the Navy with little difficulty by his uncle, an admiral, shows how all-important was influence. The end of his naval career is no less a comment on conditions in the Navy of his day. After a most successful first voyage in a happy ship Clarence finds himself at the mercy of a tyrannical captain and bullying fellow-midshipmen.

Captain Brydone was one of the rough old description of naval men, good sailors and stern disciplinarians, but wanting in any sense of moral duties towards their ship's company. His lieutenant was of the same class, soured, moreover, by tardy promotion, and prejudiced against a gentleman-like, fair-faced lad, understood to have interest, and bearing a name that implied it. Of the other two midshipmen, one was a dull lad of low stamp, the other a youth of twenty, a born bully, with evil as well as tyrannical propensities;—the crew conforming to severe discipline on board, but otherwise wild and lawless.

It is hardly surprising that Clarence was sickened with horror at having to be present at the flogging of seamen, and that his final undoing was the battle of Navarino, when, after having his clothes bespattered with the blood of two sailors killed at his side, the sensitive boy of sixteen was found shuddering in his berth.

Alan Ernescliffe, the betrothed of Margaret May (in *The Daisy Chain*), forms a link between the conditions of these times and those prevailing in the mid-Victorian period. Alan was the son of a distinguished officer who had fought at Trafalgar, and he himself sailed as a midshipman on his first and his father's last voyage, presumably in the latter years of William IV's reign. We are reminded that in those days 'mate' was not a title confined to the Merchant Service, when we hear of Alan's exploits: as mate he had been put in command of a captured slaver, and quelled a mutiny of the crew. Alan is not far removed, in fact, from the setting of some of Captain Marryat's thrilling tales. Ethel May, when discussing the hopes of an engagement between the impecunious Alan and her sister, Margaret, thinks it still in the realm of possibilities to amass a fortune by means of prize money: 'Look here—it would all be very easy; she should stay with us, . . and he go to sea, and get lots of prize-money.''

With Harry May we are approaching more modern times. He is not cast straight from home into the midshipmen's berth, but is sent at twelve years of age to a naval school at Portsmouth. All the same, it is a very youthful Harry who embarks on his first voyage under Alan's tutelage, to experience before he was eighteen an escape from a burning ship and a sojourn on one of the South Sea Islands, tending the dying Alan. The Navy was still no place for any but the tough of fibre. We do not hear, round about the year 1850, of Harry's passing any examination before being appointed to a ship, but things have changed by the time Sam Merrifield,[1] some ten years later, is offered a cadetship. No influence on the part of his father (a naval captain who has gone through the Crimean War), and the latter's friend (an admiral), will absolve Sam from the ordeal, terrifying to one whose brain was the reverse of academic, of answering questions in mathematics and other useful subjects. Poor Sam for days follows his sisters' governess round with his Euclid in his hand,

[1] In *The Stokesley Secret*.

but his perseverance is rewarded, and we last hear of him (in *Modern Broods*) as a captain, very worthy but restricted in outlook.

The last sketch in Miss Yonge's naval portrait gallery is that of Ernley Armytage, who marries Gillian Merrifield. He forms a contrast to her narrow-minded cousin Sam, for Sam could never be imagined admiring a girl with aspirations to a university career and embarks on matrimony somewhat grudgingly. Armytage is a man of easy geniality and adventurous disposition, ready for all experiences, as he shows when in *Strolling Players* he spends his leave on tour with an amateur theatrical troupe. These aberrations do not, however, prevent him from being a distinguished officer, decorated during the fighting in Egypt. We feel that, with his multiplicity of interests, Captain Armytage is one of a new generation, far removed from the somewhat grim days of the sailing-ship.

Knowing Miss Yonge's remarkable memory for conversations, one must assume that the talk of her naval characters is to some extent based on fact. Their conversation is larded with the metaphors of their profession, such as "making all shipshape" and "don't lug off my figurehead," though it must be remarked that Harry May is much fonder of this kind of talk when an aspirant naval officer than after he has become the real thing. Miss Yonge is, indeed, not the only author to put such expressions into the mouth of the Navy, for Miss Austen makes Admiral Croft say, "I wish Frederick would spread a little more canvas, and bring us home one of these young ladies to Kellynch." It is noticeable, on the other hand, that Miss Yonge's Army characters have no such jargon of their own. While the naval man by the exercise of his profession remained cut off, sometimes for a period running into years, from society, the Army officer, except when on active service, played his part in ordinary intercourse to a degree that varied according to his regiment and the place where it was stationed.

Miss Yonge generally gave a fictitious name to the regiments of her soldiers, but for her, as for other writers, a Guardsman was a Guardsman, whose glamour or eligibility was not to be masked under a paltry pseudonym. It must not be supposed, of course, that Charlotte dealt in the same species as that made famous by Ouida, for hers are comparatively sober specimens. We have the most detailed account of the life of Arthur Martindale in *Heartsease*. It leaves us with the impression that Arthur's life consisted of long periods of leave, interspersed with short spells of duty, which could usually be arranged so as not to clash with any tempting social activity, such as the Derby or a fishing holiday. During the season Arthur was apparently free to accompany Violet into Society on most evenings. The only occasion on which we hear of him in uniform was after Violet's confinement, when "she gloried in being carried to her sofa by so grand and soldierly a figure, and uttered her choicest sentence of satisfaction—'It is like a story!' while his epaulette was scratching her cheek." A commission in the Guards was certainly a luxury rather than a means of subsistence. When Arthur is hopefully discussing the allowance he can expect after his marriage, he thinks his father cannot possibly give him less than £1000 and a house, while he does not see why it should not be £1500, or even £2000. On receiving £1200 and the rent of a house in Belgravia, he considers himself very pinched for money, being a young man of extravagant habits. (When the idea had been mooted of living in the country, he had declared that he could not manage on less than £2500.) As Arthur's family increased, Lord Martindale purchased for him fresh steps in rank, so that in the course of five years he advanced from captain to colonel.

Besides being the natural environment for the son of a nobleman, the Guards was also apparently a good social jumping-off ground for the newly rich. When Ferdinand Travis (*The Pillars of the House*) is explaining to Mr Audley his father's reasons for wishing to put him into the Life Guards, he says:

"You see he is bent on my being an English gentleman. . . . He knows a man with a son in the Life Guards, who has persuaded him that it is the thing, and I don't greatly care."

"Is he prepared for the expensiveness?"

"I fancy it is the recommendation," said Ferdinand, smiling with a little shame.

Apart from her Guards officers, Miss Yonge's Army men seem able, more or less, to live on their pay. This was not always easy, as Alick Keith (*The Clever Woman of the Family*) points out to his gay sister when he urges her not to persuade the officers of her father's old regiment into giving a ball, on the grounds that the expense would fall heavily on most of them. Unless, like Alick, a man had private means, he could not generally think of marriage until he had become a major. Thus Philip Morville, a young man of twenty-three who has just obtained his captaincy, does not dare to ask Laura Edmonstone's parents for her hand, and enters into a clandestine engagement with her (*The Heir of Redclyffe*).

Miss Yonge's pictures of Army life faithfully mirror its developments over the long period covered by them. They begin in the days of commissions obtained by purchase or by nomination, as in the case of Philip, who had got into the Army through the influence of Lord Thorndale, the father of one of his friends. In the novels written after 1870 there are, of course, many comments on entry into the Army by examination. In *The Three Brides* (1876) we note the emergence of a new phenomenon, the Army crammer, named most appropriately Mr Driver. After Mr Driver has successfully got Charles Charnock into Sandhurst, Lord Rathforlane, who will at first not listen to the entreaties of the scholarly Terence for a university career, sends him to the cramming establishment for coaching in mathematics, which Terence so much dislikes that they haunt him when he is delirious with fever. (The importance of mathematics for the Army entrance examination makes one wonder what would have happened to Arthur Martindale, who was incapable even of working out correctly the cost of a ticket to the Lake District, if he had been called on to face such an ordeal.) The arguments against examinations are set forth in *Magnum Bonum* by Mr Ogilvie, when he is talking over with Caroline Brownlow the bullying which her small son Armine has had from his cousin Robin, on refusing to do the latter's French exercises:

> I can't help seeing in that unfortunate boy the victim of examinations for commissions. Boys must be subjected to high pressure before they can thoroughly enter into the importance of the issues that depend upon it; and when a sluggish, dull intellect is forced beyond endurance, there is an absolute instinct of escape, impelling to shifts and underhand ways of eluding work.

To which one is tempted to answer that one doesn't wish to be at the mercy of "sluggish, dull intellects" in times of national stress!

The pros and cons of another development of the latter half of

Victoria's reign are well ventilated in *Beechcroft at Rockstone* with the introduction of the family of Captain White, who had been an officer, raised from the ranks, in General Sir Jasper Merrifield's regiment. Captain White has been dead for a few years, but we see this somewhat conventionalized figure through the eyes of his children and Gillian Merrifield—a man of the lower middle class who has taken to soldiering after a boyish escapade, self-educated, and endowed with the character and good sense which had gained him the esteem of his general. Against these 'pros' must be set the 'cons,' in the shape of his wife, a once beautiful but now slovenly and whining Maltese, married in his non-commissioned days. One feels that the Whites' family life can hardly have been pleasant even before the father's death reduced them to great poverty. The mother's coarse-grained nature must have jarred sadly on the gentle instincts Kalliope has inherited from the father, and which have been fostered by a good education and intercourse with the Merrifield family. All problems are here solved by Mrs White's timely death and the adoption of the children by their father's rich cousin, but in real life the social problems of the former ranker in snobbish Victorian days were acute. Kalliope was a beauty who could triumph over the prejudices against her origin, but we hear of a much more typical example when Rosamund Charnock, in *The Three Brides*, describes the sad case of a daughter of a former sergeant coming to the regimental ball dressed in colours enough to set anyone's teeth on edge. No one deigns to notice her, until Julius Charnock and Lord Rathforlane take pity on her and ask her to dance.

One point that strikes us forcibly about the Army in the days before the Crimean War had drawn people's attention to the appalling condition of the medical service is the fact that a man could buy a commission whatever his physique. Arthur Martindale, even when well, shows signs of the delicacy of lung which nearly kills him, and, when partially recovered from his desperate illness, he contemplates retaining his commission, although the doctor has warned him against living in London. Again, Gilbert Kendal, in *The Young Stepmother*, has always been a delicate youth, but there is no hesitation about sending him out to the Crimea. It is no wonder that a comparatively innocuous wound is enough to demolish him.

The twentieth-century intellectual, when not actually a pacifist, is inclined to look on war as an evil necessity forced upon the world by those of more barbarous mould, and on the Army as a corollary to be accepted without enthusiasm. Those of us who have grown up since 1918 are constantly struck by the very opposite sentiments voiced by Miss Yonge's characters. She herself was surely expressing the gospel preached by her father, when, speaking of Albinia Kendal, she refers to "one of the professions which she thought alone worthy of man's attention, the clerical and the military." Even "the clever woman," on the delightful occasion when, all unconscious, she lectured Alick on the exploit which had gained him the V.C., in attempting to prove the difference between heroism and pugnacity, can say quite indignantly, on being accused of pacifism, "I think war the great purifier and ennobler of nations, when it is for a good and great cause." Rachel, laying claim to strength of mind, pours scorn on a sentimental attitude, but other characters are more typical of their period in their romantic view of the soldier. Jane and Adeline Mohun, in general no sentimentalists, appear to regard their brother-in-law, Sir Jasper Merrifield, who had won great honour in the Crimea, somewhat as the hero of an Arthurian legend, and the fulfilment of all the glamorous visions of their sister's youthful days. This view persisted for another generation, for in *Magnum Bonum* (1879) Sydney Evelyn can look coldly on her admirer when, on his mother's losing her fortune, he contemplates leaving the Army and taking to doctoring:

> But oh, Lucas, let it be any sacrifice but that of your sword! Think how we should all feel if there was a great, glorious war, and you only a poor creature of a civilian, instead of getting lots of medals and Victoria Crosses and knighthood—real knighthood.

The Militia too could be looked at through a haze of Victorian sentiment, though it is worthy of note that the elders of a family do not share the romantic view of the young ones. In *Dynevor Terrace* Louis Fitzjocelyn can say in all seriousness in the year 1847, when subterranean growlings were making themselves heard all over Europe:

> "It is a time when a display of loyalty and national spirit may turn the scale. I am resolved to let no trifle prevent me from doing my part."

"You are quite right," cried Clara. "You ought to take your vassals, like a feudal chief! I am sure the defence of one's country ought to outweigh everything."

"Exactly so. Our volunteer forces are our strength and glory, and are a happy meeting of all classes in the common cause."

After Fitzjocelyn has made his injured ankle worse by riding to the yeomanry exercises, Clara compares "the prostrate figure in blue and silver to all the wounded knights in history or fiction," while his hard-headed father is full of contempt for his foolish exertions:

> He could have better understood a youth being unable to forego the exhibition of a handsome person and dress, than imagine that anyone of moderate sense could either expect the invasion, or use these means of averting it.

In *The Trial* we come to the Volunteer movement of 1860, when Louis Napoleon was thought to have dangerous territorial ambitions. On the night of his return from a voyage, when all the family are assembled to greet him, Harry May remarks:

> "If all I heard at Plymouth is true, we may have work handy at home."
>
> "At home you may say," said his father, "*Dulce est*, etc., is our motto. Didn't you know what a nest of heroes we have here to receive you? Let me introduce you to Captain Ernescliffe, of the Dorset Volunteer Rifle Corps; Private Thomas May, of the Cambridge University Corps; and Mr Aubrey Spencer May, for whom I have found a rifle, and am expected to find a uniform as soon as the wise heads have settled what colour will be most becoming."
>
> "Becoming! No, papa!" indignantly shouted Aubrey: "it is the colour that will be the most invisible in skirmishing."
>
> "Grey, faced with scarlet," said Hector decidedly.
>
> "Yes, that is the colour of the invincible Dorsets," said Dr May. "There you see our great authority with his military instructions in his hand."
>
> "No, sir," replied Hector, "it's not military instructions, it is Crauford's general orders."
>
> "And," added the Doctor, "there's his bride working the colours and Mary wanting to emulate her."

The argument between the enthusiastic young people and the sceptical doctor is clinched by Harry, who says that, even if the

E

enemy ships could emerge from their bases, they would never succeed in giving the British Navy the slip.

When Harry May is discussing with his sister the choice of a career he says:

> I don't know what else to be, Margaret. I should hate to be a doctor—I can't abide sick people; and I couldn't write sermons, so I can't be a clergyman; and I won't be a lawyer, I vow, . . . so there's nothing left but soldiers and sailors, and I mean to be a sailor.

This comprehensive review shows us how limited was the choice of professions open to a youth of gentle birth round about the Victorian half-century.

Having seen how the Church and the Services fare in Miss Yonge's presentation of the life of her day, we must now consider her lawyers and doctors. Law and medicine offered the greatest possible contrasts between the man at the bottom and the man at the top of the tree. Charlotte's intimacy with the Coleridge family kept constantly before her eyes the high rewards awaiting the successful barrister. Although the law courts had such a fascination for her that she constantly transports her readers thither for long spaces of time, she is more chary of describing those whose lives are given to the practice of the law, and the only full-length portrait we have of a barrister is that of Uncle Geoffrey Langford, in *Henrietta's Wish*. He is the son of a small country squire, and his considerable fortune and high position in London society are due entirely to his own exertions. We know, however, of this side of his life from hearsay, and see him only during vacation at his parents' home, where he is recognized as the big man of the family, everything being referred to him, from advice on important business matters to the smallest details of domestic or farm management. He is obviously a man who may go even farther, for his niece and daughter discuss his future, building castles in the air of his being Lord Chancellor, though Beatrice remarks that she will be content with Parliament for the present, since she has "been told too often that high principles don't rise in the world to expect any more."

The law was obviously a refuge for those whom the prejudices of the times barred out from activities which would be open to them to-day. Even as a schoolboy, as we see him in *Scenes and Characters*, Maurice Mohun's whole soul was set on scientific pursuits. When we meet him again as a middle-aged man, however, we hear that his father would not hear of his reading science, so that he had taken to the law as a means of subsistence, which gave him ample leisure for his scientific hobbies. As his sister says:

> But when we were young there was a good deal of mistrust of anything outside the beaten track of gentlemanlike professions, and my dear old father did not like what he heard of the course of study for these lines. Things were not as they are now. So Maurice went to Cambridge, and was fifth wrangler of his year, and then had to go to the bar. It somehow always gave him a thwarted, injured feeling of working against the grain.

The law, even pursued half-heartedly, appears to have provided the wherewithal for life in a solid house in a London square, a maid with leisure to attend to his daughter's toilet, and a German governess to educate her. Maurice Mohun, like many other barristers who have met only with moderate success, was glad when a Government appointment took him out to the Fiji Islands, where his interests were apparently scientific rather than legal.

Charlotte Yonge provides us with slight sketches of nearly every type of solicitor. Well above the line of gentility comes the respectable family lawyer, admitted to social intercourse with his clients. At the nadir of the Underwoods' fortunes their lawyer, Mr Staples, appeared to Felix and Lance to live on quite a grand scale, when he entertained them in his comfortable house with its trim gardens and drove them in his smart gig. The Staples family was quite 'county,' to judge by the guests and the style of their entertainment at the picnic, where Gertrude May so much shocked Felix by going barefoot. One of their daughters was the wife of the local M.P., though he did not meet with Charlotte's complete approval, being only a self-made man and a Radical.

On the whole, however, Miss Yonge does not appear to entertain a very high regard for lawyers, for Mr Staples is the exception rather than the rule. Mr Moss, in *Heartsease*, is a most unpleasant specimen who has feathered his nest at the expense of Lord St Erme, whose agent he is. His would-be genteel son,

Albert, with his unfortunate taste in chenille waistcoats and his toadying ways towards his aristocratic brother-in-law, is even more unpleasing. Every one is surprised that his daughter Violet can be so superior to such relations, though externally her up-bringing in a charming house inside Wrangerton Park seems to have been similar to that of the daughters of any professional man. As Mrs Nesbit spitefully remarks of her match with Arthur, "This would never have happened, if every country attorney did not bring up his daughters to pass for ladies!"

Even more provincial than the Mosses are the Meadows family, in *The Young Stepmother*, the relicts of another country-town attorney. Mrs and Miss Meadows have an outlook bounded by fancy-work (specimens of which adorn every available space in their sitting-room) and local gossip—of their vicar, a man who adored his wife: "I wish he would allow his poor delicate wife more butcher's meat; and I don't think it looks well to see the Vicarage without a man-servant." In retrospect we gather that Mr Meadows was not a man of the highest stamp, while his still extant partner, in his capacity of trustee to Mr Meadows's grandson, is an example of the Victorian slum landlord at his worst. He encouraged the most outrageous overcrowding and the existence of nine low beer-shops in one small lane:

> His whole conscience in the matter is to have a large sum to put into Gilbert's hands when he comes of age. Why, he upholds those dens of iniquity in Tibbs' Alley on that very ground!

Although the medical profession could not aspire to the same pinnacle in Miss Yonge's esteem as the clerical and military, it nevertheless held a secure place in her likings. The hereditary practice, which had been passed down for two hundred years in the Yonge family until it had come to her Uncle James, had the dignity of age, and was obviously the precedent for that of Dr May, which is once described contemptuously as "the throne" by Tom, its unwilling heir. Dr May has a sturdy independence and downright manner, contrasting favourably with the fawning suavity of some of his fashionable colleagues, which often masks their lack of skill in diagnosis. One of the most endearing traits of Dr May is his clinging to old habits and prejudices, though never resenting banter on the subject of his foibles. The fever epidemic in *The Trial* is a case in point. The travelled Dr Spencer holds the modern view on defective sanitation as the cause of disease, but Dr May is quite unwilling to be convinced:

"I've nearly quarrelled with Spencer. Oh! he is in high feather! he will have it that the fever rose up bodily, like Kuhleborn, out of that unhappy drain he is always worrying about, when it is a regular case of scarlet fever, brought in by a girl at home from service; but he *will* have it that his theory is proved." . . . It must be owned that Dr May was not very sensible to what his friend called Stoneborough stinks. The place was fairly healthy, and his "town councillor's conservatism," and hatred of change, as well as the amusement of skirmishing, had always made him the champion of things as they were; and in the present emergency the battle whether the enemy had travelled by infection, or was the product of the Pond Buildings' miasma, was the favourite enlivenment of the disagreeing doctors, in their brief intervals of repose in the stern conflict which they were waging with the fever.

All the same, Dr May aids his old friend in his prime object of cleansing Stoneborough:

Baths and wash-houses were adroitly carried as a monument to Prince Albert; and on the Prince of Wales's marriage, his perseverence actually induced the committee to finish up the drains with all the contributions which were neither eaten up nor fired away! Never had he been more happy and triumphant; and Dr May used to accuse him of perambulating the lower streets snuffing the deodorized air.

One suspects that Dr May would not have accepted antiseptic surgery with alacrity: he was one of those hasty people whose possessions are always anywhere but where they should be, and his consulting-room was so untidy that his precise son Tom was almost ashamed to see patients there.

Since Dr May had inherited a fair patrimony, it is impossible to assess how much of his income was derived from his profession. We are reminded that the Victorian doctor was paid in cash, when we hear of his turning out £50 from his pockets and a drawer in his dressing-room to be sent to the bank; but we do not know how long it had taken him to amass this sum. The May family lived comfortably, though not luxuriously, and there always seemed to be enough to spare for such purposes as a university education for one son or Eton for another. Socially the Mays were the élite of their little town, and could aspire to county society, though, to her mortification, Flora was often forced to decline invitations at a distance, because her father refused to keep a closed carriage, for the characteristic reason that he enjoyed communing with the moon and stars when returning from his rounds in his gig.

Just as Miss Yonge seemed to fear great success in the world of high society for her heroines, she was chary of allowing her favourite doctors to become fashionable practitioners. She draws a most unflattering picture of Sir Matthew Fleet, a contemporary of Dr May, who has pursued his career with hard-headed selfishness until he has achieved knighthood and a considerable reputation as a specialist. When there is a difference of opinion between the fashionable London doctor and one who has been content with a more restricted sphere, she generally allows the latter to be in the right. Thus Sir Matthew's flattering prognostication of Margaret May's recovery proves to be wrong; and some forty years later Tom May, by then a professor, but also keeping on his father's practice, gives a correct diagnosis of heart disease, while the London specialist plays up to the wishes of his clients and scorns Tom's views, which are, however, borne out by the patient's immediate death. Miss Yonge clearly believes in the consultant who, even if he has gone far in his profession, has the workaday background of the general practitioner. Besides Tom May, there is Dr Joseph Brownlow (in *Magnum Bonum*), who holds an appointment as lecturer at a London medical school and at the time of his death is on the verge of a big discovery, yet devotes most of his energies to patients in the Bloomsbury district, then far from fashionable. Some fifteen years after his death Dr Ruthven, one of his former pupils and by that time a physician of some repute in a fashionable quarter of London, has followed up hints gleaned from Dr Brownlow and worked out the discovery. Dr Brownlow's son, Lucas, and his nephew, John, have both just qualified, after gaining all the highest possible awards, and Dr Ruthven wishes to take one of them as his assistant. Miss Yonge is obviously disgusted by his preference for John on account of the latter's engagement to the sister of a viscount. Although John is an estimable young man, she makes it abundantly clear that Lucas has chosen the better part in his renunciation of the lady (Lucas has hidden his love, so that John may woo her) and the fashionable practice in order to make a home for his mother and combine medical research with a hospital appointment.

One of the most noteworthy differences between the medical faculty of Victorian times and that of our own is the inferior status of the 'surgeon' compared with that of 'physician.' This is nowhere better illustrated than by the contrast between the Mays and the Wards. Dr May had studied at Cambridge and Edinburgh, while his son Tom had held an honorary appointment in a Paris hospital after doing brilliantly at Cambridge and London. Henry Ward, on the other hand, had merely 'walked the hospitals,' though this was an advance on his father, who had become a surgeon after a period of apprenticeship. The Mays were, as we have seen, received by the county, but the Wards' social life is restricted to the narrow town society. The difference between the two families is rather one of prestige than of style of living, for the Wards have launched out into a spick-and-span villa, complete with conservatory, and aspire to the giving of dinner parties, which the Mays attend somewhat as a condescension. The refinement and accomplishments of Averil Ward are resented by the town as presumption on the part of her family. Her brother, Henry, is a fine example of acute inferiority complex. His frock-coat and top-hat, the regulation garb of the Victorian doctor, is self-consciously genteel, and he never loses an opportunity for aggressive assertion of his right to equality with the Mays, father and son. Henry's self-sufficiency, indeed, had allowed the fever epidemic to get a firm hold. Dr May says:

"This young lad comes down . . . full of his lectures and his hospitals, and is nettled and displeased to find his father content to have Spencer or me called in the instant anything serious is the matter."

"But you are a physician, Papa," said Mary.

"No matter for that, to Mr Henry I'm an old fogie, and depend upon it, if it were only the giving a dose of salts, he would like to have the case to himself. . . . Poor Ward, who has run to me in all his difficulties these thirty years, didn't like it at all; but Mr Henry was so confident with his simple epidemic, and had got him in such order, that he durst not speak."

When at last Tom May's love for Averil gets the better of his prudence and his dislike of the social status of her family and, after treating her with ironic courtesy on every occasion, he suddenly veers round and proposes to her, she gives expression to the prevailing view in her refusal of him. Full of wounded pride, she remarks:

> "I understand how much a country surgeon's daughter is beneath an M.D.'s attention, and how needful it was to preserve the distance by marks of contempt."

Even lower in the scale than the surgeon was the 'parish doctor.' He was often in the literal sense the direct successor of the 'leech,' for it was the parish doctor who was called in to apply leeches during Mervyn Fulmort's illness after the physician had prescribed this treatment. His family lived on a very different scale from that of the man with a successful practice. The father of Christabel Fosbrook, the governess in *The Stokesley Secret*, was a parish surgeon in London, and was so poor and hard-worked that he was only able to take his family for a day to the Zoo or one of the parks as a rare treat, while Christabel's earnings, of which she kept back only a scanty portion, were a welcome relief to her parents. She had never in her life been out of London, and the visit of one of her young sisters to Stokesley was obviously a holiday unprecedented in the annals of the Fosbrook family.

On the question of women doctors Miss Yonge progressed surprisingly. The "clever woman" was, round about 1860, regarded with horror, because her interest in medicine led her to the practice of homœopathy, in which she failed so lamentably that she felt herself to be guilty of the death of her *protégée*, Lovedy Kelland. Some ten years later Janet Brownlow announces her intention of studying medicine to fit herself to work out her father's discovery, since none of her brothers at that time seemed likely to turn in that direction. She broaches the project to her mother:

> "Be a lady doctor, Janet!"
> "Mother, you are surely above all the commonplace, old-world nonsense."
> "I don't think I am, Janet. I don't think your father would have wished it."
> "He would have gone on with the spirit of the times, mother; men do, while women stand still."

Although Mrs Brownlow disapproves of Janet's aspirations, she gives in and allows her to study medicine at Zürich. Tragedy comes on her when, having made hasty notes from her father's papers, she hands these on to Dr Hermann, the charlatan whom she marries, being persuaded that she cannot carry out the experiments without male assistance. Hermann demolishes several patients by his semi-comprehension of the formula, while Janet is capable of seeing his folly. She is allowed to end her life, expiating all her faults by heroic exertions in combating a terrible epidemic. At last the skill of a female practitioner has won Miss Yonge's grudging approval! The final stage of Charlotte's progress is marked by the fact that she marries Harry, the son of Sir Jasper Merrifield, to a lady doctor, whom he met on his way out to Ceylon. How much, however, this may be due to the influence of Christabel Coleridge, who collaborated with her in writing *Strolling Players*, we do not know.

The rise of nursing from an occupation for a Mrs Gamp to an honourable calling for a lady is also mirrored in Miss Yonge's books. It seemed unthinkable to a Victorian family to send for a professional nurse if there were a competent servant or female member of the family available. Even a young girl of eighteen, like Averil Ward, although completely lacking in experience, was expected to nurse her parents, two brothers, and two little sisters, all stricken with a deadly fever. The Anglican sisterhoods provided some of the earliest training-schools for nurses, and thus the lessons in nursing, given first to Sister Constance and later to Angela Underwood at the convent at Dearport, were a reflection of actual happenings. Angela subsequently trained at a London hospital, where she came into conflict with a matron who did not like "lady nurses"—probably also a reflection of reality.

When Harry May was reviewing all the professions open to him he might well have added the Civil Service and teaching as fit for men of gentle birth. Miss Yonge does not deal largely in Civil Servants. The only representative of the Home Civil Service of whom she tells us much is Frank Charnock, in *The Three Brides*. He is one of the new generation who, after doing well at the university, enters by competitive examination. The life he leads differs little from that of the Civil Servant of to-day. After carrying out his official duties he has ample leisure and energy to supplement his income by essay-writing and to live a pleasant social life in Hampstead. In *The Young Stepmother* the East India Company and its servants play some part. Mr Kendal came of a family whose "connexions were Indian." After being educated in England, at sixteen he returned to India, and by the time he was about twenty-four had made enough money to get married. With the help of his first wife's moderate fortune he was actually able to retire when just past thirty. The nepotism practised within "John Company" is shown by the fact that on his retirement Mr Kendal received a promise that his twin sons, then aged seven, would be given places, one in the Civil Service and the other in the bank of Kendal and Kendal at Calcutta. The latter was apparently the less attractive alternative, since the second Mrs Kendal always took care to emphasize the fact that her husband had been a Civil Servant, not a banker. Mr Kendal had been Resident at a small native court remote from British society, so, on his return, he is quite out of touch with English life. By nature a scholar, he had devoted his energies to Oriental languages, instead of to the classics, which usually absorbed the interests of Englishmen given to intellectual pursuits, and this meant that he rarely met anyone capable of sharing in his pursuits. His gradual assumption of the duties of a member of the leisured classes in England forms one of the chief *motifs* of the book.

Miss Yonge was always interested in children and their education, and her pages abound in schoolmasters. They range from an Eton housemaster, the brother of Captain Merrifield, down to Mr Potts, who teaches in a "Commercial Academy," and whose very real love of the classics does not, in Philip Morville's censorious eyes, make up for the false quantities with which he has corrupted Guy's Latin. We have grammar schools of every calibre. The headship of the small grammar school, worth about three hundred a year, which Jem Frost so imprudently takes (*Dynevor Terrace*) in order to rush into matrimony, should by rights, we are told, have been filled by a worthy man who had formerly been an "usher," and not by a "scholar and gentleman." The headmaster of Stoneborough Grammar School, on the other hand, held a very different position in society. Dr Hoxton kept his carriage, and was given to much dining out, and his wife aspired to social leadership in the town, so that Flora May in her maiden days was glad enough to be chaperoned by her; while Charles Cheviot, his successor, was thought to be a highly suitable match for Mary May, though he had no resources beyond the school. Stoneborough, indeed, appears to have been one of those ancient grammar schools which, instead of declining in modern times, was likely to attain the status of a minor public school. Even in the early days of the nineteenth century it had been able to inspire Dr May with the appropriate old-school-tie attitude: "Dr May had never lost a grain of the ancient school-party loyalty that is part of the nature of the English gentleman."

The great change which we note in the schoolmaster, as the century progressed, is the fact that it was no longer *de rigueur* to be in Holy Orders. This change is regarded with regret in the case of Dr Ryder, the headmaster of the school to which the Underwoods go, since, though he is a man of lively intellect, his beliefs are so unsettled that Mr Underwood solemnly charges Felix to remove his brothers to "schools where older systems prevail." Mr Ogilvie, who has been appointed head of Kenminster Grammar School (*Magnum Bonum*) for the express purpose of modernizing it, meets with more approval, since he is a religious man who ultimately becomes a clergyman. The changes he introduces, presumably during the eighteen-sixties, consist in lectures on science and a more all-round education, to supplement the time-honoured classical curriculum. (This was clearly needed by the boy who informed him that "Magna Charta" was the first map of the world, and by another who said that it was a new sort of cow invented by Henry VIII, which Mr Ogilvie supposed was "a happy feminine to the Papal Bull!") Mr Ogilvie was an admirer of educational innovations, since he highly approved of the system on which Caroline Brownlow taught her children, which has a most modern sound. These children had learnt about Magna Carta by seeing it, while they were taught ancient history by acting it, and were encouraged to keep a museum of curiosities collected by themselves.

Miss Yonge gives us yet another new educational phenomenon in the shape of an inspector of schools, who appears in *The Pillars of the House* more or less concurrently with the Education Act of 1870. Rupert Cheviot was a patronizing young man, very highbrow and Oxford, and one can well imagine the unfortunate teachers being inspected by him feeling, as Ethel May did when her beloved Cocksmoor underwent an inspection, "like a toad under a harrow."

Since Miss Yonge gave most of her girls a home education, and when she did send them to school obviously regarded this course as a *pis aller*, we can hardly consider teaching as a 'career' for ladies until the period covered by the last few years of her life. In the books written during the eighteen-nineties her prejudices in this respect seem to have been largely overcome, and she looks forward boldly to a 'brave new world.' She has fully acquiesced in the expediency of High Schools, and even of women's colleges, though we do not know whether she shares the view of Gerald and Dolores (*The Long Vacation*) on the superiority of the brains of the less genteel:

> "The upper tradesmen's daughters come off with greater honours at the High School than do the young gentlewomen."
> "Very wholesome for the young Philistines," said Gerald. "The daughters of self-made men may well surpass in energy those settled on their lees!"

In *Modern Broods*, her last novel, Miss Yonge does not think it beneath the dignity of Dolores Mohun, the cousin of the Marquis of Rotherwood, to become a scientific lecturer in girls' schools. Here also she puts into the mouth of a speaker at the High School prize-giving all the current views on the education and future of women:

> The female population eagerly listened while she painted in vivid colours the aim of education, in raising the status of women, and extending their spheres not only of influence in the occult manner which had hitherto been their way of working through others, but in an open manner, which compelled attention; and she dwelt on certain brilliant achievements of women, and of others which stood before them, and towards which their education, passing out of the old grooves, was preparing them to take their place among men, and temper their harshness and indifference to suffering with the laws of mercy and humanity, speaking with an authority and equality such as should ensure attention, no longer in home and nursery whispering alone, but with open face asserting and claiming justice for the weakest.

Miss Yonge had progressed far since she had condemned the emancipated doings of Mrs Duncombe in *The Three Brides*, published in 1876, though even here one can sense an almost involuntary admiration for her efficiency, which shows up the muddle-headed procedure of the menfolk.

When it became known that Felix intended to restore Vale

Leston Church at his own expense, people recollected having 'heard something of young Underwood being in trade, and concluded that he had made a good thing of it." If it came out, however, how narrow was the scope of his business, they would probably not have been so complacent, for the extent to which a man polluted by mercantile origins could penetrate into society depended on his bank balance. In the early days of the nineteenth century a rich merchant obviously felt himself to be the inferior of the poor professional man, as we see when Mr Castleford offered employment to Clarence Winslow, after the latter had been cashiered from the Navy: "Then, quite humbly, for he knew my mother especially had a disdain for trade, he asked what my father would think of letting him give Clarence work in the office for the present." When this proposal had been accepted, "it was impressed on Clarence that the line of life was inferior; but that it was his only chance of regaining anything like a position." And regain a position Clarence did, but first he had to become extremely rich.

In the Fulmorts (*Hopes and Fears*) we have the typical City man in the process of conversion into 'county.' Mr Fulmort is a big distiller, whose first step upwards has been to marry the heiress of Beauchamp, a country house which he proceeds to 'improve' into a mansion. His elder children are snobbishly ashamed of the source of their wealth, and feel embarrassed at any allusion to it, as when Augusta reports that "People in society actually asked her about the schools and playgrounds at Mr Fulmort's distillery; there had been an educational report about them. Quite disgusting!" Mervyn's great object is to forget the family business as much as possible and to be regarded entirely as the squire and man of fashion, until he reforms and countenances the schools and playgrounds mentioned by Augusta. The Fulmorts live in great state, and like to show visible signs of their wealth. When Phœbe, who, unlike her elder sisters, has none of the *nouveau riche* about her, goes out for the evening with some white "marabouts" in her hair, instead of a "magnificent ruby bandeau" Augusta had wished her to buy, the latter remarks, "How is any one to believe in her fortune if she dresses in that twopenny-halfpenny fashion?" It is not to be wondered at that the Fulmorts remained on the outskirts of Society, as we are clearly shown when the more worthy Phœbe, who is staying with

Miss Charlecote, is introduced into the fashionable Charteris circle, which, we are given to understand, is quite beyond the Fulmort mark. "The Fulmorts were in bondage to ostentation; the Charterises were lavish for their own enjoyment, and heedless alike of cost and of appearance."

Though a big manufacturer or City merchant could win his way into polite society, the retail trader was in mid-Victorian days quite beyond the pale. This is nowhere better brought out than in *The Pillars of the House* by the contrast between the social positions of Felix and Tom Underwood. In the desperate straits to which the family is reduced just before his father's death, Felix, at the age of sixteen, accepts an offer of work at a guinea a week from a bookseller and editor of the local paper, *The Pursuivant*. Mr Underwood remarks in anguish of spirit, "I did not know how much pride there was left in me till I found what a bitter pill this is!" He makes Felix look the matter squarely in the face:

> This is not as if it were a great publisher . . . with whom there would be no loss of position or real society; but a little bookseller in a country town is a mere tradesman, and though a man like Audley may take you up from time to time, it will never be on an absolute equality; and it will be more and more forgotten who you were. You will have to live in yourself and your home, *depending* on no one else.

How revolutionary was the notion is shown even more clearly by the reactions of Mr Froggatt, the bookseller, who had made the suggestion to Felix "as a sort of jesting compliment," which he hardly expected to be taken seriously:

> Good Mr Froggatt, an old-fashioned tradesman, with a profound feeling for a real gentleman, was a good deal shocked at receiving Mr Underwood's message. He kept a reading-room and was on terms of a certain intimacy with its frequenters, such as had quite warranted his first requests for Felix's good-natured help.

The fatal step is taken, and the Underwoods are to all intents and purposes social outcasts. Felix is so conscious of having gone down in the scale that he even makes his family address his letters with 'Mister' instead of 'Esquire.' They are even further degraded when they accept Mr Froggatt's offer of free quarters over the shop. As the snobbish Lady Price remarked, "Of course, after this, Miss Underwood did not expect to be visited," though she veered round some years later, on learning that Felix had become heir to Vale Leston, and was assiduous with her invitations. Felix himself fully acquiesced in the contemporary estimate of his social position, for it was a severe struggle for him to refuse the offer of a clerkship in the firm of his cousin, Tom Underwood, a merchant trading with South America. His low status has just been impressed on him by a girl, the object of his calf love, and he says, "But when it is brought home that we have slipped down two degrees in the social scale, it is tempting to step up one again." By which he presumably means that his father, the impecunious curate, had been two steps higher than his own present degraded state, while his cousin Tom, for all his riches and the possession of a town and country house, occupies only the intermediate stage.

The Underwoods had become identified with the tradesman class by mischance, but we have other examples of the status of those born into this stratum of Society. The snobbery of a little town is made abundantly clear by the fact that the second-rate 'young ladies' of Bayford refuse to collaborate as Sunday-school teachers with a certain Clarissa Richardson, a bookseller's daughter, until the example of Albinia Kendal has made it respectable. There is a parallel state of affairs in Stoneborough, which rouses the indignation of Dr May, when reported to him by Flora and Ethel. The Sunday-school teachers in their fine watered silks take exception to the uncivilized Cocksmoor children, complaining that

"it is positively improper to place ladies in contact with such squalid objects."
"Ladies!" cried Ethel. "A stationer's daughter and a banker's clerk's! Why do they come to teach at school at all?" "Because our example makes it genteel."

Flora, being sure of her position, can take a ragged child and pin up the gaps in her clothing, while the would-be ladies imagine they show their gentility by exaggerated refinement.

Lancelot Underwood, the brother who succeeds Felix in the business, provides an excellent historical picture of the gradual breaking down of the barriers that went on during the latter half of the nineteenth century. He goes into the business at sixteen, when he has no particular social aspirations, and it is only after the family has gone back to Vale Leston that the gulf between his position and the circles in which they now move worries him. He confides in Dr May:

"I did not know what I was giving up."

"In position?"

"Partly. I was a mere boy, and did not see the difference as I do now that I have been with Will Harewood at Oxford, or when I come here. I keep out of it as much as I can, for it's just a mockery to go and mix with their friends here, and talk to a pretty girl, when I know she would not touch me with a pair of tongs at home."

"More shame for her, then. Have you no society at home?"

"Oh yes, plenty of nice fellows—professionals, I mean, and a dinner with the upper-crust now and then," said Lance, laughing; "not much in itself, but making me cock of the walk in our own line—trade, I mean. Nice girls there are, too—if one had seen nothing else—but then, they keep out of the way, and the others make themselves such fools."

The solution of Lance's difficulties is his marriage with Gertrude May, a girl whose defiance of convention cheers him from the moment when he hears of her shaking hands with the chemist, a friend of her brother's who had not nerve enough to finish his medical course, "under the very shadow of his purple jars." Gertrude and Lance set up housekeeping in the country, well out of sight of the shop, and are received by polite Society. We next meet Lance some fifteen years later, just after Queen Victoria's first Jubilee in 1887, and hear that he

had entirely got over that sense of being in a false position which had rendered society distasteful to him. Many more men of family were in a like position with himself than had been the case when his brother had begun life; moreover he had personally achieved some standing and distinction through the *Pursuivant*.

By now he has no need to live genteelly in the country, but he and Gertrude have unblushingly gone to live over the shop, which has become so large that it has absorbed the house next door.

The Pursuivant had all along been the feature in the careers of Felix and Lance, redeeming them from unmitigated retail trade. In the days of slower communications a local paper was probably more eagerly read than it is nowadays, and the tone of

The Pursuivant was raised by reviews from the pens of the intellectual Bill Harewood and of Geraldine Underwood. Such was its reputation that Lance had been able to turn it from a weekly into a daily paper. Miss Yonge characteristically fits the politics of a paper to the gentility of its editors. *The Pursuivant*, a staunch upholder of Church and State, was in the hands of the well-connected Underwoods, while its Radical rival was written in the worst journalese by a low-down demagogue. One feels sure that Felix did not go in for the somewhat modern publicity of the journalists who haunted Stoneborough in *The Trial*, when he had to write up what the Press described as "The Blewer Tragedy." They rightly recognized in Mrs Pugh one avid of publicity, and she "was continually enduring the great shock of meeting people in shops or in the streets, whom she knew to be reporters or photographers." The public obviously does not change in its craving for vicarious excitement, for "the illustrated press sent down artists, whose three-legged cameras stared in all directions . . . and the furniture at the mill would have commanded any price."

'Trade' is fairly well represented in Miss Yonge's stories, but industrial concerns play little part in them. We hear something of mining in *Dynevor Terrace*, first in England and then in Peru. The mines at Illershall are of the model kind which appeal to the philanthropic Fitzjocelyn, with a chaplain and evening classes, including the lectures on chemistry which so delight Tom Madison. Tom makes such progress that he is sent out to superintend some silver-mines in Peru, where he acts as mentor to the Cornish miners, in true Victorian fashion reading the service with them on Sundays, and educates himself still further, so that he ends up as a superior clerk with the magnificent salary of £180 a year.

When manufacture was bound up with scientific research, it was apparently an occupation for a gentleman, since all had been well with Edward Williams (*The Clever Woman of the Family*), when he had owned a manufactory of patent glass from a formula invented by him. We hear of this period of his life, however, only in retrospect. It was the fact that he had left too much in the hands of his dishonest manager, Madox, that brought about his ruin, so perhaps Mr Williams did not himself come much into contact with his workpeople. Direct participation in factory management was not apparently considered fit for a man of

F

family, for Percy Fotheringham, when wishing for an occupation which would both support Theodora and use all his energies laments that a factory inspectorship would hardly be compatible with an "Honourable" for a wife.

In Miss Yonge's last books we see reflections of the same change of attitude with regard to industry as to trade. Mr White, the rich quarry-owner, is allowed to marry Adeline Mohun, who takes him rather as a last chance, though she is enamoured of his wealth and his lovely Italian villa, overlooking the quarries. It is another portent of the times that Wilfred Merrifield, her nephew, is only too glad to accept a clerkship at the marble works. In the good old days he would probably, by the exercise of his aristocratic relations' patronage, have served his country most inefficiently in the Army or Civil Service; but from these callings he was by the end of the century debarred by competitive examinations, which he was quite incapable of passing.

CHAPTER IV

THE POOR

.T is rather interesting to speculate whether Miss Yonge ever read Disraeli's *Sybil*, and, if so, what she made of its opening chapters. Her probable reaction would have been a deliberate losing of her mind to 'unsafe' speculations on the social questions raised by this grim picture and an indulgence of wishful thinking as to the effects of numerous mission churches with large funds, set up in the midst of the seething mass of corruption. When she does touch on such problems, it is generally because she wishes to show how they reacted on a character she is describing, rather than from a burning desire to expose social injustice to the general gaze. Of the "Two Nations" of Disraeli's sub-title Miss Yonge's eye rests more frequently on that to which she herself belongs, and when she looks at the second 'nation,' it is generally from the point of view of a visitor from another sphere. This is even more the case with the urban poor, whom she knew only from hearsay, than with her own country people. Almost the only instance where we see the social reformer rather than the mission priest at work is in *The Clever Woman of the Family*, and there Rachel's efforts at ameliorating the lot of the lacemakers is represented as ending in disaster, because she set to work without the sanction of the clergy.

We are shown that a cottage industry in a healthy seaside town could be almost as soul-destroying as life in a big factory, and we sympathize with Rachel when, in talking of a young lacemaker who had taken to domestic service when her health gave way, she stigmatized "a system that chained girls to an unhealthy occupation in early childhood and made an overstocked market and underpaid workers." The evils of the 'system' are illustrated by the sad tale of Lovedy Kelland, whose mother, a small milliner, "had not sacrificed her little girl to the Moloch of lace, but had kept her at school to a later age than usual in the place."

The school visitors thought highly of Lovedy, for "the girls were in general so young, or so stupefied with their work

[*i.e.*, lacemaking], that an intelligent girl like Lovedy Kelland wa
no small treasure to them." On her mother's death, however
Lovedy was not allowed to stay on until she could become a pupi
teacher, but was forced to work with her aunt,

> the most able lacemaker in the place, a hard-working woman, wh∢
> kept seven little pupils in a sort of cupboard under the staircase. . .
> For ten hours a day did these children work in a space just wid∢
> enough for them to sit, with the two least under the slope of th∢
> stairs, permitted no distraction from their bobbins, but invaded by
> their mistress on the faintest sound of tongues.

Poor Lovedy's fingers had not been trained early enough, and
her incessant tears spoilt her thread, so that "Mrs Kelland decidec
that she'd never get her bread till she was broke of her buke
which breaking was attempted by a summary pawning of al.
poor Lovedy's reward books." When the Sunday-school teache∢
tried to remonstrate she "was nearly frightened out of her wit⌐
by such a scolding as only such a woman as the lace mistress coulc
deliver." The fate of this young lady throws a sidelight on the
real feelings of the poor towards district visiting and dictation
from the clergy.

> It was not really a poor population. The men were seafaring and
> the women lacemaking and just well enough off to make dissent
> doubly attractive as an escape from some of the interfering alms-
> giving . . . and sundry houses were forbidden ground to district
> visitors.

Rachel Curtis, coming of a local landowning family, stood on a
different footing:

> Old feudal feeling made Rachel be unmolested when she came
> down twice a week, opened the door of the blackhole under the
> stairs, and read aloud, something religious, something improving,
> and a bit of a story, following it up by mental arithmetic and a
> lesson on objects, which seemed to Mrs Kelland the most arrant
> nonsense in the world, and to her well-broken scholars was about
> as interesting as the humming of a blue-bottle fly; but it was poor
> Lovedy's one enjoyment, though making such havoc of her work
> that it was always expiated by extra hours, not on her pillow, but
> at it.

Rachel very sensibly decides that the remedy would be to elimi-
nate the middleman and draw off some of the lacemakers into

other occupations, but in her attempt to provide these she comes
to grief.

Rachel's efforts to brighten the wits of the lacemakers are
paralleled by those of Lord St Erme to educate his miners, which
met with greater success. He has provided a reading-room,
stocked with books, prints, and newspapers, where he and his
sister go for two nights a week to read with the men, give them
lectures, or teach them singing.

> There's a lad now learning to draw, whose taste is quite wonder-
> ful. And if you could have seen their faces when I read them
> King Henry IV! I want to have the same thing at Coalworth for
> the winter—not in summer. I could not ask them to spend a
> minute they can help, out of the free air and light; but in winter
> I cannot see those fine young men and boys dozing themselves into
> stolidity.

As the nineteenth century nears its close, we come to the era
of 'slumming.' In *That Stick* (1892) Miss Yonge sent Bertha
Morton, the cousin of Lord Northmoor, to work off her restless-
ness in this way, though she described it slightingly as "philanthropy, not greatly tinged with religion." Bertha states her
intentions in words which are a fine sample of the development
of slang:

> I care for my neighbours, of course, after a sort, but the jolly
> city sparrows of the slums for me! . . . I've spotted my own special
> preserve of match-girls, newsboys, etc., and Mr Hailes is going to
> help me to get a scrumptious little house, where I can get to it by
> underground rail.

The popularity of slumming is even better brought out in
The Long Vacation, where it is taken up with ardour by Emilia
Vanderkist, especially since she shares the pursuit with her
cousin Gerald, a devotee of the settlement work just coming into
fashion among Oxford undergraduates. Emilia's uncertainty as
to the ultimate object of her investigations sheds a good deal
of light on the value of the Society girl's charitable efforts. She
says:

> "Do come out with me. I want to go into Ponter's Court, and
> Fernan won't let me go alone."
> "Have you any special object?" said Gerald lazily, "or is it to
> refresh yourself with the atmosphere?"

"That dear boy—that Silky—has been taken up, and they've sent him to reformatory."

"What a good thing!"

"Yes, only I don't believe he did it! It was that nasty little Bill Nosey. I am sure that he got hold of the lady's parcel, and stuffed it into Silky's cap. . . ."

"But if he is in a reformatory, what then? Are we to condole with his afflicted family, or bring Bill Nosey to confess?"

"I thought I would see about it," said Emilia vaguely.

Gerald, in contrast to Emilia, is a logical reformer, holding rather Socialistic views. He chafes at the narrowness of the sphere open to him as a small landowner, and questions his right to refuse to allow a china-clay factory to be set up on his estate for the sake of preserving its amenities: "Why should all that space be nothing but a playground for us Underwoods, instead of making work for the million."

Although Miss Yonge does not enter into the bigger social questions, she makes no attempt to palliate the iniquity of the slum landlord and the promoter of gin palaces, one of the worst evils of her period. It was largely the realization of the source of his family's wealth which drove Robert Fulmort to devote his fortune to set up a slum mission. As he explains to Phœbe:

> You and I, and all of us, have eaten and drunk, been taught more than we could learn, lived in a fine house, and been made into ladies and gentlemen, all by battening on the vice and misery of this wretched population. Those unhappy men and women are lured into the gaudy palaces at the corners of the streets to purchase a moment's oblivion of conscience, by stinting their children of bread, that we may wear fine clothes, and call ourselves county people.

Robert's panacea for all this misery is religion and education, though we hear too of practical expedients such as soup kitchens. The description of two thousand slum children going to the Forest Show at Mervyn's expense throws many sidelights on the life they lead. The pinched and stunted little Londoners are turned loose into a hayfield, but only the

> petted orphans venture to tumble about that curious article upon the ground. Two little sisters, however, evidently transplanted country children, sit up in a corner where they have found some flowers, fondling them and hugging them with ecstasy.

When it is time for the children to set out on their five-hours' train journey back to London, the prize-winners shower on them their produce and flowers.

Many a family will have a first taste of fresh green country meat to-morrow. . . . If any nosegays reach London alive, they will be cherished to their last hour, and maybe the leaves will live in prayer-books for many a year.

We are given no more than general descriptions of the misery of the London slums, but we learn from precise details that these can be nearly as bad in a small country town. In *The Young Stepmother* we read of houses with broken pavements, doors that will not shut, and ceilings through which the rain streams in. In two cottages there were twenty-three people, seven of them being lodgers, and seventy-five in the whole block of houses, while, needless to say, there were no drains, and the smells were horrible. Twice in five years these houses had been the starting-point of a terrible fever, which had spread alarmingly, killing off even some members of the family who owned them. Yet the trustee who administered the property would not sanction any expenditure on them. The dire results of a disregard of sanitation are also set forth in *The Three Brides*, which depicts a period some quarter of a century later than that described in *The Young Stepmother*. Here there is an attempt on the part of Mrs Duncombe to wake the conscience of the townspeople and local gentry in the matter, but their complete obtuseness is voiced by Mr Bowater, when he says:

There's been nothing amiss in my time. . . . Perfectly healthy in all reason! Ay! You may laugh, young folks, but I never heard of any receipt to hinder people from dying; and let well alone is a safe maxim.

In consequence of their attitude Mrs Duncombe makes a single-handed attempt at amelioration, which, however, proves fatal. Unaided by male advice, she evolves a drainage system so imperfect as to cause a terrible visitation of "typhus." Miss Yonge is not the only Victorian author to mistake for typhus the disease commonly caused by an infected water-supply, typhoid or enteric; Charles Kingsley's novel *Two Years Ago* turns on a similar visitation due to apathy and neglect among the population. It is, indeed, a fact that in such epidemics of 'fever' the infection beginning in slum property must eventually take its toll of victims from among those who are better off, if these are likewise careless of sanitation. The Victorians were amazingly slow, we feel in retrospect, to see the means of ending this recurring menace.

The reign of Queen Victoria covers the development of rail ways. In one of her stories of village life, *The Railroad Children* Miss Yonge gives us a picture of the desolate lives of the navvies who moved from place to place when engaged on their construction. She tells us that they often made for themselves "huts of mud or clay, roughly thatched with fern or reed, and so low, as to look more like the burrows of some animal than the habitations of men and women." We are taken inside one of these huts:

> The small window was so dull with dust and cobwebs, that light was needed from the open door to see clearly the few articles of furniture that the single room contained. At one end were two beds . . . at the other, two stools, a chair, a cupboard, . . . a table strewed with crumbs and smeared with butter, and a chest, upon which were placed a few cracked and dirty cups and plates.

Against this squalid background we are shown ragged and dirty children, and women, adorned with curlpapers, who spend their Sunday mornings gossiping. The story deals with three children who on their father's death are transplanted from this uncivilized and heathen world to the country paradise inhabited by their grandfather:

> There was a path up the middle, bordered with flowers, and leading to the door of a cottage with a thatched roof, and black timbers showing at the gable ends. At the side was a long, low shed, the front covered with red China roses. [The kitchen had a] sanded stone floor, oaken dresser-table, and arm-chair, handsome clock and bright display of crockery.

This brings us back to the village scene in which Miss Yonge felt so thoroughly at home. As we have seen, few of her novels ignore it entirely, but it dominates nearly all the stories she wrote for the edification of her Sunday scholars. One of these, *The Carbonels*, takes us back to the days Charlotte knew only from her parents' reminiscences. We have a most interesting

escription of the introduction of machinery and the Jack Swing
iots:

The beat of the flail on barn floors was a regular winter sound at
Uphill . . . but to get all the corn threshed and winnowed by a
curious revolving fan with four canvas sails, was a troublesome
affair, making farmers behindhand in coming to the market. And as
soon as he could afford the venture the Captain obtained a machine
to be worked by horse-power, for steam had hardly been brought as
yet into use even for sea traffic.

Captain Carbonel was one of the sensible landlords who saw to
t that his men had work in winter in place of the threshing by
₁and, but all the same some of them were ready to help Jack
ᵢwing with his machine-breaking and rick-burning, "for they all
₁ate that there machine that is to starve poor folk in winter time."

They all disguised themselves, some blackening their faces with
soot, others whitening them with chalk and some putting on the
women's cloaks, bonnets, or aprons.
"We are come for your good," said Jack Swing, or the man who
passed for him, wearing a long, Punch-like nose. "There will be
no living for poor folks if those new-fangled machines be allowed to
go on, and them Parliament folk vote out all that makes for the
people."

No wonder the Carbonels, after all their kindess to the villagers,
ᵥere mortified that the latter should turn against them.

It was hard to make allowance for the bewilderment of slow minds,
for sheer cowardice and for the instinct of going along with one's
own class of people.

Jot all landowners were such innovators as Captain Carbonel, for
ᵢonora Charlecote (*Hopes and Fears*), hating steam, still kept
he flail as late as the eighteen-fifties "as the winter's employment in the barn." For the most part, however, we hear, in the
ᵢater tales of village life, of intelligent farm labourers who were
elected for instruction in dealing with the steam-engine, by
hen in general use.
Captain Carbonel did not meet with opposition only in his
ᵢttempt to introduce machinery. The old farm bailiff

growled at first and foretold that nothing would come of "thicken
al'"; that the mangled-weazel . . . would not grow; and that the

cows would never eat "that there red clover as they calls apollyon."
But when the mangel swelled into splendid crimson root and the
cows throve upon the bright fields of trifolium, he was as proud
as any one.

The villagers were just as suspicious of schemes for their own
good. Coal was so difficult to get that they were forced to rob
the woods and hedges, to the fury of one of the landowners, who
threatened to take vengeance by withholding his yearly donation
of blankets. ("As if it would do them any good to make them
colder," cried Dora.) And yet when the Carbonels and the other
landowners clubbed together to fill a barn with coal, which was
sold to the villagers at sixpence a bushel, they said, "Depend on
it, the Captain made a good thing of it." In spite of all these
hindrances and the fact that Uphill was a lawless place, where
Cobbler Cox, the Constable (surely a lineal descendant of 'the
Watch'), was more "skeered of the rogues than the rogues was of
he," the Carbonels really did achieve something, so that the
doctors at the infirmary said that they knew an Uphill person
by the tidier clothing. This was chiefly owing to the weekly club,
which provided decent garments, conducive to attendance at
church. A very similar state of affairs is described in *Chantry
House*, which deals with the same period. Here, however, there
was no infirmary to fall back on for medical treatment, and the
cottagers of Hillside depended almost entirely on "Madam
Fordyce" and her medicine chest.

Miss Yonge's tales of village life cover a period of some fifty
years, so that we can watch the progressive betterment in the life
of the agricultural labourer. As late as the eighteen-seventies
there was still apparently considerable hardship. In *The Three
Brides* Joe Reynolds, aged ten, was able to go to school only when
he could not pick up an odd job—"bird-starving, stone picking
and cow-herding," since he could not get taken on as carter-boy,
not being "so lusty as some on 'em." Even more fortunate little
boys, able to stay longer at school, seem very glad to do any small
job that will bring them in a few pence. A little sugar or treacle
or plain bread is a treat, while the purchase of a penn'orth of
"Gibraltar rock" (a striped and glutinous sweet) is an event.
Sufficient milk is by no means general, and one feels sympathetic
towards the little girl who was sent to fetch milk, given gratis to
her delicate little sister, and could not resist a sly lick herself,

ince presumably the healthy members of the family lived on
kim milk. In all the accounts of the philanthropic activities of
Miss Yonge's characters we are constantly struck by the gratitude
f the poor for what would seem very small mercies—the tippets
nd bonnets contrived out of scraps, and the cast-off dresses and
hoes, which are regarded as a great prize. The insufficient diet
f the poor is shown up by the fact that it was esteemed an act of
neritorious self-denial to renounce one's helping of pudding, as
Norman May did, and carry it off to a poor family. The 'hungry
forties' are well depicted in *Scenes and Characters*, and no scene
ives us a better idea of the poverty of the farm labourer, even
n a model parish, than the description of 'gooding.'

> St Thomas's day was marked by the custom called . . . "gooding."
> Each mother of a family came to all the principal houses in the
> parish to receive sixpence, towards providing a Christmas dinner.
> . . . With a long list of names and a heap of silver before her,
> [Lilias] sat at the oaken table by the open chimney in the hall,
> returning a nod or a smiling greeting to the thanks of the women
> as they came, one by one, to receive the little silver coins, and warm
> themselves by the glowing wood fire. . . . Agnes Eden appeared, in
> order to claim the double portion allotted to her mother, as a
> widow. This was the first time that Mrs Eden had asked for the
> gooding-money, and Lilias knew that it was a sign that she must
> be in great distress.

This was indeed the case, for her neighbour, Mrs Grey, while
waiting to have a purple stuff frock measured off for her little
girl, told Lilias that "not a bit of butter, nor a morsel of bacon,
as been in her house since Michaelmas." This incident brings
ut, too, the extraordinary goodness of the poor to one another,
or we hear how

> Andrew Grey had dug up and housed her winter's store of potatoes
> . . . and little Agnes often shared the meals of his children. The
> Greys had a large family, very young, so that all they did for her
> was the fruit of self-denial.

n the tales of village life we are constantly meeting with similar
cts of kindness. Perhaps one of the most pathetic of these is
he story of the nine-year-old boy (*Langley Little Ones*) who gives
hirty shillings, the result of years of careful saving of his small
arnings, to his grandmother to pay her rent, when her geese,

the sale of which was to have provided the money, are stolen. How narrow was the margin between paying one's way and absolute want is shown by the fact that there is no alternative between the acceptance of David's gift and the old woman's having to give up her clean and picturesque cottage, which "had a nice garden too, with double daisies and thrift and violets along the paths, and vegetables beyond, also three or four stocks of bees."

In the later books there is less of this extreme poverty to be met with, but the most tangible sign of increasing prosperity is in sartorial changes. In *The Carbonels* women working in the fields in the eighteen-twenties are described thus:

> The one that was best off had great boots, a huge weight to carry in themselves: but most had them sadly torn and broken. Their skirts, of no particular colour, were tucked up, and they had either a very old man's coat, or a smock frock cut short, or a small old woollen shawl, which last left the blue and red arms bare: on their heads were the oldest of bonnets, or here and there a sun-bonnet, which looked more decent.

Many of the children of these women came to school stocking less and unkempt. The stage following the poverty-stricken garments of the early days of the century was that of the decent print or stuff frock, with an extra ribbon or so for Sunday, which was often the result of anxious contriving. In the eighteen-forties the acquisition of fresh trimmings for the bonnets to be worn at Whitsun was an important matter even in the family, not of a labourer, but of a smallholder. The Lee children all appeared "in their striped pink frocks and white tippets . . . and their straw bonnets, the fresh bright straw set off by the dark green of the ribbons" (*Langley School*). In the eighteen-fifties the English villager still retained something of peasant naïveté, and we read of a boy buying at the fair this object of historic interest: a

> neck-handkerchief . . . bright blue, with gay pictures of the Queen, Prince Albert, Louis Napoleon, and the Sultan, at the corners, and London, Paris, Constantinople, and Sebastopol, along the sides.

In the last quarter of the century we come to the age of sophistication, where the villagers have begun to ape their betters. By 1880 a coachman's daughters go to the school treat in thin white frocks, ulsters, and 'clouds' (thin shawls, worn in the evening to cover the bare head); while in the last story of village life, *Founded on Paper*, we meet with young men in neat tweed suits and their womenfolk in equally fashionable garments. Another striking contrast is the Sunday-school treat of the 'eighties. There are no more paltry home-made gifts, but Christmas-trees with such presents as drums, fairy dolls, knives, monkeys, neckties, and "scissors like birds"; instead of solid buns the children are each given an elaborate bonbon (*Langley Adventures*, 1883). We also hear of a summer treat where the children are taken by train to see Porchester Castle (was this reminiscent of Miss Yonge's own doings?) and for a row on the sea, while in *Our New Mistress* (1888) the schoolchildren are sent to a pantomime.

Over the whole period one is struck by the difference in the way of living of the labourer and the artisan, working farmer, or small tradesman. Nowadays their standards have been levelled up by the rise in wages, but then a man 'bettered himself' by becoming his own master. The comfort of the farm labourer's existence varied, of course, according to locality and circumstances, but we hear frequently of cottages bare of all amenities, and even in bad repair. Compare with these this description of the bed-room of the invalid son of the village postmistress and keeper of the general shop (*Friarswood Post-office*):

> There were spotless white dimity curtains round the lattice window; and the little bed, and the walnut of the great chest . . . shone with dark and pale grainings. There was a carpet on the floor, and the chairs had chintz cushions; the walls were as white as snow, and there were pretty china ornaments on the mantel-piece; many little pictures hanging upon the walls, and quite a shelf of books upon the white cloth, laid so carefully on the top of the drawers.

In fact, it frequently strikes a modern reader how much he would prefer the white walls and pre-Victorian furniture of the cottager to the elegant wallpapers and 'modern' furniture of the gentry.

Miss Yonge's contacts with the poor were confined to the school and intercourse with the domestic staff. As one would expect, she views this not very objectively, but through the eyes of the mistress. We have the most intimate portraits of the old nurse, who seems often to have become part rather of the family for whom she works than of her own. The life of the servant in a fashionable household does not, on the whole, interest Charlotte so much as the humdrum existence of the average maid. We do not learn many details as to wages, though we know that Caroline Brownlow (*Magnum Bonum*) gave her cook eighty pounds, a sum to be spoken of with bated breath, while, at the other end of the scale, a girl would be sent out to be taught her job as kitchen-maid for nothing but her keep, with injunctions to eat all she could and 'grow stout.' The average wage was from twelve to sixteen pounds or less. Charlotte's views on servants are probably those expressed by Dr May and Ethel, in *The Daisy Chain*, when they point out to Meta the enormity of not letting her maid, Bellairs, have a night off to visit her sick mother. (Meta herself is convinced of the right course, but fears the strictures of her fashionable aunt at the sight of her hair done by a less skilled hand.) It is probably much more important to Charlotte that Meta, besides learning to do without a maid, promotes the attendance of the domestic staff at family prayers and herself reads with the younger maids. Our modern notions are frequently outraged by the treatment meted out by Miss Yonge's characters to domestics, but no tale can be more revealing than that of Anne Cleft, in *Lads and Lasses of Langley* (1881). Anne has been an exemplary servant, but has never been able to save, because her feckless relations are always borrowing money from her. She has to undergo a serious operation, for which her mistress pays, but before she can be fit to go back to work she will have to spend some time in a convalescent home, costing seven shillings a week. Of this her mistress, who is by no means well off, will find two shillings, but Anne has no means of raising the other five shillings until her nephew in the nick of time repays her loan to him. Before this happy solution her employer's brother-in-law ventilates the question:

> Such things can never be remedied till some one makes a stand. The relations prey on her. She is weak and saves nothing, trusting to your weakness. You are weak, and maintain her when your wages should have put her in a condition to maintain herself, and thus you are giving a premium to improvidence and unscrupulous borrowing.

Emma, the cook, who overheard this conversation, "thought it just, but hard." (Emma and Alice, the other maid, would have liked to provide the other five shillings, but could not, the one having a helpless father and the other an orphan niece to keep.)

It must be added that the mistress never thought of saving the money by having one maid less, but lamented having to pay a temporary housemaid; yet she was described as a good woman and a kind mistress. One can hardly forgive even Miss Yonge for complacent acceptance of such a lamentable state of affairs.

The most striking contrast to the lack of progress in the conditions of domestic service is provided by the startling evolution of elementary education over the same period. In the eighteen-twenties the 'dame school' was almost the only means of education open to the poor, and in *The Carbonels* we hear of one kept by an old lady, who was so infirm that she did nothing but mumble and shake, and had to leave the work to her granddaughter, Lizzie. When the Carbonels came to look at the school, this girl "stamped at some to enforce her orders, shook the rod at others, and set up the smallest like so many ninepins . . . on one small bench." Five children, who paid fourpence instead of twopence a week, were privileged to have a whole and sound form near the fire, and could spell words of one syllable, while there was one show scholar, of whom Lizzie explained:

"She be in her Testament, Ma'am"; . . . and accordingly a terribly thumbed and dilapidated New Testament was put into the child's hand, from which she proceeded to bawl out, with long pauses between the words, and spelling the longest, a piece of the Sermon on the Mount, selected because there were no names in it.

The only thing properly taught was needlework, which some of the bigger girls did quite respectably. The Carbonels took steps to put an end to this state of ignorance by setting up a school in the wash-house, which was used only for one week in five, when "two women, in high white muslin caps and checked aprons, came to assist the maids in getting up the family linen."

A tub was set on the Saturday, with ashes placed in a canvas bag on a frame above; water was poured on it, and ran through, so as to be fitted for the operations which began at five o'clock in the morning, and absorbed all the women of the establishment, and even old Pucklechurch, who was called on to turn the mangle.

There is a similar dame school in *Chantry House*.

The next stage in education is represented by the ousting of the dame and the setting up of a school by the local gentry or clergy. The type of school depended, of course, largely on the means of the benefactors, who sometimes could not afford to pay a mistress but did all the teaching themselves, as the May girls did, when they started by the modest hire of a cottage room to educate Cocksmoor. They thought their fortune made when they were given ten pounds a year to pay a mistress, Cherry Elwood. The latter had been in superior service, until she was lamed by an accident, and was able to teach nothing but sewing, reading, writing, and very elementary arithmetic. When a school was built at Cocksmoor, Cherry was sent for a few months to a training school to render herself more fit for it. The village schools established in the eighteen-forties nearly all appear to have had teachers whose acquirements were on a par with Cherry's, and to have depended for more ambitious teaching on visiting gentry, who, as we have seen, were often very erratic. When a girl, on a visit to her grandparents in the country (*Henrietta's Wish*), gave lessons on grammar, her aunt remarked of the mistress, "How she must be scandalized by the introduction of a noun and a verb!" The children, for the most part, left school very early, for the thirteen-year-old gamekeeper's daughter at Langley is spoken of as staying on beyond the average age. Here is her school:

> The girl's school at Langley was a pleasant room . . . it was of flint stones with black mortar, and red bricks at the corners, and the windows in arches at top, and glazed in a honeycomb pattern. There was a projecting window at the end with a wide seat in it, where the upper girls used to sit when they were about any work requiring good light. . . . Then there was a chair near it for Mrs Wright, the mistress, and a table, round which the classes stood to say the Catechism, or to read; and all along one side of the room was a sloping desk where they wrote their copies. The walls were hung with beautiful pictures of birds and beasts.

Even though many of Miss Yonge's teachers surpassed the attainments of Cherry Elwood—a number of them, indeed, by the 'fifties and 'sixties having been trained—not all parents favoured the village school. We hear of the cobbler in *The Carbonels* sending his little girl to "Miss Minifer's genteel academy, where she learnt bead-work and very little besides," while the parents of Clementina Fielding, who think themselves a cut above the village and dress her up in tawdry finery, take a lot of persuading before they will let her go to Langley

School. Even in one of the stories dealing with the eighteen-eighties (*London Pride*) the 'genteel academy' still existed, for a coachman's daughter, coming with her father to London, expressed a desire to be sent to one, where fancy-work and dancing were taught for a shilling a week; but he is too sensible to be taken in and sends her to the 'parish school.'

With the passing of the Education Act of 1870 the final stage in the evolution of the Victorian Elementary school was reached. In her early days Miss Yonge's chief concern had been that the lower classes should have some kind of instruction. Now it is her aim and object to save them from the 'godless education' of the Board school. Sometimes this can be achieved by such simple means as the provision of a separate room for the hat-pegs, which was required by the School Board at Cocksmoor (a far cry from the one cottage room of the original school), but at others it demands the raising of sums such as two thousand pounds for the building of new schools. Thus we have the great bazaar, justifiable in such a cause, of *The Long Vacation*. The products of these schools are very different from the simple children, grounded in 'the three R's,' of earlier days. The youngest White boy (*Beechcroft at Rockstone*) was apparently fit to go straight to a Woodard school after receiving his early education at the expense of the State. He had, of course, the refining influence of his elder brother and sister at home, but the reverse was true of Ludmilla, the half-sister of Gerald Underwood. Such of her refinement as did not come naturally to her she owed to her education at the elementary school in Mr Flight's parish. She was sufficiently ladylike and well spoken to arouse the incipient jealousy of Dolores at Gerald's apparent admiration of "a pretty face, especially in the half-and-half class," before she knew that they were brother and sister.

The contrast between the teachers of the new order and the old is best of all brought out in *Our New Mistress, or Changes at Brookfield Earl*, published in 1888. When Jessie Martin, the product of a training college, comes to be headmistress at Brookfield Earl, the widowed niece of the former mistress, known as "Governess Betsy," stays on to teach the infants. In view of her unfortunate experiences during an inspection, it is not surprising that Betsy fights shy of attempting any examination. Having prepared a lesson on "a dog," she became flustered on being

G

asked to give one on "a table," and made the children say it "was often spotted, had two eyes, claws, and was very faithful to follow its master wherever he went." For all this, the villagers commiserated Betsy for not being made headmistress, and she herself "had enough to say about the uppishness of these young things that had been to them fine Colleges, and thought they knew better than them as were mothers." Jessie, on the other hand, was a well-read young woman, with the speech and manners of a lady, and most modern in her educational methods. She has a horror of corporal punishment, but by quiet firmness revolutionizes the discipline of the school, cures the children of learning out loud, and teaches them to attack their work intelligently, while she introduces Kindergarten methods, with singing games, for the Infants. It is interesting to note the shifting of Miss Yonge's sympathies in this book. Instead of looking at village affairs through the eyes of the daughters of a former vicar, who teach in the school in the approved manner, she sees things from Jessie's point of view, and agrees with her in resenting their interference. The conclusion is that, when efficient teachers could not be found, the lady did well to supplement their instruction; but when there were teachers of equal education with herself, and, moreover, with better methods of teaching, she will do well to stand aside.

We have seen something of the education and daily life of the villager, but Miss Yonge does not neglect to present him also on festive occasions. In her last stories he is not so very different from the older farm labourer we know to-day, but the earlier tales give us delightful glimpses of a more picturesque age. The pleasures of the lower orders are, of course, always set within certain bounds, and are generally watched over by the clergy. Speaking of past days in *The Carbonels*, Miss Yonge says:

> To be a steady and religious youth was a more difficult matter in those days than at present, for harmless outlets for youthful spirits had not been devised, and to avoid mischief it was almost needful to abstain from almost all the company and pleasures of a country lad.

Even fifty years later she makes one of her characters remark philosophically that, so narrow was the scope of permissible relaxations, a well-conducted young man of the artisan class was bound to be something of a prig, and this dictum probably represents her own sentiments. We do not, of course, see the lower classes at their illicit merrymakings, which are only mentioned as snares to tempt the unthinking. The sixpenny hop, frequently held at a public house, seems to have been one of the temptations most difficult to resist. The reasons for withstanding it are set forth by Mrs Grey, in *Langley School*, when she tells her daughter that dancing is all very well for young ladies who are carefully chaperoned, but the village girl is exposed to the dangers of a solitary return after dark from such diversions. Thus it is only the servants of careless people like the Fulmorts who frequent these entertainments, and it was at such a dance that the untrustworthy housemaid met the men who were planning to commit the burglary.

Respectable diversions are, however, provided lavishly by Miss Yonge. There are frequent references to harvest customs, such as the supper and the bringing home of the last sheaf, but she obviously prefers such as have an admixture of religion. The picture painted by Frank Willoughby, in *The Castle Builders*, of his uncle's parish was worthy of Hursley itself:

Old Jem Churcher rings the harvest service bell at half-past five, and all the people come to church before they go out to the fields. That would be what you would call like a picture, Emmie, seeing them all come out from under the church gateway with their reap-hooks, and their little wooden kegs of beer. Yes, and just this very time—'tis eight, is not it?—he will be ringing the curfew; and nobody stops a bit in the field after that, but in they come . . . to church; and you can't think how pretty it is coming out, to see the porch and the church-yard all heaped up with their sheaves of gleaning.

Christmas, of course, had its appropriate festivities. Some of the tales of village life are here documents of quite historic interest. We have the contrast of the carols of the Bramley and Stainer era with the traditional carol, of which strange versions were extant, such as:

Rise up, rise up, brother Divers,
And come along with me;
There's a place in hell prepared for thee,
To sit upon a serpent's knee.

And there is the mummers' play, of which Miss Yonge gives

fragments in *The Christmas Mummers,* similar to Hardy's version in *The Return of the Native:*

> There were tall helmets. . . . High and bright they stood up, so as to make the boys look taller; and round the edge were sewn a number of long narrow slips of coloured paper, to hang down over the faces, and serve instead of the masks and vizards which mummers used to wear in the grander days long gone by. Bows of ribbon everybody got where he could, to be sewn on over the white trowsers, shirt sleeves, or white canvas frocks.

The summer had its festivals too. On May Day the children made their bright garlands and carried them round the village in the quest for pennies. But dearest of all holidays was Whitsun, when it was a point of honour for rich and poor alike to have some new bit of finery to show off. The Whit Monday Club Walking has been preserved for us by Hardy's account of it in *Tess.* We will round off our picture of village life with Miss Yonge's picture of this ceremony:

> At half-past ten the rude music of the band of the Friendly Society came pealing from the top of the hill, then appeared two tall flags, crowned with guelder roses and peonies, then the great blue drum, the clarionet blown by red-waistcoated and red-faced Mr Appleton, the three flutes and the triangle, all at their loudest, causing some of the spectators to start, and others to dance. Then behold the whole procession of labourers, in white round frocks, blue ribbons in their hats, and tall blue staves in their hands. In the rear, the confused mob, women and children, cheerful faces and mirthful sounds everywhere.

CHAPTER V

THE CHURCH

W HEN in 1829 the Winslow family took possession of Chantry House (in the novel of that name) they were both shocked and amused at the state of affairs revealed to them on their first visit to Earlscombe church. From their point of vantage in the family horsebox pew in the chancel, made snug on cold days by the stove whose pipe found a vent amidst the floriated tracery of a window, they peeped through the curtains at the "three-decker," where the clerk, making wild shots at Biblical names and long words, performed a monotonous duet with the curate. It was also the duty of this clerk to box the ears of any unruly member of the group of village children, who sat in slovenly fashion on the chancel steps, and, when the time came for the anthem, to join the bassoon and clarinet in the gallery and take his part in raising a tune so strange that the Winslows could scarcely conceal their amazement. Mr Mears, a hack curate, worn out by his work as a schoolmaster during the week, was forced to spend his Sundays in delivering, morning and afternoon by turns at Earlscombe and the neighbouring town, the same sermon, so indifferent that, as Mr Winslow drily remarked, it would hardly bear repetition.

The village of Earlscombe itself was no better than could have been expected from such indifferent pastoral care. The school was kept by an ignorant though picturesque old dame, whose hereditary claim to the office had outweighed her utter incompetence. So brutalized were the villagers that Emily Winslow was forbidden to carry out her schemes of cottage-visiting. In fact, Earlscombe presented suitable material on which to show, as Charlotte Yonge loved to do, the miracles wrought by the ideals of the Oxford Movement. Miss Yonge wrote *Chantry House* when she was already old enough to enjoy dwelling on the past, and when sufficient time had elapsed to show in due perspective the early phases of the religious changes in which her whole being was bound up. It therefore gives the best historical survey of these changes, whereas her other novels are rather documents showing history in the making.

With the utter darkness of Earlscombe is contrasted the dawn of better things seen in the neighbouring village of Hillside, under the care of its benevolent squarsons, Parson Fordyce and his son, Parson Frank. To us the "grinder organ" which fulfilled their notions of ecclesiastical propriety seems just as sad a falling off from the fiddle, bassoon, and clarinet of Earlscombe as the scholarly discourses and snowy surplices of the Fordyces were an improvement on the uninspired utterances and soiled garments of the poor curate. The ousting of rustic orchestras from the churches appears to have been a fairly general measure, by no means confined to clergy of extreme 'Puseyite' tendencies. It is constantly referred to in the works of Miss Yonge as the necessary preliminary to the introduction of more seemly worship, and is a phenomenon recorded by other Victorian novelists, finding its most famous expression in Hardy's *Under the Greenwood Tree*. Charlotte Yonge's clergy were never strengthened in their desire to see an organ installed in their church by the fascinations of a potential organist such as Fancy Day, but they felt the sterner urge of convinced theory. Thus the rift between vicar and instrumentalists was not usually so quickly healed as it was at Mellstock, and Charlotte records with some regret the occasional secession of a deposed fiddle to non-conforming bodies, and the prejudice which had to be faced in slowly building up an effective choir. But even the parish of Hillside had in 1829 progressed only as far as the grinder organ, with its repertory of metrical psalms.

The history of Parson Frank Fordyce is that of the birth of the Oxford Movement. His father was a man of exemplary life and a benevolent parish priest, but his pastoral duties did not prevent his being a keen rider to hounds. Under the influence of his wife, whom the worldly stigmatized as "methodistical," Parson Frank's first step upwards was to forswear all the field sports he loved so well. Those who try to fit the history of the various movements in the development of the English Church into watertight compartments often fail to realize that the Evangelical movement reacted on those whose views, expressed in *Tracts for the Times*, appeared to be its direct antithesis. Hillside and Earlscombe were in the Hannah More country, and the first

mistress in the school set up by the Winslows had been taught
as a child in the school at Cheddar. Men such as Parson Frank
learnt from pious Evangelicals to establish their spiritual relations with the Deity, but are represented as deepening these
relations through channels not favourably regarded by their
teachers. During the years when Frank Fordyce was apparently
leading the life of a well-to-do country parson the ferment of
Tracts for the Times was working, and with the deeper feelings
aroused by the death of his daughter Ellen in the mid-eighteen-
thirties the final stage of his development was reached. On leaving
Hillside he devoted his energies and fortune to a neglected Lan-
cashire parish. The Oxford Movement had gone beyond its
tentative beginnings and was in full swing.

The first stage of the Oxford Movement is reflected in Miss
Yonge's earlier works, *Chantry House* being a retrospect. Fortunately Miss Yonge considered it irreverent to weigh the pros
and cons of dogma and to make free with the name of the
Almighty in a novel, so we need not look in her books for exposi-
tions of the teaching of the Movement from the lips of its pro-
tagonists. Such characters are rather the fruits by which it
should be known, and though their practical activities are fully
shown, we have to infer from these much of their beliefs.

In the early phases of the Movement the two features most
stressed by Charlotte Yonge were church-building and school-
teaching. It was characteristic that the theme of *Abbeychurch*,
her first English work, should be provided by the consecration
of a new church. The church-building *motif* finds its chief
expression, however, in *The Daisy Chain*, where the building
of Cocksmoor Church is linked with the tale, so fraught with
romantic pathos for the Victorian reader, of the love of Margaret
May and Alan Ernescliffe. Although the church was the fulfilment of Ethel's vision and the reward for her constancy and
perseverance, it was built with Alan's money as a memorial of
the happiness of the lovers who appear to the reader so ill-
starred. This church, with its roof shaped like the timbers of a
ship, to symbolize the fulfilment of a sailor's vow, and with
Margaret's betrothal ring set round the stem of the chalice,
seemed the acme of romance. On hearing of the lacework spire,
through which the blue sky could be seen, dominating heath and
hillside, and of the windows exulted over by each individual

donor, the reader conjures up a vision illuminated with the medieval glories of Gothic architecture. Then, with a shock of surprise, he realizes that Cocksmoor could only have been a lifeless imitation of the Gothic past, and that the windows would to-day be the object of almost universal scorn.

When a church already existed, Charlotte Yonge's right-minded persons contented themselves with "beautifying" or "rendering more seemly" the existing fabric. The first objective against which their destructive zeal was directed was the church seating. A high pew to them was never a fine piece of old oak or a good example of Jacobean carving, but a temptation to somnolence or unseemly behaviour. This wholesale destruction of pews was frequently a clear case of the triumph of principle over conservative sentiment and æsthetic feeling. Dr May so clung to the past that his sense of "ecclesiastic propriety" was hard put to it to reconcile him to the loss of the old pews, and even of the gallery, an object which the nineteenth and twentieth centuries unite in regarding as an excrescence. Charlotte herself probably had a stifled regret for the banished pews, for Lady Merrifield, who was often a vehicle for her own sentiments, confessed in her latter years that the idea of churchgoing in the abstract always brought before her mind's eye the Beechcroft church of her childhood, with its high pews, before it had known the hand of the reformer.

The Sunday school was by no means an innovation of the Oxford Movement. Keble and his followers saw that the Evangelicals were right in recognizing in the children the most hopeful objects for their teaching. The difference between them lay in the way they taught. The two methods of approach are contrasted in *The Castle Builders*, where Emmeline and Kate ill-advisedly become involved in the activities of a school, run by an Evangelical committee of laymen. Such bodies, in the eyes of Miss Yonge, lacked the proper sanction of the Church. Similarly, the Ladies' Committee at Stoneborough, which was such a thorn in the flesh of Ethel May, ruled unchecked over the Sunday school and all other charitable institutions in the town, until finally subdued by the tact of Dr Spencer. As did Trollope in the case of Mr Slope, Miss Yonge rather cruelly indulges her prejudice against Evangelicals by frequently hinting that those who professed this form of religion were not

drawn from the best social circles, though she later made full
amends by the impeccable gentility of the Low Church Miss
Hepburns in *The Pillars of the House*. Emmeline and Kate have
their eyes finally opened to the enormity of teaching without the
sanction of the Church by the ill-bred meddling of a certain
member of the committee, who takes exception to their substitu-
tion of teaching on the Catechism for exposition of the Scrip-
tures, and tells them that the Catechism has been made "a
party badge." The girls are also regarded with suspicion on
account of their connexion with Lord Herbert Somerville, one
of the lights of the High Church party.

This viewing of the Catechism as a party badge was no doubt
the outcome of its use by the High Church clergy as a vehicle for
conveying to the people generally their own views on the efficacy
of the Sacraments as set forth for the educated man in *Tracts
for the Times*. It was certainly put to this use by Miss Yonge
herself in her "Conversations on the Catechism," published in
The Monthly Packet. *The Castle Builders* is, indeed, pure
propaganda on the subject of Confirmation and the Sacrament,
though, in spite of its avowed object, it manages to be very good
reading. The story culminates in the Confirmation of Emmeline
and Kate, who had allowed themselves to lose one opportunity
after another for reasons quite insufficient in the eyes of Miss
Yonge. Confirmation was important as the key unlocking the
door to full Christian privileges. Emmeline and her sister are
made to see the full enormity of their ways when, after narrowly
escaping death by drowning, it is brought home to them that it
would have been due to nothing but their own negligence if
they had been forced to meet their Maker unfortified by the
sacrament which their more spiritually-minded stepbrother
had received on the very morning of the accident.

This insistence on the strength to be derived from participation in the Holy Communion is a prominent feature of nearly all
Charlotte Yonge's books. Where a Mrs Sherwood would stress
faith in the Atoning Blood as the essential of the deathbed Miss
Yonge, though not disregarding this article of belief, prefers a
scene in which the friends of the dying man kneel by his bedside
and share in his last Communion. Streams of tears were shed by
the Victorian reading public over the deathbed scene in that
Victorian best-seller *The Heir of Redclyffe*. Guy is dying in

circumstances which would appear to ensure his well-being in a future life, having taken the fatal fever while tending his former enemy, but Charlotte does not allow him to die until a priest has found his way to the remote Alpine village where Guy is lying and has performed the last rites of the Church.

In Guy is found an exaggeration of the tendencies fostered by the inner side of the Oxford Movement, as distinct from its outward manifestations of church-building, teaching, and ritual. The modern reader may find him unconvincing, but such authentic records of the spiritual state of the followers of the Movement as Hurrell Froude's *Remains* show the same morbid consciousness of sin over the slightest fault. Froude could write in all seriousness in his diary for 1826:

> *September* 29. I cannot say much for myself to-day. . . . Looked with greediness to see if there was a goose on the table for dinner.
>
> *October* 4. I had an impulse, too, to let it be thought here that I had had only three shots, when I really had had four; it was very slight, to be sure, but I felt it.
>
> *October* 21. Meant to have kept a fast, and did abstain from dinner; but at tea ate buttered toast, when I knew it was bad for me; yet all the while was excusing myself with the notion that I ought to prepare for the journey that I should have to-day.

When we note that Mr Froude, though living an apparently blameless life, remarks that he has "forsaken the Lord," or "I stand in my naked filthiness before Thee," we can recognize the stuff of which the Heir was made.

Another type dear to Charlotte Yonge is the weak person made strong through the comforts of religion. She expressly states that such was the idea on which were built up the characters of Louis Fitzjocelyn in *Dynevor Terrace* and Violet in *Heartsease*. The quality of Louis's religion is chiefly brought out by the way in which his father, a rigidly correct statesman of conventional religious habits, reacts to it. Lord Ormersfield is inclined to regard the piety of his son as emotionalism, and cannot believe that it will cure him of the faults of his volatile nature. He is at last, however, forced to admit that the devotional habits on which Louis orders his life have given him stability and made him a respected and useful member of society. In Violet the reader is allowed to watch the spiritual development which turns the unimaginative piety of a schoolgirl into the deeply felt religion which sustains the heroine and her family through many trials. The common denominator most apparent to the modern reader in all these records of religious experience is an excess of morbid self-questioning. Its more sacred aspects are veiled in decent reticence, so that we rarely get unblushing dissertations on pious emotions as in so much other literature of the age. We hear frequently of little manuscript books of private devotions, such as that kept by Lord Fitzjocelyn under his pillow during his illness, but their contents are not laid bare. In addition to manuals of prayer, both new and old, published and unpublished, all of Miss Yonge's well-educated characters read, mark, learn, and inwardly digest every word of Keble's *Christian Year*. Even the profane Owen, in *Hopes and Fears*, can come out with an apposite quotation, likening the green and white of a girl's first party dress to the snowdrop of one of the poems. The same emotion which expressed itself in admiration for *The Christian Year* also finds an outlet in an exaggeration of the Wordsworthian cult of moralizing over natural beauties. Miss Yonge herself could on occasion write with straightforward appreciation of beautiful scenery, but many of her characters seem incapable of allowing themselves a simple enjoyment of nature, but can see in it only a symbol of some rarefied emotion. Those "Bekenntnisse einer schönen Seele," the diary of Helen Fotheringham, the "beautiful soul" whose influence pervades *Heartsease*, though she is dead before the opening of the novel, are typical. She writes in the diary kept for the edification of her lover:

This morning was a pattern one for February, and I went out before the brightness was passed, and had several turns in the walled garden. . . . The frost last night was not sharp, but just sufficient to detain the dew till the sun could turn it into diamonds. There were some so brilliant, glancing red or green in different lights, they were quite a study. It is pleasant to think that this pretty frost is not adorning the plants with unwholesome beauty, though the poor little green buds of currant and gooseberry don't like it, and the pairs of woodbine leaves turn in their edges. It is doing them good against their will, keeping them from spreading too soon. I fancied it like early troubles, keeping baptismal dew fresh and bright; and those jewels of living light went on to connect themselves with the radiant coronets of some whom the world might call blighted in their early bloom, and deprived of all tha life was bestowed for; but how different is the inner view, and how glorious the thought of the numbers of quiet, commonplace sufferers in homely life, like my currant and gooseberry bushes who have found their frost has preserved their dewdrops to be diamonds for ever.

By the eighteen-fifties many of the practices advocated for the past twenty years by 'Puseyite' clergy had become fairly general In Miss Yonge's earlier novels her clergy think they have brough about a great reform when they introduce monthly, instead o thrice yearly, celebrations. These services take place generally after Matins, and, when an "early service" is mentioned, thi means the daily Matins, which was yet another plank of the reformers. Violet Martindale told her husband that she had no Sunday book to read, and would feel uncomfortable if she missed Evensong, and so prevailed on him to plough through the rain with her to church. Yet it was only after she had come, in religious matters, under the influence of her brother-in-law John (formerly the betrothed of Helen, whose diary has been quoted) that Violet was conscience-stricken at having missed her Christmas Communion just because she felt too shy to stay on without the unthinking Arthur. *Heartsease* has few happen ings which date it, but it seems to belong to a period somewha earlier than 1854, the actual date of publication. In most o those books which appeared during the 'fifties and 'sixties it is possible to deduce a celebration at least monthly, and frequently weekly. *The Pillars of the House* gives the most precise informa tion about the details of churchgoing. Here Alda, when living in the household of the comparatively Low Church Tom Under wood, stays to late Communion, while her brothers Felix and Lance go to early celebrations at their more advanced church When Lance was spending a week-end in London, in the middle of the eighteen-sixties, he goes even higher in the ritualistic scale and enjoys an orgy of religious dissipation, consisting of a Choral Eucharist, followed by sung Matins.

In all Charlotte Yonge's pattern parishes daily Matins and Evensong were as important as frequent celebrations. All her right-thinking characters found weekday churchgoing a source of great spiritual refreshment. It was one of the signs that Albinia Kendall (*The Young Stepmother*) had firmly established

er influence over her stepdaughters, when they took to climb-
ng the hill up to the church every day. The May family also
ell more and more into the habit of frequenting the Minster
n weekdays, after Mr Wilmot had introduced seemly worship
here. One of the first moves of Julius Charnock, in *The Three
Brides*, when appointed to the family living some time during
he eighteen-seventies, was to provide daily services. This did
not always come easy to his junior curate during the days of his
unregenerate diaconate, when cricket often seemed much more
attractive than churchgoing. Nor did the sight of his three dogs
ooking appealingly at him from the vestry door help him to get
hrough the service.

During the latter half of the century the "grinder organ" of
Parson Fordyce, with its limited repertory of metrical psalms,
had become but a memory to the elders, and the young people
were zealously promoting the introduction of *Hymns Ancient
and Modern*. When Averil Ward remarked with amazement in
1860, "But *does* anyone approve of the New Version [of Tate
and Brady]?" Dr May answered, "Don't come down on me. . . .
I know it all; but the singing psalms are the singing psalms to
me—and I can't help my bad taste—I'm too old to change."
As with the old pews, the Doctor clung to what had been endeared
by long association. He speaks, for instance, with obvious emotion
of a metrical version of the Twenty-third Psalm: "Ethel, they
sang that Psalm the first Sunday I brought your mamma home."
It is, however, to the musical Underwood, rather than to the
unmusical May, family that we must turn for a correct impression of mid-Victorian development in Church music. They
provide us with discussions in which the cathedral use of Minsterham, with its generally accepted repertory of chants and anthems,
is contrasted with the Gregorian chants, which must have been
an innovation, as yet rare, in the slum parish of Robert Fulmort
(*Hopes and Fears*). The hold that *Hymns Ancient and Modern*
was gaining is well illustrated by the fact that the invalid
Ermine Williams should take pleasure in teaching her little
niece and the small maid to sing "The Strain upraise of Joy and
Praise" for Trinity Sunday.

Just as the innovations in ritual and services of the eighteen-
thirties and -forties had become widely accepted habits by the
eighteen-fifties and -sixties, so ideas that had seemed chimerical

and far-fetched during the early period were being translated into reality as the century progressed. Charlotte Yonge's early books are tinged with the sentimental medievalism engendered by a passionate devotion to Scott's novels. One of its most popular aspects was a yearning for the monastic life, without any real conception of what this involved. Emma Brandon's pious vapourings and her dream of restoring to its original purpose the Priory of which she is the heiress in the prosaic nineteenth century are typical of this trend. The very fact that she can be taken in by the talk of the specious Mark Gardner, when he reduces her aspirations to absurdity through his exaggeration of them, shows them up as nebulous. Emma is at last brought to reality when she is saved from joining her even more extreme-minded friend Theresa Marstone in conversion to Rome, and she contents herself merely with bringing up orphans instead of founding a sisterhood. Such institutions had to wait for a later age and more worthy founders. The first hint of the practical realization of the dream is in *The Heir of Redclyffe* when Guy leaves the Miss Wellwoods five thousand pounds to found a sisterhood, though it is not clear whether this is to be merely an institution for nursing and teaching or a full-blown convent. It is certain, however, that the uninitiated were ready to attribute any excess to the 'Puseyites,' and that popular gossip exaggerated this legacy into the means for establishing a chantry to pray for the soul of Guy's grandfather!

By the year 1854, in the early chapters of *The Pillars of the House*, the Sisterhood at Dearport was already a going concern. Lord Herbert Somerville, the consumptive curate of *The Castle Builders*, had since died and left his fortune and his wife as a legacy to found a sisterhood. The former Lady Herbert, now Sister Constance, comes to nurse Mr Underwood in his last illness and to minister to his stricken family, and at most crises in their history the Underwoods fall back on the Sisterhood for practical assistance. The feature of convents most appreciated by the general public was the training given there in nursing. Even Dr May, who accepted most religious innovations somewhat against the grain, was full of praise for the two nuns who had been sent to deal with the Stoneborough fever epidemic, and only registered a mild protest by calling them "Those gems of women" or "Miss What d'ye-call-her," instead of Sister

Katherine and Sister Frances. By the eighteen-seventies sister-hoods appear to have attained to a certain popularity even in fashionable circles. Lady Susan Strangeways, who let none of the pious practices of an advanced ritualist debar her from being thoroughly in the swing socially, talked with pride of her eldest daughter, who had taken the veil. In *The Three Brides* yet another activity of convents is brought into prominence—the retreat, which appears to have been used by Lady Susan as a kind of spiritual rest-cure after the London season. Although such practices were apparently accepted by a certain section of fashionable society, represented by the Strangeways, they were still anathema to the old-fashioned, such as Sir Harry Vivian, so that his daughter, Eleonora, had to attend the retreat without his knowledge.

Bound up with the question of the monastic life was that of the restoration of property, diverted at the time of the Reformation from the religious orders. Charlotte Yonge herself did not sentimentalize over the dissolution of the monasteries, and she gives an unbiased picture of their state in her Tudor story, *The Armourer's 'Prentices.* Many of her characters, however, are filled with a sense of hereditary guilt when they enjoy the revenues of Church lands. The sentimenal Emma Brandon can even reflect with pious horror that she might "die in the guilt of sacrilege." But it was left for Felix Underwood to give proof that his sentiments were genuine. Other characters might express regret, but Felix had the strength of mind to continue in trade and cut down all luxuries, until he was able to restore to the Church the income derived from the lay Rectorship of Vale Leston. Felix was a thoroughly practical man, so the restoration took the sensible form of endowing a new parish in an outlying part of his estate, on which the suburbs of the nearest town had encroached.

Although convents are frequently mentioned by Miss Yonge, none of her male characters enter Anglican monasteries. The nearest approach to such institutions countenanced by her are clergy houses for celibate priests, such as that founded by Robert Fulmort in *Hopes and Fears,* in the reaction from his love affair with the worldly Lucilla. Here vicar and curates lived a simple life in the heart of their slum parish, together with a few privileged lads, like Clement Underwood, who formed a small choir school. It is doubtful whether Miss Yonge thoroughly approved of priests' being cut off from the normal atmosphere of home life. Indeed, she took care to place within reach of the clergy house the old city home of Honora Charlecote, where choirboy and curate alike could enjoy the gentle influence of a cultivated woman. This was Clement's holiday resort in his boyhood, and, when he had risen to be vicar, his own incumbency was given a propitious start by the presence in that same house of his sister, Geraldine. When Miss Yonge portrays a celibate priest, he often seems an individual instance where celibacy was the right course. Robert's spiritual growth had set him above the weaknesses of humanity, and his strength must be devoted to the service of mankind, not confined to the cherishing of one woman. In the case of Clement Underwood, the sight of his dying father, leaving ill provided thirteen children, at least four of whom had been produced when he was already suffering from tuberculosis, might well have given him a bias towards a celibate priesthood.

If a fairly general characteristic of the earlier exponents of 'Puseyite' teaching was an exaggerated medievalism, their chief snare in the eyes of Miss Yonge was the Church of the Middle Ages in its nineteenth-century form. Those who take a wrong turning find that it leads them Romeward. But in the second phase of her writing, apparently, the more potent danger was 'doubt.' Several characters in the novels of the middle period lament that Oxford, which had once been the inspirer of lofty sentiments and the spur to action, had become a place of trial, where the faith of the undergraduate was tested by unchristian argument. In the earlier novels doubt was represented as a weed of foreign growth, which had not yet taken root on British soil, and was stigmatized under the name of "Germanism." A girl in *The Two Guardians*, one of the tales in which what one critic called the "âpre Puseyism" of Charlotte's youth was most rampant, went so far as to die of love on breaking off her engagement with a young man who, though "so clever, so sensible," and thinking Christianity "the best and most beautiful form of religion yet promulgated," qualified this view by considering it all very well "for women and weak-minded people," and capped all by talking "of the Old Testament as if it was just like Greek mythology." Miss Yonge evidently recognized this view as a heresy of German manufacture, since she makes the German

overness, whom the resourceful Theodora Martindale got rid of
y means of a faked ghost, shock her pupil by calling the book of
Ĵenesis a "schöne, mythische Geschichte" and the prophets "the
Iebrew avatars." By the middle period, however, doubt had
pread far beyond the Fatherland, and was lying in wait to
orture Norman May when the arguments of the lax Harvey
Ânderson, though triumphantly refuted by Norman in public
lebate at Oxford, returned to haunt him at moments when he
vas left alone with his morbid thoughts. Norman spoke later to
Ĉthel of his wrestlings of the spirit as if they had been the crisis
•f a desperate illness, and so deeply did he feel the gravity of
.uch symptoms that he determined to avoid any danger of a
ecurrence of the religious distempers engendered by the Oxford
atmosphere, by removing himself to the distant mission field.

The weeds of doubt had apparently spread widely by the
eighteen-sixties, when they were choking the mind of Rachel
Ĵurtis 'The Clever Woman of the Family' who had merely caught
.ap a few of the prevalent ideas from periodicals. What these
loubts were is a matter for speculation, for Miss Yonge was not
willing to expatiate on such shocking matters for fear of unset-
tling her own faith or that of her readers. The modern reader
suspects that the doubts, spoken of with bated breath by Rachel
when she had come to a more submissive frame of mind, would
really resolve themselves into the views held by a Broad Churchman of the eighteen-sixties. A short stay at the parsonage of
Mr Clare and a few discussions with that saintly priest were
quite enough to dispel Rachel's doubts for ever.

The "doubts" of Miss Fennimore, the highly intellectual
governess of the Fulmorts, in *Hopes and Fears*, come into a
different category, being the result of ignorance rather than sins
against the light. She came of a Unitarian family and had high
moral standards, based on a liberal and philosophical interpretation of "Christianity, modified by the world's progress." Influenced by her admiration for the spontaneous religious habits
of her pupil Phœbe, Miss Fennimore is led to re-examine the
foundations of her beliefs, but is not finally convinced of her
errors until she sees the dire effects of her own precepts when
Bertha, the youngest sister, at the age of fifteen attempts to
elope with a man of evil character, and has to go through a brain-
fever before she is cured of the flippant attitude to religious

H

matters engendered by Miss Fennimore's system. After the governess has been received into the Church and expiated her past errors by a year's work in Robert Fulmort's slum parish she is allowed to go back to his sisters and resume her studies with them "on safer ground." Many years later we meet Miss Fennimore again in *The Pillars of the House* as the joint head with Bertha, whose fortune provided the necessary funds, of the school which gave a free education to Robina and Angela Underwood. Miss Yonge is less chary of allowing Miss Fennimore to formulate her religious views than she was in the case of Rachel Curtis, apparently having no fears that they would have a baneful effect on the faith of either authoress or reader. Nowadays such views might well be expressed by any Churchman of liberal outlook, and would shock none but a fundamentalist or extreme Anglo-Catholic.

It is, of course, impossible to pin down within clearly defined dates the various phases in the development of some institution especially in the case of a body such as the Church of England which admits such varied shades of opinion and practice. It can however, be stated with some degree of accuracy that the High Church party passed in Miss Yonge's lifetime through three phases. With the first two she progressed joyfully, step by step but as the third developed she was growing old, and was inclined to straggle along in the rear. So long as the innovations did not strike at the very root of her beliefs she was prepared to look with tolerance at the doings of the innovators, even if she could not go along with them wholeheartedly. As she characteristically expressed it by the lips of Dr May and Ethel, while one generation had established the Knights of the Round Table, it was left for the next to progress to the search for the Holy Grail. In the novels of Miss Yonge's old age we see the latest developments in the Church darkly through the glass held up to them by the older characters, who express her own views. Geraldine Grinstead (*née* Underwood) helps us to form an idea of her nephew, Gerald Underwood, as a typical representative of the rising generation. His religious views, which caused a certain feeling of anxiety to his aunt, are never expressly defined, but the reader with some knowledge of the period would certainly deduce them to be those which fluttered the ecclesiastical dove-

tes when Dr Gore edited *Lux Mundi* in 1890. These views
generally went with the "Christian Socialism" of the Oxford
undergraduate of Gerald's day, and of this he was a decided
exponent with his slumming activities and reaction against the
Underwood conservatism.

While Gerald and his set went beyond Miss Yonge in dogma,
another section of his contemporaries satisfied their urge for
innovation by external changes. In the late eighteen-seventies
the Strangeways girls had shocked a village congregation by their
crossings and genuflexions, but by the end of the eighteen-
eighties and eighteen-nineties the ritualist was to be met with
quite often. When Geraldine painted one of her famous
academy pictures, representing Lance as *The Acolyte*, some time
during the eighteen-sixties, an Evangelical lady was glad to be
assured that the vestments and ornaments had been made out
from a book. Some twenty years later Geraldine could probably
have drawn much of her setting from life had she visited
St Kenelm's Church at Rockstone, where the Reverend Augustine
Flight indulged his taste for the ornate, which was slightingly
designated by Adeline Mohun as "Quite oppressed with ornament. City taste, you know." Mr Flight had devoted the money
his father had made in the City to transmogrifying a tin taber-
nacle into a church complete in every ritualistic detail. Even
when St Kenelm's was first mentioned (in *Beechcroft at Rockstone*) it was over-ornamental; but some half a dozen years later
it was being still further beautified by mural frescoes, representing very fanciful and black-letter saints. The ceremonial at
St Kenelm's was such as befitted this setting and the musical
tastes of the incumbent. All this is in keeping with the unattached nuns, Sister Beata and Sister Philomena, described thus
by Jane Mohun:

> They are what my brother calls Cousins of Mercy. The elder one
> has tried two or three Sisterhoods, and being dissatisfied with all
> the rules, I fancy she has some notion of trying to set up one on her
> own account at Mr Flight's. They are both relations of his mother,
> and are really one of his experiments—fancy names and fancy rules,
> of course. . . . So they act as parish women here, and they do it
> very well.

In Jane's words we sense a slight strain of malice, which is absent from the following description of rather similar parish arrangements in a growing industrial town:

> St Ambrose Road was dominated by a tall and beautiful spire according to the original design. They turned and looked in at the pillared aisles, stained glass and handsome reredos.

A former church worker sums up the situation thus:

> [The new vicar] has three curates and a house of sisters and works the parish excellently . . . his womenkind are rather grand—quite out of our beat and in parish work I am only an estimable excrescence.[1]

The characters in Miss Yonge's later novels are often slight sketches, not to be compared with the full-length portraits of her more vigorous years. Their value lies in the rounding off of the picture of the Victorian period and in the comments she herself makes through the mouth of her elderly characters pointing out developments and contrasts. One of her most frequent comments on the latest aberrations of the extreme ritualist was that his reverence was often only technical, and that he missed the true awe of the spirit felt by her generation in the presence of holy things. She noticed that two girls could behave in church with demonstrative devotion, with many crossings and genuflexions, and yet indulge in mundane and flirtatious talk the very moment they had passed the sacred threshold. In Miss Yonge's eyes the new type of Anglo-Catholic was inclined to fritter away his energies in laying too much stress on the outward trappings of religion. This is brought home to the heroine of *Nuttie's Father*, when, after contact with a wider circle, she meets again the youth whose ritualistic views she once shared:

> She was tired of Gerard Godfrey! Had he always talked of nothing but "the colours," chants, E.C.U. classes and teetotalism? Whatever she began, it always came back to one or other of these subjects and when she impatiently declared that she was perfectly sick of hearing of the use of Sarum, he looked at her as guilty of a profanity.

Again, when Armine Brownlow, in *Magnum Bonum*, was in bondage to the ultra-ritualistic sister of his vicar, he was sent out in pouring rain, in spite of his delicate chest, to fetch tassel and cord of the correct colour for the banner, which was to figure

[1] *Nuttie's Father*.

n a Harvest Festival procession. Armine later recovered from
his aberrations, and, though still a ritualist, was allowed by Miss
Yonge to become the "cynosure curate" for the young ladies of
fashionable watering-place.

Another of the changes which struck Miss Yonge sadly was the
diminished zeal of the modern girl for Sunday-school teaching.
Lady Merrifield recalled the days of her youth, when every girl
regarded her schoolchildren as "the prettiest and cleverest in
nature," and wrote little pink books about them, in which the
good ones either died young or were rewarded by living in a
clergyman's family; whereas her daughters, even the old-
fashioned Mysie, taught in Sunday school only from a sense of
duty. The C. M. Yonge enthusiast often wonders whether this
sense of disenchantment, hanging about her later descriptions of
many activities of the Church which had seemed a veritable
romance in the early novels, was an echo of reality, or whether
the golden haze thrown over the first phase of the Oxford
Movement merely existed because the young Charlotte had the
gift of making her reader see things through her own eyes. The
truth lies possibly somewhere in between these two hypotheses.
A movement in its beginnings often attracts the adventurous,
pioneering spirit, while the enthusiasm of the originator, once it
has won general acceptance, is toned down into the lukewarm
benevolence of the commonplace supporter. It is instructive to
compare the May family with their descendants and those of
their friends in Miss Yonge's last few novels. A Gillian Merrifield unwillingly reading to an invalid girl has succeeded to an
Ethel May burning hot with enthusiasm for her work among the
poor of Cocksmoor.

What of Ethel's other romance, the mission field? She was
happy to see her favourite brother, Norman, renounce a brilliant
career to go out to New Zealand, while Meta Rivers felt that all
her aspirations were being fulfilled when she accompanied him
as his bride. She cast over all his activities the romantic aura
of the period of the *Idylls of the King*, and wrote quite sincerely,
when describing the mundane manufacture of a knapsack for
her missionary: "I do like such a good tough bit of stitchery, to
fit my knight out for the cause." To sense the different outlook
of the two ages we should compare the missionary meeting in the
town hall at Stoneborough on the day when Norman proposed

to Meta, where Miss Yonge so well succeeds in conveying th
tense emotion and enthusiasm of the audience, with the S.P.G
meeting at Vale Leston in *The Long Vacation*. In the degenerat
fin de siècle days it was apparently necessary to offer a weddin,
in high life as a bait to secure a large audience for our old friend
Norman, now a bishop, and Leonard Ward.

The same disenchantment hovers over the clergy of the lat
nineteenth century. They seem very commonplace men com
pared with their predecessors. Their social status was on th
whole not so elevated. A Lord Herbert Somerville, that aristo
cratic and handsome young curate, with the hectic flush whicl
made him even more interesting and attractive, had given plac
to an Alexis White, the son of an officer risen from the ranks
who reaches the priesthood not by the university, but by way o
a theological college. Similarly Robert Fulmort and Clemen
Underwood are followed in the clergyhouse by Gerard Godfrey
a clerk in a humble way, who has achieved Holy Orders afte
serving an apprenticeship as lay reader.

It must be confessed that Miss Yonge herself in all her work
expresses a preference, either avowed or tacit, for clergy of higl
family. In *The Clever Woman of the Family* the Williams sister
were inclined to wince at the slight lack of refinement in M
Touchett, who was the son of a minor canon, and, though a
Oxford man, "had only been at a Hall." In no book is the asse
of gentility more stressed than in *The Pillars of the House*
Mr Underwood, though living in the utmost poverty, never los
the air of the country squarson, which he should have been ha
justice been done him, and Miss Yonge delights in letting u
know that years of insufficient food and drink had not spoilt hi
discriminating palate for the old port, contributed by his eve
more aristocratic fellow-curate to Felix's birthday picnic. I
spite of the sad necessity which drove Felix into trade, the Under
wood family preserved their air of breeding and a conviction tha
good blood was a possession of which no external circumstance
could rob them. Even at their fortune's lowest ebb they coul
look down on Mr Mowbray Smith, the product of a provincia
university, who overlaid his lack of breeding with tuft-huntin,
snobbery, and when Felix took Clement to Vale Leston he felt
justifiable pride in being able to produce a clergyman brother s
obviously a scholar and a gentleman, while old Fulbert brough

rward his son's brother-in-law, who looked more like his farmer indred than a cleric.

In all Miss Yonge's novels clergymen appear, whether in the refront or in the background, but in no other novel is the hurch so much bound up with the fortunes of the characters as a *The Pillars of the House*. It justifies her boast that the great im and object of her writing was *Pro Ecclesia Dei*. The Under-ood family is rooted in the early phase of the Oxford Movement, hich saw the beginning of the ministry of Mr Underwood, *ère*, while it puts forth shoots, still vigorous at the close of the entury. Clement, a ritualistic prig in his youthful days, has ecome a tolerant and sensible middle-aged clergyman, whose hole attitude to the rising generation bears out the wise words Miss Yonge wrote in *Womankind*, when she herself was be-oming elderly:

> We enjoy progress as long as we go along with it, but there often comes a time when the progress gets beyond us. And then! are we to be drags, or stumbling-blocks, or to throw ourselves out of the cause altogether? . . . A welding together of the new and the old is the thing needful. Not that the young should treat everything old as worn out and ridiculous. It has been the strength and glory of England that she has been built on her old foundations instead of sweeping them away; but when we pass the bounds of our own youth, we have to bear in mind that it is narrow intolerance on the part of the elder generation which provokes the younger into a general overthrow as soon as they have the power.

BOOK THREE

FAMILY CHRONICLER

CHAPTER VI

JOHN KEBLE: DOMINANT INFLUENCE

DURING Charlotte's youth the Oxford Movement had been approaching the Yonge family through Sir William Heathcote, Mr Bigg-Wither, and Dr Moberly; but the dominant influence of her life was to arrive in 1836 in the person of John Keble, who was in that year presented to Hursley by his old pupil Sir William. Fate had clearly intended Charlotte to be caught up in the toils of the Movement, for the August of 1823 in which she was born was part of that memorable Long Vacation when Keble indoctrinated his pupils Hurrell Froude, Isaac Williams, and Robert Wilberforce with his principles. The seed then planted had grown apace, and, when Charlotte was only just entering her 'teens, it was bearing a vigorous crop of tracts and sermons. The Mr Slopes might preach Sabbath Day observance and salvation by a faith that could save even the deepest-dyed sinner who at his last moment experienced conversion; but the Mr Arabins, with learned arguments culled from deep readings of the Early Fathers and Caroline divines, were yearly gaining ground on them. So long as the tractarians did not threaten their loved temporalities, the Dr Grantlys of the Church too came in time to accord their dignified, if somewhat aloof, patronage to the Movement. If they might continue in their old and decorous ways, it mattered not if earnest young curates preached Laud's doctrines on the efficacy of sacraments, and even went to the unheard-of lengths of holding a monthly Communion service instead of keeping to the three times yearly enjoined by the rubric. These serious-minded clergymen did not only concern themselves with regeneration by means of the sacraments. They had come to the conclusion that zeal must no longer be the prerogative of the Evangelical or Methodist, but that the whole body of the Church must be shaken out of its dignified somno lence. Every year an increasing number of earnest young men nurtured on the milk of Newman's sermons and the meat of Dr Pusey's discourses, were launched on parishes all over the country, where they proceeded to stir up the apathetic, exhort the sinner, and permeate the Sunday school with a good Trac tarian atmosphere. They also, if they were gentlemen of fortune or had some wealthy admirer of the Movement at their back set about building or restoring churches in that particular style which makes us wonder why the Almighty should have allowed this outbreak in religious fervour to coincide with such an un fortunate period in architecture.

If Newman and Pusey gave the greatest intellectual stimulus to the Movement, it was Keble who furnished the perfect example of what a parish priest should be. Coming of a family of Non-Jurors who had quietly held to the teaching and ideals of the seventeenth-century divines, he had been bred up by his father to an unusually high standard of parochial activity. Nature and home atmosphere had made of Keble one of those rarely attractive characters that must inspire affection even in those who dissent from their views. Keble fulfilled the ideal, beloved of the Victorian, of being "strong as the lion, pure as the dove"—lion-like in the convictions that would never allow a relieving shade of grey in black or white, that held uncom promisingly to a certainty of eternal punishment for the wicked, and could speak of a Divorce Bill as " a Bill for legalizing adultery," and say "that it would be a gain to this country, were it vastly more superstitious, more bigoted, more gloomy, more fierce in its religion, than at present it shows itself to be"; dove-like in his gentleness and charm in ordinary intercourse, and in the vein of poetry that had found expression in *The Christian Year*. His true humility had prompted him to turn his back on Oxford, where he had won every possible distinction and where his reputation was at its height, and to give himself up to cheer his father's last years and minister to rustics. Such was the man who came to Hursley to be the deepest and most abiding in fluence on Charlotte Yonge's character and life.

From the moment of Mr Keble's arrival at Hursley the Yonge

mily took to him and his wife and sister, and were soon on
rms of the warmest friendship with them. There were various
les of the Movement and its prophet that made their special
ppeal to Mr and Mrs Yonge. Mrs Yonge was undoubtedly most
tracted by him as the author of *The Christian Year*, and, like
r daughter and many other pious ladies, probably knew many
the verses by heart. Mr Yonge, for his part, was taken up by
e practical side of the Movement. He cherished a fatal
ssion for amateur architecture, and had long had designs on
e picturesque old church with its ivy-covered boarded tower.
is true that the new railway was to run perilously near it, and
at the village had grown in the opposite direction—an excuse
fficient in Mr Yonge's eyes for building a new church on the
ain road in the centre of the village. As soon as he had found
r William Heathcote and Mr Keble ready to support him, he
it his whole soul and every spare penny into the undertaking.
he ascetic side of Mr Yonge that scorned all but the most Spar-
n equipment in his dressing-room, that abjured wine in hopes
averting hereditary gout and allowed fishing and shooting to
merely holiday relaxations, found a congenial aspect of the
ovement in the stress it laid on self-denial. He proceeded to
ve money for the church by giving up the journey to Puslinch
r some five years and denying himself snuff. Of personal
pervision he was no less prodigal; and, equipped with a know-
dge of military drawing and an admiration for York Minster,
felt himself competent to act as architect. Many a day was
ent in riding about inspecting different kinds of stone, viewing
ires not too ambitious for the funds in hand, or tracking down
d carvings for altar-rails and pulpit in antique shops in back
reets of London. The results prove Mr Yonge to have had more
ir as a connoisseur than as an architect. At Whitsuntide 1837
lian, aged seven, and much embarrassed by sentimental
urmurs from old ladies of "Pretty dear!" laid the first stone.
Mr Keble had many interests in common with Mr and Mrs
onge, but to Charlotte he was all in all. Soon after his arrival
Hursley he began to prepare her for Confirmation, and in her
found a pupil capable of appreciating his lore. If *Conversa-
ns on the Catechism*, which Charlotte Yonge began writing
me fifteen years after her own Confirmation, echo the instruc-
ns she then received from Mr Keble, we can only stand

amazed at the intellectual powers imputed to a girl of fourtee
or fifteen. A solid foundation of Bible history, references to th
Early Fathers and English divines, the history of the Churc
(as interpreted by the Tractarians), with excursions into th
comparative study of liturgies, apparently formed the programm
of the discussions. But perhaps the 'conversations' are mor
formidable than their originals; certainly Charlotte regarded th
hours spent in the quiet study at Hursley as moments of refresh
ment, both intellectual and spiritual.

As well as absorbing from Keble the theory of religion Chai
lotte was also concerned with its practical application in he
efforts to do her part in raising funds for the new girls' scho
which, it was felt, should accompany Mr Yonge's nineteenth
century Gothic church and the new boys' school. One day
when she and her mother sat racking their brains to get mor
money, they hit on the expedient of making a little book of th
French stories written for M. de Normanville and selling it i
aid of this charity. It was thus that *Le Château de Melvil*,
saw the light. In this book the story of the Melville girls is use
as a framework to hold various tales, which are mostly transl
tions of favourite nursery stories. The plot is laid in the peric
of the Napoleonic wars, which had for Charlotte a romanti
attraction through her father's tales. But the main interest fc
us must lie in the characters of the Melville girls, the fir
creatures to be born of Charlotte's lonely wanderings in the fiel
and copse at Otterbourne. It is amazing how alive they are fc
the productions of a girl of fifteen, and that in a foreign tongu
(though we must allow for her master's corrections)—curiou
Pauline, who listens at the door, and on its sudden opening fal
into the room on her nose; lazy Emilie and her bosom frien
in whose affected manners and sensibility Charlotte pokes fu
at the boarding-school miss of the previous generation; even th
virtuous Henriette, who saves her sisters by her presence of min
when they are all cut off by the tide. The year 1838, which sa
the publication of *Le Château de Melville* as well as Charlotte
Confirmation, was clearly one of the landmarks in her history

The years between the printing of this small book and her fir
efforts in English fiction were tranquil ones. For Charlott
there was no solemn 'coming out' from the schoolroom into
butterfly drawing-room existence. In fact, the girl who sti

id algebra with her father at the age of twenty-two never seems to have quite emerged from the atmosphere of the school-room, and the transition is imperceptible from the days when she wrote her exercises for M. de Normanville to those when she herself produced text-book upon text-book for the young. For one thing, the repression of her childhood and the refusal to give her a just estimate of her assets both in looks and brains eventually rendered her shyness quite irremediable, and strangers were apt to think her proud or bored—an utterly erroneous impression. The contrast of her manner towards her intimates gave them all the more pleasure; among them she did not restrain her natural vehemence. At times, indeed, she even became a little overwhelming, and, when mounted on one of her literary or historical enthusiasms, she would soar away, leaving her earthbound listeners panting after her. At the least approach, however, to formal society, Charlotte would arm herself with the well-bred impassivity into which she had been schooled, and prepare to encounter formidable strangers with all the courage she could muster. Yet she was always ready to observe, and to lay up such observations, on the humours and peculiarities of the society in which she found herself, and to store her retentive memory with phrases and turns of speech that took her fancy. Moreover, there was no reason why she should not have been a social success. Richmond's portrait of her at twenty-one shows her as a slim, pretty girl with good features and large dark eyes, her face softened by her ringlets and by the pensive droop of the head. When congenial society woke the dark eyes and mobile mouth into animation, Charlotte was a very charming person, the more so from her complete unconsciousness of her own attractions.

The social functions at which she felt most at home were those of a religious or an informal nature, such as a missionary festival or church dedication. These she described in long letters to Anne Yonge, and later reproduced in her books. Then there was the annual feast given by the Kebles to the united Sunday schools of Hursley and Otterbourne. It was Charlotte's delight to march proudly to church with her flock of demure little girls in their fresh cotton frocks and bright garlands. Next came the satisfaction of setting those children of the 'hungry 'forties' down at the long tables on the vicarage lawn and plying them with a substantial tea. There was no room for shyness as she ran to and fro among them or escaped to the merry tea laid in the dining-room for the helpers. Afterwards she would watch the animated scene in the park, where the boys played cricket and the girls formed picturesque groups under the trees. The day ended with singing on the twilit lawn. Years later, in *Musings over the "Christian Year,"* Charlotte Yonge wrote of these moments, so dear both to her and to Keble himself:

> How exquisite it used to be to stand on the terrace in the fresh evening scents of early summer, the grey church tower rising among the flowering shrubs—the weeping gold chains of the laburnum and the crimson tufts of the shumach, with straight dark horizontal bars of cedar thrust between, the stars gradually gleaming out, or a round full moon rising, and the children's voices, softened in the open air, pealing out in "God save the Queen" and finally in Ken's Evening Hymn; the universal hum of "thank you, Ma'm," Mr Keble's public "good-night" and the cheers of the boys dying away with the trampling feet in the distance.

Charlotte did not even despise the more worldly joy of dancing, when it formed part of a *fête-champêtre*. The Heathcotes were in the habit of giving entertainments of this kind which moved her to such mirth that she would bubble over into doggerel verse to celebrate the occasion. Such was the dance on the lawn which ended the beating of the parish bounds, or the heir's coming of age, where the merrymaking went on with waltz, quadrille, and Highland fling, until the evening ended with a glorious display of fireworks. Charlotte felt herself much more at home going up the middle and down again in the country dance on the lawn than in the artificial light of the ballroom, where self-conscious-ness would stiffen her limbs into ungainliness, and where there was the unfortunate necessity of making polite conversation to her partners. But the kind of party which she most enjoyed and where she chiefly shone was one when the evening was spent in playing paper games. This could be a highly intellectual and amusing pastime when the players included clever people like the Yonges and their friends—Moberlys, Coleridges, Dysons, and Kebles. For Mrs and Miss Keble were almost as delightful as the master of the house himself. Both were ladies of culture, and indulged in a degree of refined invalidism which endued them with an appealing charm. Mrs Keble, with her

elicate complexion, clear hazel eyes, and fine features, dressed
in the soft stuffs and bright colours that her husband loved, was
acknowledged by all to be a fit wife for a poet. She had a
charming faculty of setting shy people at their ease, and was
always ready to discuss books with Charlotte or lend her drawings
to be copied. It was a great occasion when Charlotte wrote to
Anne in 1839:

> I am going to Hursley to-day to stay with Mr Keble, in the hopes
> of hastening the departure of this tiresome cold. I like the thought
> of the visit very much, though it being the first time of my staying
> out by myself, how I shall manage winding up my watch remains
> to be proved.

Sophistication did not come early in those days.

When Charlotte was about twenty she was introduced to
another delightful Tractarian household, which was an extraordinary replica of the Keble *ménage*. Mr Dyson, who had been
up at Oxford a friend of Keble's and of Sir John Coleridge's, and
one of the inner circle of the movement, had become Vicar of
Dogmersfield, near Winchester, and settled there with his wife
and sister, Miss Marianne Dyson. Miss Dyson was a great
invalid, lamed by rheumatism and a sufferer from headaches,
but she had a strong and clear, if not original, intellect, and she
was a competent authoress of children's stories. She also set on
foot a small boarding school in Dogmersfield for girls of the
lower middle class, which it was her great hobby to supervise.
Although Miss Dyson was some fifteen years older than Charlotte, it was not surprising that they immediately struck up a
great friendship, in which Marianne evidently acted as mentor,
for Charlotte's nickname for her was "Driver," while she herself
was the "Slave." Soon an unbroken stream of letters began to
flow from Otterbourne and Dogmersfield, and Miss Dyson
accompanied every step of Charlotte's literary career, each new
development in the plot of all the earlier books being discussed
with her.

It was largely due to Miss Dyson that Charlotte Yonge's
passion for school-teaching bore literary as well as practical fruit.
For teaching Charlotte had a brilliant gift. In the classroom the
cloak of shyness fell away, and she could give out her personality
unobscured. Miss Coleridge, who later often watched her lessons,

tells us that "she taught in school like the most sympatheti
and cultivated of day-school teachers, conveying an immens
amount of knowledge and without a trace of stiffness or shyness.'
Such was Charlotte's affection for her Sunday school that sh
spent hours in preparing her lessons, and at the end of the da
she wrote down verbatim the answers of her pupils and sen
them to Anne Yonge or Marianne Dyson, together with length
screeds on the characters and doings of the children. It was o
behalf of her own schoolchildren that Miss Dyson first made us
of Charlotte's literary-pedagogic talent. Before the days o
systematic elementary education there was little in the way o
suitable text-books for children of the class of Miss Dyson'
protégées. Charlotte was set to supply the need, and the resul
was some admirable little books. It was not long before she wa
writing *of* as well as *for* the village, and soon her tales wer
accepted by Miss Anne Mozley for *The Magazine for the Youn*
brought out by her brother, Richard Mozley, a well-know
publisher of Church writings. Thus began the lifelong series o
tales of village life which form an admirable picture of socia
development during the nineteenth century.

Charlotte's gift for fiction was helped on by her strange habi
of recording verbatim conversations that took place mostly a
Puslinch, but sometimes at Otterbourne or during visits to th
Coleridges or to Lord Seaton, as her mother's stepbrother, Joh
Colborne, had now become. The conversations are for the mos
part utterly trivial, and were recorded for no other reason tha
her wish to keep green the humours of the passing hour. T
her they were not useful exercises in authorship, but monu-
ments to cousinly affection and friendship. It was, however, thi
habit that inspired the lifelike talk of the various families sh
created.

The conversations give us such an intimate glimpse of th
everyday life of a Victorian household that we feel as though w
were peeping through a window at the family group, as it sit
lit up by the soft radiance of lamp or candle. There are the young
ladies clustered round the large table with its fringed cloth, their
curls demurely veiling their faces as they bend over their embroidery. Now they make remarks that are "either very wise
or great nonsense," and now they stop to listen to the farming discussions of the two Mr Yonges or to their mothers'

A Review of Volunteers in Stoneleigh Park, 1860

By courtesy of "The Illustrated London News"

JOHN KEBLE
George Richmond, R.A.
By courtesy of the National Portrait Gallery

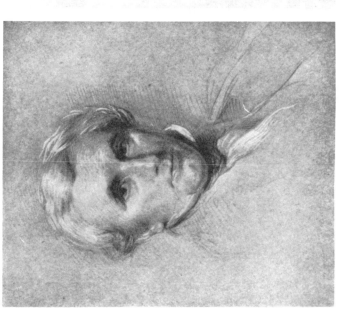

WILLIAM CRAWLEY YONGE
George Richmond, R.A.
Reproduced, by courtesy of Messrs Macmillan and Co., Ltd., from "Charlotte Mary Yonge," by Christabel Coleridge

reminiscences on what they call irreverently "old people, or the genealogy of the coffee-pot." The boys spend their time detailing the achievements of the day's fishing or shooting, or in arguments that end in their rolling about the floor like young puppies, until separated by an elder sister. Sometimes the girls come in for their share of fraternal teasing, and Julian is not slow to chaff Charlotte about her pet Sunday scholars or her habit of turning up her eyes when she is composing. She is fully capable of holding her own in their sparring—by a nonchalant indifference to Julian's doings or some annihilating remark about "little younger brothers." In the Heath's Court conversations there is none of this teasing, for Judge Coleridge himself mingles delightfully with the young people's chatter. They discuss such books as Miss Sewell's *Amy Herbert*, of which one lady staying in the house remarks that they liked it very much —"indeed, papa cried over it."

In a world where eminent judges were ready to enter into serious discussions on the merits of fiction for girls in the school-room, or where such books could move middle-aged gentlemen to tears, there was obviously scope for Miss Yonge's talents. From the Heath's Court discussions we see that from the beginning Charlotte was aware that stories inculcating the right principles had their humble part, as much as tracts or sermons, in the great movement. It was with this laudable object in view that a solemn family conclave later decided that Charlotte might be allowed to publish, though Mrs Bargus did not think writing books for money was a ladylike occupation. Mr Yonge gravely put before Charlotte three motives that might impel young authors to rush into print—"love of vanity, or of gain, or the wish to do good." Upon which she tearfully answered that she hoped she had written with the purpose of being useful to young girls like herself. At this even Grandmamma was pacified, and gave in when it was decided that her granddaughter should not take money herself, but that it would be used for some good work. It was not until *The Heir of Redclyffe* drew tears from a large reading public that Miss Yonge's pet charities struck a highly profitable seam, though the five tales that preceded it brought in a supply of gold that was not to be despised.

The connecting link in these five stories was the moral wish of the young authoress

I

to present a picture of ordinary life with its small daily events, its pleasures and its trials, so as to draw out its capabilities of being turned to the best account. . . . Each has been written with the wish to illustrate some principle which may be called the keynote.

It speaks well for Miss Yonge's gift for story-telling and character-creation that it defeated these excellent intentions so far as to cause some contemporary critics to accuse her of not making the moral sufficiently evident. Such critics would have had her adhere in this respect to the high standards of Miss Edgeworth, Mrs Sherwood, or of Miss Sewell.

In *Abbeychurch* at least, the characters are opposed black or white, with shades of grey not admitted, and the plot is slight. It is built round two incidents, the consecration of a new church (a scene of deep interest to the Yonges) and the forbidden visit of a party of giddy young people to a Mechanics' Institute—represented as a place frequented by those who "question the possibility of the first chapter of Genesis and . . . fancy that the world was peopled with a great tribe of wild savages, instead of believing all about Adam and Eve and the Patriarchs."

In spite of the faults natural in the production of a girl of twenty, there is some truth in Dean Church's opinion: "It is a very clever book, and the young lady will write well in the future . . . because every character, however simple, is perfectly distinct and living."

After the publication of *Abbeychurch* Charlotte very wisely abstained from print for three years, until *Scenes and Characters* came out in 1847. In the preface she modestly calls it a "chronicle of small beer," but for the lover of her writings it has a peculiar interest, as it is the warp of that complicated web of Mohun-May-Merrifield-Underwood history, of which the last threads were not to be woven until the end of her long life. The Mohun family had been Charlotte's dream companions since the first days when she had been old enough to take her wet day's exercise along the gravel path round the field. They had become as real to her as the Puslinch cousins themselves. It matters little that the moral aim of the story is to imbue the reader with a right conception of the importance of a sense of duty in daily life. The Mohun family were already creatures vigorous enough to take little harm from their avowed didactic purpose. The central characters were strong enough to survive over a period of some forty years, until they appeared again.

Henrietta's Wish, the next book, is chiefly remarkable for the
character of old Mrs Langford, who was obviously drawn from
Mrs Bargus. She is represented as a brisk old lady with the
prejudices of an earlier generation as well as its sound common
sense, which comes as a relief from the early Victorian mawkish-
ness of her grandchildren, Henrietta and Fred. Mrs Langford
is always entertaining, whether she is laying down the law to
her sons and daughters-in-law, who all hold her in great awe
and address her as "Ma'am," or plying her sick grandson with
nourishing delicacies, against the new-fangled advice of the
doctors. The main theme of the tale, however—that is, the dire
results of a lack of filial piety—is exaggerated beyond the taste
even of Miss Yonge's contemporary critics. In *The Two
Guardians* the crude morality of Charlotte's youth is yet more
rampant. Even in a literature rich in prigs, Marian Arundel, the
heroine, takes a high place. *The Castle Builders, or The Deferred
Confirmation*, is, in point of time, no later—it came out in *The
Monthly Packet* from 1851 to 1854, while *The Two Guardians*
was published in 1852—but the former shows that Miss Yonge's
powers were maturing, and her chief improvement lies in her
attitude towards her characters, whose destinies she has learnt
to control with greater aloofness. Both in the development of
the heroine, Emmeline, and in the portrayal of the minor
characters, such as Sir Francis and Lady Willoughby, she shows
real skill. He is a dried-up, yellow-faced little general, somewhat
fussy and worldly-wise, and most peremptory in his dealings
with his children. Having spent half his life in the East, he is
completely out of tune with the new developments, especially in
religion, that have occurred in his absence. His wife is another
type of the Anglo-Indian of those days, who often suffered
expatriation for half a lifetime, and in her the influence of
the East shows itself by a graceful lethargy of mind and body,
from which she can only be roused to read countless novels and
to adorn her comely person for society. There are also excellent
thumbnail sketches, such as that of the Miss Shaws, old ladies
such as we all have known, given to good works, who had

little aquiline faces, and there were dimples fixed into lines of a
perpetual smile on the permanently red and rather yellow cheeks,
and their heads seemed used to no occupation so much as nodding
in acquiescence with each other.

That *The Castle Builders* is by no means worthless reading is shown by the fact that it was liked by so competent a critic as Professor Palgrave.

Charlotte's first years of authorship were passed in the unruffled calm of a prolonged childhood. Obedience dictated that even the day's literary output had to be subjected to parental criticism, as each evening after dinner the family clustered round the lamp with sewing or book. Docile Charlotte never complained, but her silence was the more eloquent when, after many evenings of lectures on the plot of *Kenneth, or the Rearguard of the Grand Army* from Mr Yonge, that expert on the Napoleonic wars, Charlotte laid aside this story for some years. Even then Papa's too copious advice seems to have clogged her pen, for it is one of the weakest things she ever wrote. Moreover, besides being subjected to her own family, her literary plans and attempts were the common property of her small circle of intimate friends. Few weeks passed by that did not see Charlotte making her way along the winding lanes that led to the Kebles' home at Hursley. There she would seek the tranquil peace of Mr Keble's study and relieve her mind of her perplexities and of the sins that burdened her over-scrupulous conscience. Mr Keble was to her what she and Marianne Dyson called in their own private language, a "Pope"—that is, the spiritual guide necessary to one of the weaker sex. She confessed that she did not "know how far a woman's strength of sense and discrimination goes" and had "no certainty of not going off headlong into something very foolish, fancying it right"—a tendency she depicts in more than one of her heroines. But Charlotte distinguishes very clearly in her letters to Marianne between cherishing for her Pope a "kind of half-historical love for living saints" and making of him a *Bild*, meaning by this an ideal to be striven after—a Guy Morville, or a Galahad. Charlotte was very much afraid of live *Bilds*, and says, "I know women have a tendency that way, and it frightens me, because the most sensible and strong-minded are liable to be led astray" —again, a trait plentifully exemplified in her works.

It was not only ghostly but literary counsel that Charlotte sought, and when the conference in the study was ended she would sit by the fireside with the two ladies and her mentor, and, her eyes shining with excitement and tones vehement with

agerness, pour forth her latest plot. Or, on the long summer
venings, they would sit on the green lawn next the churchyard,
eep in some discussion on the moral aspect of the tales, until the
nadows cast by the great trees round the vicarage began to
ngthen and the bell for the daily Evensong put an end to their
alk. Keble would make such observations as, "It occurred to
ie whether, when the ladies quote Greek, they had not better
ay they have heard their fathers and brothers say things." He
ɔok the greatest care that no hint of "coarseness" should sully
he purity of Charlotte's writings. Thus he would not allow
'heodora in *Heartsease* to say that "really she had a heart,
hough some people thought it was only a machine for pumping
lood." He also transformed the "circle" of the setting sun
nto an "orb" and a "coxcomb" into a "jackanapes."

Dogmersfield was not so accessible as Hursley, but when
harlotte's friendship with Marianne Dyson was yet young the
enny post came in and facilitated almost daily effusions, by
vhich all their literary schemes might be shared and the
"Driver" urge her "Slave" to fresh efforts. Long discussions
f a new plot were apt, however, to be broken into by such
tilitarian considerations as, "Do you want to know where to
et red cloak stuff two yards wide at four shillings per yard?"
`he friendship was also stimulated by occasional visits, one of
vhich was paid in the spring of 1850. Miss Dyson was engaged
n a story depicting two characters, "the essentially contrite
nd the self-satisfied," and this was, of course, imparted to
`harlotte. This idea, involving the repentance of an apparently
lameless character, took such a hold on the girl's imagination
hat the generous Miss Dyson made her a present of the plot.
`harlotte betook herself home, her brain afire with thoughts of
he hero who was to become Guy Morville, the Heir of Redclyffe.

Scene grew out of scene with film-like rapidity. Soon little
emained of the original plan except that the virtuous hero,
iuy, was to save the life of his rival, Philip, at the expense of
iis own.[1] Most days saw the arrival of a letter at Dogmersfield

[1] Miss Dyson makes Guy rescue Philip from a marsh. It is very
ikely that Miss Yonge got the idea of Guy's death nursing Philip from
ier cousin, John Yonge. He stayed at the Hotel Bodenhaus, Splügen,
n 1844, and may well have told his sisters the story suggested by the
ollowing entries in the visitors' book:

with fresh news of the Morvilles and Edmonstones, of whom
Charlotte speaks as if they are mutual friends about whom she
retailing some gossip: "I have found out what the offence wa
that made Guy bang the door." And "Sir Guy Morville has ju
arrived at Hollywell and Charles does not know whether to lik
him or not." Or again:

> I am getting really fond of Philip, and Mamma says people wi
> think he is the good one to be rewarded, and Guy the bad on
> punished. I say if stupid people really think so, it would be ju
> what I should like, for it would be very like the different mora
> caught by different people from real life.

She shows her own attitude towards her characters when sh
writes:

> I have been reading Mr Hurrell Froude over again; I am su
> that he is wrong when in that essay on fiction he says the auth
> has no pleasure in it and feels the events and people are under h
> own control. I am sure I don't, and what Guy and Philip ma
> choose to turn out I cannot tell, they seem just like real acquai
> tances.

But what were the elements in *The Heir of Redclyffe* tha
made it *the* novel of the moment? The faint image of Guy i
the mind of the average reader recalls him as a hero who too
a whole chapter dying, and whose character was on a par wit
his soulful appearance as depicted by Kate Greenaway in th
Macmillan illustrated edition. Yet, putting aside the bitten li
and flashing eye that accompanied manifestations of Guy'
unbridled temper, we are most struck by his readiness to accus
himself of sin, and his habit of repenting where we can see littl
or no blame. It is a weakness of the book that the plot shoul
turn on the fact that Guy, roused by Philip's meddlesom
accusations to one of his celebrated exhibitions of rage, and feel
ing that he would like to come to grips with that priggis
youth, should inwardly convict himself of murder, and thereupo

---

"4 *June*, 1834. If any persons be disposed to pass by Riva and Colic
to the Stelvio, they should be informed that in June, July and August
most pestilential fever prevails in the marshes of those places."

"Died in this house on the 13th August 1835—Thomas Allo
Osborne, Esq., aged 34. He had a long illness and, on his death, hi
wife was fetched home by her two brothers, Aretas Akers and J. Ramsa
Akers."

adopt an attitude of *mea culpa, mea maxima culpa* that gives
colour to the charges against him, and makes him accept his
punishment as an act of expiation. Yet, as we saw, we have only
to turn to such a work as the *Remains* of Hurrell Froude, which
had enjoyed a tremendous vogue in Tractarian circles during
the two years before the *Heir* was written, to find a parallel in
reality. Charlotte, while conceiving the character of Guy, had
set about re-reading the *Remains*, and had little need to exag-
gerate her hero's perverse and morbid introspection.

One of the most interesting aspects of Guy's character is the
attempt to work out in it the great problem of heredity, the
visiting of the sins of the fathers upon the children unto the
third and fourth generation. Miss Yonge's treatment of the
theme is characteristic. Guy is a Morville of the family sprung
from one of the murderers of Thomas à Becket. In the seven-
teenth century a descendant, Sir Hugo Morville, wickedly
seized lands to which he had no right, and thus set up a feud
with the younger branch of the family. In the civilized nineteenth
century Guy and Philip, the representatives of the two branches,
of course would not dream of continuing the feud; but all the
same an antipathy exists between them, which Miss Yonge
would have us believe to be "a strange ancestral enmity"—
though one feels that Philip's galling attitude towards Guy needs
no such high-sounding explanation. Guy's hot temper may
certainly have been inherited; at any rate, he considers his
banishment to Redclyffe and the breaking off of his engagement to Amy as reparation for the sins of his ancestors as well
as for his own evil passions.

It is also interesting to consider the works that influenced
Miss Yonge's treatment of the motive. These are, in all probability, the story told in the introduction to *Guy Mannering*
(Charlotte knew her Scott from cover to cover) and, more
especially, the *Sintram* of de la Motte Fouqué. This romantic
tale, built round Dürer's *Knight, Death, and the Devil*, had
kindled the imagination of the England of the thirties and
forties, and more than one translation had appeared. It is not
surprising that Charlotte, who had grown up with the Dürer
engraving brought by her father from Paris in 1815, should have
her fancy taken by the fashionable book. She had the happy
inspiration to make Guy see in Sintram a man pursued by a like

fate, and allowed him to work out his salvation in a way which
parallels Sintram's expiation. As Sintram wrestles with his devils
in the solitary castle of Mondenfelsen, so Guy is banished to his
red sandstone castle, romantically situated on a crag against
which beat the waves of the Atlantic.[1] In Amy, Guy sees a
Verena—though in Sintram she is the mother and not the lover
of the hero—whose prayers and sweet influence will help him
to conquer his doom. The Heir finally dies of fever caught while
he is nursing Philip, and the ancestral guilt is thus expiated.

The extraordinary popularity of *The Heir of Redclyffe* is most
revealing of the taste of the public of the eighteen-fifties. It
drew tears from elderly professors. Young officers in the Army
felt a copy to be a necessary part of their equipment, while
Dante Gabriel Rossetti, William Morris, and their friends looked
on Guy with such veneration that they determined to take him
as their model. A young Guardsman, playing "Confessions,"
actually wrote down as his prime object in life to make himself
like Sir Guy. Even as late as 1865 undergraduates displayed a
remarkable enthusiasm for Miss Yonge when she visited Oxford.
Guy's death moved people in all corners of the world, from Jo
in *Little Women*, who sat with her book in the attic, eating russet
apples and weeping, to the bride of an English bishop, who, to
the consternation of her husband, was found by him in tears
over it on their honeymoon.

The Heir of Redclyffe appeared at a fortunate moment. By
1853, when the book came out, the Oxford Movement had passed
out of its more academic phase, and its ideas were already attract-
ing a wider public. As we have seen, Guy was an absolute
expression of the ideal hero for the Movement both in his life
and in his death. The fact that the opportune arrival of a clergyman enabled him to die duly fortified by the last rites of the
Church endeared his deathbed to Tractarians. Even in his
historical and literary affections Guy was the perfect reflection

---

[1] For those who have any wish to locate Redclyffe, it may be of
interest to note that Miss Yonge herself states in her *Cameos from
English History*, vol. i, p. 156, that the murderers of Becket fled to
Morville's castle in Cumberland, where it was said the very dogs would
not approach them. Cf. *The Heir of Redclyffe* (Macmillan edition,
p. 289): "it was said the very dogs crouched and fled from the sacri-
legious murderer." This seems to disprove an idea held by some people
that Redclyffe was in North Devon.

of the tastes engendered by the Movement—King Charles, whom he regarded as a saint; Malory, with Sir Galahad as his favourite hero: *I Promessi Sposi*; and Keble's lectures, given while he was Professor of Poetry, which Miss Yonge makes Guy and Charles translate out of their original Latin.

In Amabel also the public saw the perfect heroine nurtured at second hand on the popular influences that had shaped Guy. Alice Meynell, in her introduction to the Everyman edition of *The Heir of Redclyffe*, aptly described her by quoting the Elizabethan phrase for a good wife, "in all things his sweet ape." There is about Amy a haze of sentimentality that endeared her to a society prone to that vice. There was a thrill of pleasurable emotion in the picture of Amy in her wedding-dress at Guy's funeral, and of the pathetic young widow with her fatherless baby going to Redclyffe to act the ministering angel to Philip. In fact, all the last chapters of the book, which, from the point of view of artistic construction, should never have been written, provide much matter for the sentimental reader, as well as for those who love a clearly pointed moral.

For us Guy and Amy are not ideals of perfection after which we would strive, so we cannot feel in them the same reality with which their contemporaries endowed them. There is, however, plenty in *The Heir of Redclyffe* that must carry conviction for us as it did for its first readers. The minor characters are drawn with much humour and insight—Mr Edmonstone, who is so well imagined that we regret that Miss Yonge was sparing of the comic relief he affords; Charles, whose caustic sayings mitigate the sugary parts of the tale; to say nothing of the dog, Bustle. The book abounds, too, in pieces of happy description. There is the detailed, if somewhat romanticized, picture of Redclyffe, the vivid account of the storm and shipwreck in the bay, and the slightly sketched Swiss scenes of the honeymoon. Above all, there are the intimate glimpses where we catch a family unawares in its home setting, in which not even the great novelists of the period excelled Miss Yonge. With the very first words of the book we walk straight into one such scene:

> The drawing-room of Hollywell House was one of the favoured apartments, where a peculiar air of home seems to reside, whether seen in the middle of summer, all its large windows open to the

garden, or, as when our story commences, its bright fire and stands of fragrant green-house plants contrasted with the wintry fog and leafless trees of November.

The stage is set for the appearance of the various members of the Edmonstone family: Charles, the invalid, on his sofa, surrounded by books for his desultory perusal; Laura, her curls veiling her drawing; and then Amy, laughing behind her camellia, which Philip so characteristically breaks by knowing how to carry it better than she does. *The Heir of Redclyffe* is certainly not a book to be dismissed as a piece of mere sentimentality suitable only for elderly ladies.

Before the *Heir* ran the gauntlet of public opinion, it had to make its rounds to Dysons, Kebles, and Coleridges, who were all ready with their comments, which Charlotte received with becoming deference. The future Lord Chief Justice Coleridge said that, when Philip came to Oxford to inquire into Guy's expenditure, Guy should have kicked him downstairs, while Julian Yonge went so far as to say that he would have horse-whipped him round the quad. Finally, when the manuscript had been exposed to all this local criticism, Mr Yonge set to work to give the sentences a final polishing, on the grounds, one supposes, that a man *must* write better than a woman; or, it may be, because he felt this to be the natural exercise of parental authority. Then he put the book into his bag and set off for London and the publishers, for it seemed to Mr Yonge indelicate that a young lady should enter into direct negotiations with Grub Street. His own knowledge of the publishing trade was, how-ever, slender. On Sir John Coleridge's advice he took the book to Mr Murray, who turned it down on the ground that he did not publish novels. With Mr Parker it fared better, and a contract for *The Heir of Redclyffe* was signed, the book appear-ing early in the next year.

Although this was Charlotte's first attempt at a real novel, she did not concern herself much about its fate. It was as though Guy had gone with Mr Yonge on a visit to London, from which he might at any time return. "If only Guy could have seen Mr Keble to-day, how he would have enjoyed it," she writes. Nevertheless, Charlotte was well pleased when the parcel of complimentary copies arrived and she could send "the dear Guy" to Marianne, writing

his mother's name in the first that came out. . . . I hope she has him
by this time and is satisfied with the son she gave me to educate,
who has been one of my greatest pleasures for two years and a half.

The printed copies of the novel renewed all the discussions
which the Yonges and their circle had enjoyed over the manuscript. The Kebles and their curates apparently knew whole
speeches from it by heart, and after a visit from one or other of
them Mrs Yonge writes, "It seems almost as if Guy and Amy
had been here themselves this morning, so much have we talked
of them." Mr Keble was reading the book out aloud to his ladies;
but, when he had seen them take their candles and retire to
bed, he would steal back, poke up the fire, and read on with
avidity. Even when he did tear himself away from his young
disciple's enthralling production, he was not always quit of the
subject, for twice Mrs Keble talked in her sleep to warn Guy and
Amy to shun the fever-stricken area.

Charlotte, who was already deep in *Heartsease*, was too much
occupied with her writing and her parish avocations (letters on
her literary schemes were apt to end with "Penny Club awaits
me") to concern herself much with the reception of her book—
beyond the circle of her friends and relations. It came as a
complete surprise to her that *The Heir of Redclyffe* sprang into
such immediate popularity, and that every day brought her
"some fresh peacock," as she calls the newspaper puffs and letters
of congratulation that poured in. Even the unworldly Charlotte
could not help being elated, so much so that she sought an opportunity of speaking to Mr Keble about the sin of pride. When
Charlotte had poured out to him in his study all her fears of
vainglory, he said, "Yes, my dear, I have been thinking a great
deal about you now." Years later, Miss Yonge described how

he told me "a successful book might be the trial of one's life";
showed me how work (even of this sort) might be dedicated; how,
whenever it was possible, I could explain how the real pith of the
work came from another mind; and dismissed me with the con-
cluding words of the 90th Psalm (the which has most thankfully,
I own, so far been realized).

The Heir of Redclyffe was not the only scheme of importance
that emanated from Dogmersfield. In the August of 1850 the
Dyson family began talking about the lack of a suitable magazine

for the schoolrooms of the upper classes, and it was not long before Charlotte's letters to Marianne were full of plans for such a publication. Mr Mozley was already bringing out *The Magazine for the Young*, edited by his sister, for a large public of Sunday-school children, and now he showed himself quite willing to cater for the devoted young ladies who instructed them. The Mozleys and Dysons were unanimous in their choice of Charlotte as editor, and she for her part was delighted with the new venture. In November 1850 its name and contents were still in the air; yet in January 1851 the first number made its appearance. Those were golden days for editors, when such trifles as a few days' delay in the appearance of a periodical or the casual addition of a dozen pages or so were of no consequence. The friends of the new magazine could hardly introduce it to the public under their own private title of *The Codger*—so called because it was intended to please "steady old codgers." They luckily eschewed such suggestions as *The Maidens' Manual*, and it was known through its long course of nearly half a century as *The Monthly Packet*.

The aims of this periodical, as set forth by its editor in the preface to the first number, were undoubtedly, and rather terrifyingly, moral. It was intended to help young people from fifteen to twenty-five to form their own character, "not as a guide . . . but as a companion in times of recreation, . . . to make them more steadfast and dutiful daughters of our own beloved Catholic Church of England."

As usual, Charlotte's prefatory bark was worse than her bite, for the welcome introduction into the schoolroom of *The Castle Builders*, as well as of *The Little Duke*, in the first numbers, more than compensated for the mental effort required for the assimilation of the *Conversations on the Catechism* that accompanied them. Midway between these two extremes hover the "Cameos" from history, called thus because "they are to present scenes and heroes in relief," and intended to be a complement to schoolroom history. It was to the young ladies of the schoolroom that *The Monthly Packet*, with its gentle instruction and its innocent romances, was to bring such joy, for their reading had hitherto been but scantily provided for. Yet on occasion it found its way from the schoolroom to the parental study, and to this day there still exist neat rows of bound volumes collected by Tractarian grandfathers and great-uncles.

As editor of *The Monthly Packet* Miss Yonge had definitely taken possession of the pulpit from which she was to preach Keble's ideas to the young-ladyhood of England for so many years. Yet the preacher could forget herself in the playfellow who had not lost touch with the child's little world. She was more ready to unbend in the schoolroom than in the drawing-room, and the family that did most to keep fresh her contact with youth was that of Dr Moberly. Alice, the eldest of his dozen children, was twelve years younger than Charlotte, but, as time went on, she grew more and more companionable, and was in great demand at Otterbourne. She would spend the morning painting or illuminating in the drawing-room under Mrs Yonge's supervision, while Charlotte sat writing at her own table, constantly bursting out with some indignant opinion which was met by her mother's dry comments. The younger girls too were welcomed at Otterbourne. Both Mrs and Miss Yonge loved natural history, and taught their young visitors how to take an intelligent interest in flowers and birds, while Charlotte was always ready to amuse them with her shells or pour into their willing ears the plot that was occupying her at the moment. On one occasion she even went so far as to draw them a picture of Phyllis Mohun, to satisfy their eager desire to know what she really looked like; and another time, when an artistic Moberly was filled with a longing to illustrate *The Heir of Redclyffe*, Charlotte was quite ready to help and criticize.

Such a kind and understanding grown-up friend is a treasure to any schoolroom, and the Moberly children were always delighted when Charlotte turned up at the Headmaster's house in College Street, in the course of a shopping expedition in Winchester. On one of these occasions she had found the children rehearsing a play of Miss Edgeworth's, and this started her on writing historical playlets for them. In *The Mice at Play* Charlotte actually starred as Queen Philippa, in honour of whom, she tells Alice, she "will try to grow as fat and dignified" as she can. Something of the child lingered long in Charlotte, and she tells Alice, "You cannot think how I shall enjoy the fun of the rehearsals."

CHAPTER VII

MATURITY

THE year 1854 brought sorrow to the Yonges over and above their personal share in the national grief at the happenings in the Crimea. These too came very near them, for Julian, who had joined the Rifle Brigade in 1852, was now ordered out to the Front. Mr Yonge was in his element during the February days before Julian sailed, as he lavished on him counsels remembered from his own soldiering days, and equipment that could only be completed in time for his departure by dint of his father's most strenuous efforts. The week of bustle and hurry ended with a last long day with Julian at Portsmouth. Late that night Mr Yonge returned home, weary and depressed. To the terror of Mrs Yonge and Charlotte, he had a seizure at ten o'clock in the evening, and they passed a fearful night by his bedside.

The next day, when the use of his limbs and power of speech had come back to him, Charlotte, who had little experience of illness, took courage, and was able without misgiving to enjoy a last walk round the field with Julian, who had been sent from Portsmouth for one more glimpse of his family before he sailed. She even wrote her usual chatty letter to Marianne Dyson, in which details of Mr Yonge's symptoms are mingled with parish gossip. The shock was all the greater when, at six o'clock on the second evening after he had been taken ill, Mr Yonge had a second seizure, and was dead before medical or spiritual help could be called. Charlotte was able to pull herself together and read the commendatory prayer, but when Mr Bigg-Wither arrived in time only to minister to the living, she admits that, though he meant well, the strain of having to listen to 1 Corinthians xv was very great.

Even while still numb from the shock, Charlotte did not forget the friends either of the real or of her imaginary world. She wrote to Marianne:

> My trouble has come; he had a second attack and died at six to-night.

Mamma is too like Amy, excited with thankfulness. I dread what it will be; I don't think we half believe it yet.

You will write to me; perhaps I may write to-morrow, but I can't tell. We have Mr and Mrs Keble helping us to-night. Oh what will the waking be!

For Charlotte, indeed, the waking was from the days of a protracted childhood into an adult existence no longer ordered according to her father's commands. This submission, the duty of all good Victorian daughters, had been, indeed, Charlotte's pleasure, for her father was to her the greatest of heroes. For thirty years her first thought at every juncture had been to watch the expression in her father's dark eyes; their "beaming smile" was her greatest happiness, while their "warning glance" was her chief dread. Hero-worship of Mr Yonge absorbed such of Charlotte's emotions as were not taken up by her literary creations and by religion. We should expect, indeed, that the blank felt on his death would be much greater than it appears actually to have been, but it must be remembered that the theology of the period encouraged the consolation of thinking of Mr Yonge gazing benignly from heaven, watching the joys and sorrows of his daughter's life. At each decision to be made Charlotte consulted Papa's *manes* mentally, just as much as she did Mr Keble in the flesh.

It was thus not long before Mrs Yonge and Charlotte began outwardly to recover from their loss. Downright, good-tempered Anne Yonge came on a long visit to Otterbourne, and helped them to pick up the broken threads of their existence. Even the anxiety about Julian in the Crimea could not mar the pleasure of the long walks and talks in Anne's company. Then there were always books to be written, and these Mrs Yonge enjoyed almost as much as her daughter. Not long after Mr Yonge's death, she was writing:

I think Charlotte is the one person who has more pleasure from her books than I have. We never tire of talking of them before they are written, and correcting the MS. and the proofs. I have just read the first volume of Guy again, but cannot venture upon the second (that containing the death scene and Amy's grief for her husband). My thankfulness increases, I think, that Charlotte's guide was spared to her till the dangers from a first success were over. I do not see that she loses her unselfconsciousness, and, if there is a danger, we have Mr Keble.

The two main literary schemes of the moment were *Hearts
ease* and *The Daisy Chain*, the first part of which was already
delighting the readers of *The Monthly Packet*. If anything, the
contemporary vice of sentimentality is even more rampant in
Heartsease than in *The Heir of Redclyffe*, though it may be only
its sickly title that makes us think so. This title is a play on the
name of the heroine—Violet—who by the end of the book has
brought heart's ease to its most stormy characters. But Violet
herself is by no means as unreal as a mere outline of the story's
events might make her appear, and before she has progressed
too far along the paths of righteousness she is both natural and
delightful. The sentimental piety of some of the characters, the
celerity and completeness with which Arthur Martindale,
Violet's husband, reforms under her influence, and the im-
possibly diabolical nature of Mark Gardner, Arthur's tempter,
are the weak points of the book. What, indeed, should the carefully guarded Charlotte know of villains?

Heartsease provoked nearly as many tears of delighted sensibility as the *Heir*. Charles Kingsley, after wiping his eyes a
dozen times before he got through it, was so much charmed that
he wrote off immediately to congratulate Mr Parker on having
published such a "delightful and wholesome novel," which is
"wise and human and Christian, and will surely become a
standard work for aye and a day." Kingsley thought it spoke
well for the public taste that the sales were so immense, and
tells Parker not to mind if some of the critics are not so much in
love with virtue as was the general public. But their verdict
was so favourable that the novel even found its way out to the
Crimea. Its scenes of peaceful English life, though these include
a fire and a mining disaster, brought relief to Lord Raglan from
the tragedy around him, as he read it just before his death.

Although *Dynevor Terrace* was not published until 1857, it is
not out of place to mention it here, as its hero, Louis, Viscount
Fitzjocelyn, follows closely in the footsteps of Guy and Violet.
(Miss Yonge was soon to outgrow her romantic affection for
high-sounding titles, and *Dynevor Terrace* was almost the last
book where the aristocracy fill the centre of the stage.) The
weakness of the book, as even contemporary readers felt, was the
excessive filial piety which impelled Mary, the heroine, to drag
out five years of exile in Lima with her vicious father, Mr Pon-

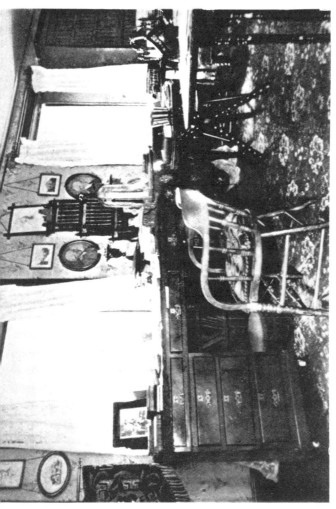

CHARLOTTE M. YONGE'S WRITING-TABLE IN HER ROOM AT ELDERFIELD

Photo W. T. Greene

Reproduced, by courtesy of Messrs A. R. Mowbray and Co., Ltd., from "Charlotte Mary Yonge," by Ethel Romanes

144

A VICTORIAN WEDDING (1855)

By courtesy of "The Illustrated London News"

nby, and a flighty young Spanish stepmother. In the end, of
ourse, all is for the best; Mary finds herself able to accept Louis,
ho began proposing as a brotherly cousin, but develops into a
assable lover, and with whom she has been in love from the
eginning. In spite of this reward of constancy, however, the
arlier submission is overdone. There is a subplot, recounting
he marriage of Louis' proud and fiery cousin, Jem Frost, to the
ristocratic Isabel Conway, and her gradual awakening from the
isions and manufacture of sentimental historical romances to
he reality of poverty and household cares. In *Dynevor Terrace*,
s in *Heartease*, the various threads of the tale are skilfully woven
ogether. Miss Yonge never fills us with the fury that some even
f the greater Victorian novelists arouse, when they drag us
way from the main theme of a book into some irrelevant by-way.

It is strange that Mary Ponsonby should not have had more
fe in her, for, as Miss Yonge told Marianne Dyson, her charac-
er is meant to recall Anne Yonge. Miss Coleridge considered
hat, in Mary, Charlotte was glorifying comparative dullness, so
s to rebuke in herself any tendency to intellectual pride, on the
ame principle by which Shakespeare, according to Dowden,
lorified the practical Henry V because his own mind was more
kin to that of Hamlet. But, even if the imaginary Mary does
ack the charm of the real Anne, it is psychologically correct for
he novelist to mate her tranquillity with Fitzjocelyn's mercurial
emperament. *He* is certainly the most convincing of the trio
f characters (Guy and Violet being the others) who exemplify
he strengthening force of religion. Miss Yonge herself once
aid, "I think I have always loved him more than Guy."

The outstanding portrait of the book is Louis' great-aunt,
Mrs Frost, a beautiful old lady who combines the sprightly
harm of the eighteenth century with the religion of the nine-
eenth. Miss Yonge admits to having drawn her from an old
ady she had known in Devonshire, but who this old lady was is
ot known. The book covers a wide area. We are carried without
pparent improbability from one English scene to another, over
o Paris in the thick of the Revolution of '48, and to distant
Lima, where Miss Yonge takes us right up into the silver-mines
n the mountains, and gives us one of the best pieces of descrip-
ive writing she ever achieved. She had a peculiar flair for
reathing life into the dry bones of guide and travel book, and a

K

Peruvian gentleman once remarked on the exactness of h—
descriptions in *Dynevor Terrace*.

The sadness caused by Mr Yonge's death had clearly n—
dimmed Charlotte's creative faculty, for it was during the ye—
1854 that she progressed with *The Daisy Chain*, the first pa—
of which came out in *The Monthly Packet* between 1853 an—
1856, when the whole was published in book form. It is wit—
this tale that Charlotte Yonge became undisputed mistress —
the *genre* that she has made peculiarly her own, that of th—
'family chronicle,' as she herself describes *The Daisy Chain* i—
its subtitle. *Scenes and Characters* was already tending in th—
direction, but it can hardly be compared with the much long—
Daisy Chain and *Pillars of the House*, which both embrace —
tremendous range of characters and great space of time.

It was almost by accident that Miss Yonge stumbled on th—
literary form that was to give such perfect scope to her power—
In 1852 she had been delighted by a request from Dr and Mr—
Moberly to be godmother to their baby daughter, who wa—
christened Margaret Helen. All remarked that Philip's sister
Margaret, in *The Heir of Redclyffe* was a most unsatisfactor—
namesake for the new baby, and that Miss Yonge ought to writ—
a story about a *nice* Margaret for her. She obligingly set he—
brains to work and conceived the character of Margaret May—
the surname being given because little Margaret Moberly ha—
been born in May. Soon Margaret's individual fate was swal—
lowed up in that of the whole lively May family, who cam—
thronging in on Charlotte.

By the term 'family chronicle' the modern novelist under—
stands a deliberate attempt to trace social development a—
mirrored in the fortunes of one particular family. Miss Yonge—
however, had no such conscious aim. It is only incidentally, an—
in so far as they are natural products of their time, that the Ma—
family hold up a mirror to it. They move in a little world whos—
confines are more or less those within which live the character—
of Trollope's novels. But while Trollope takes us into the drawing—
room and the smoking-room, Charlotte leads us into the school—
room, from which angle we generally view the life in he—
microcosm. To the real lover of Miss Yonge the May's school—
room, with its Dutch-tiled fireplace and old-fashioned furnitur—
—the drawing-room, which opens into the quiet garden with it—

ulip-tree—these are as real as the home of her own childhood.
The Mays themselves have been the dear friends of many suc-
cessive generations of young people. Ethel set many Victorian
damsels to teaching Sunday schools and working for the poor.
Nowadays we are graceless enough to love her more in her early
days, before she has conquered the harum-scarum ways that
make her so natural and lovable. All the May family have
individuality, but perhaps the chief favourites have always been
Ethel and the sailor, Harry. It must have been for his sake that
a young midshipman was able to supply from his memory the
missing page of the ship's copy of *The Daisy Chain*. But the
central figure of the family group is Dr May, who is worthy to
rank with Dr Thorne, the creation of the greater novelist, as
one of the most charming doctors of Victorian fiction. His
character bears an obvious likeness to Charlotte's uncle, Dr James
Yonge of Plymouth, an eager, impulsive man of great ability.
Charlotte tells us that the general atmosphere of merry family
life was reminiscent of Puslinch, but many little touches must
have been suggested by the Moberly family, whose schoolroom
and nursery days she was watching while actually writing the
book. The riotous dinners in holiday time, when Dr Moberly
and his youngest son would chaff each other till it ended "in a
hand-to-hand fight," were surely the model for the Mays'
Saturday dinners, where "the Doctor was as bad as the boys,"
and the Bible-reading and discussions with Mrs May reproduce
one of the customs of the Moberly schoolroom. The discussion
on ambitions with which the book opens was, indeed, intended
to be its keynote, but luckily the joy of story-telling, as usual,
relegated the moral to its proper place in the background.

Three of the great interests of Charlotte's life find expression
in *The Daisy Chain*, mainly through Ethel, who is probably the
most complete piece of self-revelation in her writings. Church-
building and Sunday schools we have already met with in the
earlier books, but the third *motif*, Foreign Missions, here strikes
a new note. It is no exaggeration to say that *The Daisy Chain*
became one of the most important pieces of propaganda in direct-
ing the thoughts of the younger generation of Tractarians to the
mission field. Harry's adventures in the Loyalty Islands and the
departure of Norman and Meta for New Zealand made of it a
positive romance. We feel nowadays a little dubious concerning

David, the perfect convert, who spent his time asking Harry "little easy first questions about the Belief," but it must be admitted that Charlotte had solid fact at her command to draw on for the missionary parts of the tale. A distant cousin, John Coleridge Patteson, decided in 1854 to go out with Bishop Selwyn. The words of his father, Judge Patteson, "God forbid I should stop him," foreshadow Dr May's attitude to Norman. In fact, "Coley" Patteson seems to have served to some extent as a model for Norman, and Charlotte tells us that his earlier voyages in his mission ship had been so suggestive of incidents fabricated in *The Daisy Chain* that the proceeds were felt to be the due of the mission, and in 1859 were dedicated to the intended college at Kohimarama. This was later called St Andrew's, after Cocksmoor Church, at which Charlotte must have felt honoured.

While she was in the thick of *The Daisy Chain*, in June 1854, Charlotte had an orgy of missionary dissipation, such as may well have served as copy for the great S.P.G. festival at Stoneborough. For Charlotte, June the 9th was to be a red-letter day, for she had her special part to play in the welcome given to Bishop Selwyn, the leading figure of the proceedings. She said, years afterwards, in her life of Bishop Patteson:

> My mother had always been eagerly interested in the Mission, and when on the day of my father's funeral something brought before her the request for the vessel (the *Southern Cross*), she said to Mrs Keble how much she should like to see the sum raised by contributions from those who liked the *Heir of Redclyffe*, then in its first flush of success. Mrs Keble, pleased to see that anything could interest her, warmly took up the idea, other friends joined and by their great kindness a sum was raised sufficient to be at least worth presenting to the Bishop.

Of course, Charlotte modestly omits to mention her own share in the subscription for the *Southern Cross*, but it is a well-known fact that a substantial part of the profits of *The Heir of Redclyffe* went towards it.

The auspicious day began with a service in the cathedral, when Charlotte had her first sight of the Bishop, looking beautiful in his lawn sleeves. Whispers of admiration passed between Mrs Keble and Charlotte, who paid him the high tribute of likening him to Mr Yonge. After the service Charlotte charac-

eristically shrank into the Moberly house to avoid the mighty
luncheon at the Warden's. The great presentation was stage-
managed by Dr Moberly so that it should be as little of an
ordeal as possible to modest Charlotte. They went to the
Warden's garden, where she was allowed to creep off out of the
way into the path by the river with Alice Moberly. They found
little Johnnie Selwyn "cutting capers on the lawn," and he was
sent to fetch his papa and mamma. When they reached the
garden, Dr Moberly had little two-year-old Maggie, Charlotte's
godchild, all ready with the envelope containing £146 10s., on
which Mrs Yonge had written: "Towards the vessel for the
Island Mission," clasped in her hands. When Maggie had
trotted up to the Bishop and been rewarded by him with a kiss
for her charmingly done part in the presentation, Charlotte was
called from her walk by the riverside and introduced to the
Bishop, who soon set the shy young lady at her ease by being
as kind to her as if she "had been Wabisana"—one of the pet
converts. She felt very proud to be taken on his arm to the
afternoon's missionary meeting. This was as delightful as all
the other happenings of the day, for she was "pitched into a
corner between the Kebles," and they could indulge in "little
whispering comments" together. They were thrilled with
emotion at the "glorious speech" of the fine-looking white-
haired Warden Barter, who was always one of Charlotte's heroes,

especially where he said what the heathen wanted was not only
money but men, not only men but gentlemen, yes, gentlemen, for
a true gentleman was the perfection of the Christian law.

Charlotte's gratification knew no bounds when, at the close
of the meeting, the Bishop came up to her and again escorted
her back to the College. This time she had a "real good talk . . .
about the doings in N.Z." At the dinner at the Warden's
Charlotte had too many friends round her to feel any constraint
at the crowds of guests assembled in the drawing-room. On the
way to the final missionary meeting of the day Charlotte and
Anne Yonge, who was on a visit to Otterbourne at the time, fell
in with the Warden and Bishop once more. The Bishop again
delighted her with thanks for the money, saying quaintly, "I
suppose I am joint heir with the Heir of Redclyffe."

The strenuous day ended at half-past nine, and Charlotte

and Anne were escorted by Mr Wither back to Otterbourne, where they found Mrs Yonge all ready to hear of the day's doings. They very much pleased her, particularly the Bishop's last saying. Altogether, the two young ladies felt almost as tired as if they had been to a ball, and the great day was thought by Mrs Yonge worthy of commemoration by the gift of a pendant to her daughter. Its appropriate design was a gold St Andrew's cross with an enamelled daisy in the centre. At the back of it was a tuft of little Maggie Moberly's hair under glass. Engraved on the cross were Maggie's initials, and the date, "June 1854."

For an illuminating contrast to the Winchester Missionary Festival, we must turn to the account of the famous Barchester meeting, at which Mrs Proudie was so much in evidence, in *Framley Parsonage*. Although Charlotte allowed Mr Clare, in *The Clever Woman of the Family*, to enjoy that novel, we feel that this flippant passage cannot have met with her entire approval. For, to her, missions represented one of the few romantic patches in a drab modern world, and those engaged in them were the inheritors of the crusading spirit.

By this time had begun the publication of that type among her books by which Miss Yonge is perhaps best known among a certain, though not the contemporary, section of her public. These are the historical tales—romances one can hardly call them—written primarily for children, but with a veracity and skill which have made them the delight of many who have passed the age of childhood. For a number of to-day's schoolchildren *The Little Duke* is the first, perhaps the only, work of Charlotte Yonge that comes into their hands, and hardly a child fails to enjoy it. This story was the first of Miss Yonge's works in this *genre*, of which some were to be written at intervals all through the author's life. The readers of the first *Monthly Packet* had been delighted by it in 1851, and, from its publication in book form in 1854, the fascination of Richard the Fearless, eight-year-old Duke of Normandy, and Osmond de Centeville, his faithful squire, was felt in every schoolroom. Generation after generation held their breath at the tense moment when Osmond carries Richard in a bundle of straw out to the stable, until both are safe out of the hands of the perfidious French. No history book could so well teach the difference between the hardy Norman and the civilized Frank as the excellent portraits of Norse-speak-

ng Fru Astrida and grim Bernard de Harcourt, contrasted with
he effete Court of Louis, King of the French. Vivid touches
emain in the memory, such as the opening in the dim, smoked-
illed hall of the castle where Fru Astrida is supervising the
preparations for the evening meal, and the coronation of the
little Duke, where he singles out Alberic as the only young thing
among all the grave nobles who come to do him homage.

Miss Yonge next turned her attention to English history,
with the production of the somewhat less popular *Lances of
Lynwood*. Eustace Lynwood captures the famous Bertrand du
Guesclin in his first battle, and is knighted by the Black Prince.
The story recounts the subsequent adventures of himself and his
nephew Arthur in Bordeaux and in the mountain castle of which
he has been given command. Miss Yonge had read to some
purpose "the bewitching chronicle of Froissart," and this, as she
tells us in the preface, supplied her background to the story.

It is worth considering here what are the characteristics of
Miss Yonge's writing that have made her historical tales popular
with so many generations of children. It is true that, as will be
explained, she tends to bring to these stories the same Victorian
outlook that is found in her contemporary writings, but this
does not worry the young, and in some respects the individual
descriptions and accounts of incidents are even better written
than in those. Her faithfulness in reproducing the scenes in her
own world which she had beheld or experienced must have been
in some ways a tie to her, and in purely imaginary picture she
could let herself go most happily.

Anticipating its publication by more than ten years, we quote
from *The Chaplet of Pearls*:

> Setting aside the consideration of the risk, the baby-weddings of
> the Middle Ages must have been very pretty sights.
> So the Court of France thought . . . at the union of the little pair,
> whose united ages did not reach ten years. There they stood under
> the portal of Notre-Dame, the little bridegroom in a white velvet
> coat, with puffed sleeves, slashed with scarlet satin, as were the
> short, also puffed breeches meeting his long white knitted silk
> stockings some way above the knee; large scarlet rosettes were in
> his white shoes, a scarlet knot adorned his little sword, and his
> velvet cap of the same colour bore a long white plume, and was
> encircled by a row of pearls of priceless value. . . . The precious

heirlooms were scarcely held with the respect due to an ornament so acquired. The manly garb for the first time assumed by his sturdy legs, and the possession of the little sword, were evidently the most interesting parts of the affair to the youthful husband who seemed to find in them his only solace for the weary length of the ceremony. He was a fine, handsome little fellow, fair and rosy, with bright blue eyes, and hair like shining flax, unusually tall and strong-limbed for his age; and as he gave his hand to his little bride, and walked with her under a canopy up to kneel at the High Altar, for the marriage blessing and the mass, they looked like a full-grown couple seen through a diminishing-glass.

The little bride was perhaps a less beautiful child, but she had a splendid pair of black eyes, and a sweet little mouth, both set into the uncomprehending solemnity of baby gravity and contentment in fine clothes. In accordance with the vow indicated by her name of Marie, her dress was white and blue, turquoise forget-me-not bound the little lace veil on her dark chestnut hair, the bosom of her white satin dress was sprinkled with the same azure jewel and turquoises bordered every seam of the sweeping skirt with a train befitting a count's daughter and meandered in gorgeous constellations round the hem. The little thing lisped her own vows forth without much notion of their sense, and indeed was sometimes prompted by her bridesmaid cousin, a pretty little girl a year older, who thrust in her assistance so glibly that the King, as well as others of the spectators laughed, and observed that she would get herself married to the boy instead of her cousin.

Similarly in narrative, she appears to have had more scope in her historical than in her contemporary work—no doubt because in the countries and periods to which she transported herself and her readers events tended to be more exciting than they could be made to appear realistically in Victorian England. Here is the escape of the Little Duke, already referred to: he is being smuggled out from the French Court concealed in a bundle of straw:

Richard, from the interior of the bundle, heard Osmond set open the door; then he felt himself raised from the ground. Osmond was carrying him along down the stairs, the ends of the straw crushing and sweeping against the wall. The only way to the outer door was through the hall, and here was the danger. Richard heard voices, steps, loud singing and laughter, as if feasting was going on; then someone said, "Tending your horse, Sieur de Centeville?"

"Yes," Osmond made answer. "You know, since we lost our

grooms, the poor black would come off badly, did I not attend to him."

Presently came Carloman's voice: "O Osmond de Centeville! is Richard better?"

"He is better, my Lord, I thank you, but hardly yet out of danger." . . .

Richard could hardly help calling out to his dear little Carloman; but he remembered the peril of Osmond's eyes and the Queen's threat, and held his peace, with some vague notion that some day he would make Carloman King of France. In the meantime, half stifled with the straw, he felt himself carried on, down the steps, across the court; and then he knew, from the darkness and the changed sound of Osmond's tread, that they were in the stable. Osmond laid him carefully down, and whispered—

"All right so far. You can breathe?"

"Not well. Can't you let me out?"

"Not yet, not for worlds. Now tell me if I put you face downwards, for I cannot see."

He laid the living heap of straw across the saddle, bound it on, then led out the horse, gazing round cautiously as he did so; but the whole of the people of the Castle were feasting, and there was no one to watch the gates. Richard heard the hollow sound of the hoofs, as the drawbridge was crossed, and he knew that he was free; but still Osmond held his arm over him, and would not let him move, for some distance. Then, just as Richard felt as if he could endure the stifling of the straw, and his uncomfortable position not a moment longer, Osmond stopped the horse, took him down, laid him on the grass, and released him. He gazed around; they were in a little wood; evening twilight was just coming on, and the birds sang sweetly.

"Free! free!—this is freedom!" cried Richard, leaping up in the delicious cool evening breeze.

It will be remembered that here Charlotte is writing for quite young children (the little Duke himself is not much more than nine years old at this time), and perhaps the fact that so much of her work was written about young people, and for that critical and discerning audience, helped to 'set' her style in such an admirable way. For, though she wrote for children, she never wrote childishly. Nor is there any talking down to her readers: none of the "my little man . . ." or "perhaps, children, you will ask . . ." to be found in her works, as there is often enough in those of her contemporaries, and in others writing for juveniles

—a style so putting-off to the children themselves. Yet the successful writer for children has to be continually in the child's place—explaining difficulties, catching the imagination with an exciting word or interesting allusion to something that the child knows, and, above all, avoiding dullness as the plague. No facetiousness and no purple-patching will avail to win the attention of the unsophisticated child—there must be good strong interest in the matter on hand, vividness, and ease in writing. And these are precisely the characteristics of Miss Yonge's writing.

Most of her historical work, however, was in the future in 1854, though we must not forget that she was throughout this period engaged, among other things, on the *Landmarks of History*, of which she had just published the series as far as Charles V. In other respects Miss Yonge was by this time at the zenith both of her powers and of her fame. She had found the medium of expression which exactly suited her, and was recognized as the interpreter of that fundamental institution the Victorian family. Naturally the family has always been a "fundamental institution," but not perhaps in any place nor at any time has it been so conscious of itself and of its own importance as in nineteenth-century England. The settled existence and the prolongation of childhood, which prosperity was making possible, may partly account for this: it may have been partly due also to the tremendous influence of the Old Testament, with its patriarchal outlook. Not that Miss Yonge—"family chronicler," as she called herself—ever preaches about the sanctity of family life (save so far as she quotes Scriptural warrant for the submission of wife and children), but she does what is far more effective; she illustrates it. It cannot be amiss to show in some detail some of the elements of which her 'chronicles' are composed.

BOOK FOUR

VICTORIAN FAMILY LIFE

CHAPTER VIII

SETTINGS AND OCCUPATIONS

M<small>ISS</small> Y<small>ONGE</small> was no impressionist. Like most of her generation, she would have held that a picture was built up from a
multiplicity of carefully chosen details, rather than dashed in by
a few broad strokes. The liberality of her description is typical
of the superabundance of her world, though it was likewise
peculiarly suited to her observant feminine nature. We have
already mentioned her record of trivial conversations, practice in
which enabled her to render in so lifelike a manner the day-to-
day talk of the households which she represented. It is the same
with the settings in which her people have their existence. She
revelled in backgrounds; she adored portraying figures. The
description given to her mother of Jane Colborne's wedding[1] is
only one example of hundreds which could be taken from her
letters. To real and fictitious scenes alike, her perfection of
detail gives a vividly pictorial effect.

Perhaps it is at the opening of her books that Miss Yonge takes
the greatest care of her settings. Before we have been for half
a page with the May family, we receive an indelible impression
of their schoolroom—its two large windows, with their wide seats
and scratched panes, looking out on the broad, old-fashioned
street of Stoneborough; the blue walls with tall skirting that
formed a shelf at the top; the fireplace, ornamented with blue
and white tiles bearing "marvellous representations of Scripture," and protected by a very tall green guard; the solid chairs,
their seats of faded carpet-work; the loaded bookcases, the piano
and the globe. The stage is set for the entrance of the family.

[1] See page 193.

The descriptions are not all so homely. Here, from a less-known work (*Nuttie's Father*), is depicted—and without the touch of malice which a modern writer would inevitably have added—a suburban street, St Ambrose Road. The semi-detached houses here

> had their entrances at the angles, with a narrow gravel path leading by a tiny grass plat to each.... [Was not Mr Dutton's], with lovely sill boxes full of flowers in the windows, the neatest of the neat; and did not the tiny conservatory over his dining-room window always produce the flowers most needed for the altar vases, and likewise bouquets for the tables of favoured ladies? Why, the very daisies never durst lift their heads on his little lawn, which even bore a French-looking glass globe in the centre.

Charlotte Yonge had a weakness—perhaps also typical of her period—for the stately homes of England, now so rarely seen intact among us. She describes with relish the opulent houses and spacious parks necessary for the backgrounds of her more distinguished personages. Here is the mansion (admittedly among the grandest of its kind) to which the heroine of *Heartsease, or The Brother's Wife* is brought, to encounter the scarcely concealed indifference or displeasure of her husband's family.

> The grand parterre, laid out in regularly-shaped borders, each containing a mass of one kind of flower, flaming eschscholtzias, dazzling verbenas, azure nemophilas or sober heliotrope, the broad walks, the great pile of building, the innumerable windows, the long ascent of stone steps, their balustrade, guarded by sculptured sphinxes, the lofty entrance and the tall powdered footmen, gave her the sense of entering a palace. She trembled, and clung to Arthur's arm, as they came into a great hall, where a vista of marble pillars, orange trees and statues opened before her.

No wonder that poor Violet was reminded of pictures of Versailles, and that, observing from her window the denizens of the terrace, she felt as if no one but peacocks had a right to be there.

(It is sad to think what this monstrous edifice had replaced. When it is burnt down, Lord Martindale says that his wife's rich aunt had insisted on his building it as an inheritance for his son, but "when I think of going home, the old red pediment with white facings always comes to my mind as it used to look up the avenue when we came back for the holidays." How many other landowners must have pulled down their Georgian houses and put up an atrocity like Lord Martindale's, which, he says, was insured for twenty thousand pounds, but that would "nothing like cover the amount of the damage!" He goes on to further reminiscences about the old house, talking of jackdaws and martens' nests, of jargonelle pears and of the stags' antlers in the hall, which old Mrs Nesbit had always so much disliked.)

As a contrast, here is a cottage interior, rather conventional, but of the kind that Miss Yonge must often have seen in her own village visits. It is her pleasant choice of words rather than any novel observation that makes this picture so effective.

> The Harpers' cottage stood in a large garden and was made of squares of timber filled up with bricks in a sort of herring-bone pattern. . . . The kitchen was a model of tidiness. The dresser was loaded with bright tins and blue-and-white crockery, with a neat cloth spread over the lower part, as white as the muslin window-blinds. The floor was as perfectly clean as if the bricks were still in their yard, the round table shone like a looking-glass, the copper kettles were almost lilac with ruddy brightness. The curtains were white dimity, and so was the broad frill that was hung over the ample chimney beneath the mantelpiece, covered with brass candle-sticks, smart white china poodle dogs, holding each a black hat in his mouth, and the like ornaments, and wherever there was room on the walls, hung or were pasted pictures in bright colours, a few small ladies and gentlemen, and several almanacs, with all sorts of shocking things going on in the picture at the top. . . . There were several Bible pictures too.

These two latter descriptions, though clever enough, seem to record chiefly external impressions, as though Miss Yonge had been a visitor rather than a dweller in either place. But here is an apartment with which one feels that she must have been completely familiar. It is inhabited by the two daughters of a parson—decayed gentlewomen, as a later age might have termed them. One has become a governess, the other an Invalid —no less a profession in itself. (Incidentally, a description of the latter by a neighbour includes the following sentence ". . . hair with threads of grey: I hope she does not affect youth; she can't be less than one or two and thirty.")

> The foundation was the dull third-rate lodging house—the superstructure told of other scenes. One end of the room was almost

filled by the frameless portrait of a dignified clergyman, who would have had far more justice done to him by a greater distance; a beautifully-painted miniature of a lady with short waist and crisp curls was the centre of a system of photographs over the mantelpiece; a large crayon sketch showed three sisters between the ages of six and sixteen sentimentalizing over a flower-basket; a pair of water-colour drawings representing a handsome church and comfortable parsonage; and the domestic gallery was completed by two prints, one of a middle-aged county-member, the other, one of Chalon's lady-like matrons in watered silk. . . . The table-cover was of tasteful silk patchwork, the vase in the centre was of red earthenware, but was enriched with real ivy-leaves gummed on in their freshness, and was filled with wild flowers; books filled every corner.

There is a story by Kipling in which a theatrical manager, for reasons of his own, brings into being a Flat Earth Society. Later, the real Believers come to the same spot in a charabanc, unpack a folding harmonium, and chant a hymn in praise of earth's flatness. The comment is: "I saw sick envy on Bat's face. 'Curse Nature! she gets ahead of you every time. I should never have thought of the harmonium.'" What modern novelist, consciously 'doing' a Victorian interior, would have thought of those gummed-on ivy-leaves?

Outdoor and country scenes were as much part of the Victorian life as the schoolroom or the parlour, especially for children. Miss Yonge introduces the twelve-year-old heroine of *The Two Guardians* in her favourite Devon scenery—a background specially apt because Marian is used to an out-of-door existence and chafes at the restraints of social life, suffering considerably from the confinement to which she is subjected by the grand family of her less congenial guardian. She misses most of all her spirited pony and the rides she used to take with her grown-up cousin, in scenery such as that described in the opening chapter:

They reached the top of the hill, and found themselves on an open common, with here and there a mass of rock peeping up, but for the most part covered with purple heath and short furze. . . . The view was splendid, on the one side moors rising one behind the other, till they faded in grey distance, each crowned with a fantastic pile of rocks, one in the form of a castle, another of a cathedral, another of a huge crouching lion. . . . On the other side, between two hills, each surmounted by its own rocky crest, lay nestled in woods the grey Church tower and cottages of the village of Fern Torr; and far away stretched the rich landscape of field, wood, and pasture, ending at length in the blue line of horizon, where sky and sea seemed to join.

Perhaps it is Miss Yonge's personal attachment to the setting of country life which made her enjoy writing the description of the Mays' picnic, on Meta's birthday, to the old Roman camp where they find the bogus antiquities. The younger children run wildly up and down the mounds, and then Meta joins Ethel and Norman in tracing out the old lines of the encampment.

Happy work on those slopes of fresh turf, embroidered with every minute blossom of the moor—thyme, birdsfoot, eyebright, and dwarf purple thistle, buzzed and hummed over by busy black-tailed, yellow-banded dumbledores, the breezy wind blowing softly in their faces, and the expanse of country—wooded hill, verdant pasture, amber harvest-field, winding river, smoke-canopied town, and brown moor, melting greyly away to the mountain-heads.

Here is another word-picture of the same part of the country:

They had, in the meantime, been mounting a rising ground, clothed with stunted wood, and came out on a wide heath, brown with dead bracken; a hollow, traced by the tops of leafless trees, marked the course of the stream that traversed it, and the in-equalities of ground becoming more rugged in outlines and greyer in colouring as they receded, till they were closed by a dark fir wood, beyond which rose, in extreme distance, the grand mass of Welsh mountain heads, purpled against the evening sky, except where the crowning peaks bore a veil of snow. Behind, the sky was pure gold, gradually shading into pale green, and then into clear light wintry blue, while the sun setting behind two of the loftiest, seemed to confound their outlines, and blend them in one flood of soft hazy brightness.

Far-view Down, as Miss Yonge imagined it, may have been in much the same part of the country as Francis Brett Young's Far Forest, the setting of most of his novels and, for instance, of Dr Bradley's earliest remembrances, with "the blue dome of Radnor Forest rising to southward and to northward the more irregular mountainous masses of the Forest of Clun." But it is curious that Miss Yonge, for all her sympathy with children, never trained herself to see with a child's eye, nor underlines

the difference between the vision of the young and the mature.
She would never have written, like her namesake:

> The child's mind was too deeply absorbed in things immediate
> to his eyes—the falling village street, with its rain-scoured surface;
> the little shops with bottles of sweets in the windows; the black-
> smith's; the baker's; the dogs that sunned themselves in the dust;
> the cats on the doorsteps; the white ducks that waddled down to their
> grayling-dimpled swimming-pool above the low weir; the bridge,
> with its piers and embrasures; the river itself, clear and swift or
> tawny with storm-water and flecked with barmy foam—to be
> aware of these present magnitudes—much less of the gigantic
> system of ridge and furrow that lay to eastward; the granite saddle-
> backs of the Clees and Comus' forest-fleeced Chase; the long fold
> of Wenlock Edge and the troughs of Temeside, Apedale and Corve-
> dale lying between.[1]

That is the description of an artist—perhaps too conscious an
artist to conceal his art. Miss Yonge's writing was a craft, not
effortless, indeed, but natural, pleasant, and so easy to read as to
make up in direct appeal for the lack of subtlety which distinguishes it from the work of a modern writer.

Often her families are introduced—or reintroduced—in their
setting, the whole forming a Conversation Piece of the kind
made so popular by Winterhalter's pictures of the Royal Family.
Here is the May family, as they reappear in *The Trial* (*More
Links of the Daisy Chain*), now nearly all grown up, when the
sailor brother, Harry, is home on leave:

> The drawing-room was a goodly sight that evening, and the
> Doctor, as he sat leaning back in weary happiness might be well-
> satisfied. . . . The youngest "Daisy" . . . was perched on the sailor's
> knee, though as he had seated himself on a low foot-stool, her
> throne was subject to sudden earthquakes . . . and the two presented
> a pleasing contrasting similarity—the open honest features, blue
> eyes and smile, expressive of hearty good-will and simple happi-
> ness, were so entirely of the same mould in the plump, white-
> skinned rosy-cheeked, golden-haired girl and in the large, powerful
> bronzed rugged sailor. . . . Those were the idle members upon the
> hearth-rug. On the sofa, with a small table to herself and a tall
> embroidery-frame before her, nearly hiding her slight person, sat
> Mrs Ernescliffe (Blanche), her pretty head occasionally looking out
> over the top of her work to smile an answer and her artistically

[1] Francis Brett Young, *Dr Bradley Remembers* (Heinemann, 1938).

arranged hair and the crispness of her white dress and broad blue ribbons marking that there was a step in life between her and her sisters[1] . . . a little behind was Mary, winding one of Blanche's silks over the back of a chair. . . . Richard and Ethel were arranging the "sick-albums" which they had constructed—one of cheap religious prints of texts and hymns, to be lent in cases of lingering illness; the other, commonly called "the Profane," of such scraps as might please a sick child, pictures from worn out books or advertisements which Ethel was colouring, Aubrey volunteering aid which was received rather distrustfully.

To get the full pictorial effect of this scene, one should remember, of course, that it is illuminated by candlelight, except that Tom, the doctor brother, is occupied with "various glass dishes, tubes and slides and a tall brass microscope" by a shaded lamp, burning (as his sister put it) "something horrible ending in 'gen.'"

What might be the occupations of other families, or of the Mays themselves at other times? For the women of the household there was, of course, always plain sewing. It was often 'for the poor.' Ethel May and her sisters did a great deal of "contriving," to produce from their worn garments tippets and dresses for the children of Cocksmoor, while Meta Rivers, who would have been the 'poor little rich girl' of a more sentimental atmosphere, is found to be in the habit of doing plain needlework, as a discipline for herself after her Confirmation. But there might also be "company work," as distinct from the less polite sewing which was generally performed in the bosom of the family. In *Chantry House* (though this is pre-Victorian in period) Miss Yonge presents the mother at tambour-work on muslin dresses for her daughter—these dresses, be it noted, to be worn both summer and winter. Margaret May, from the earliest days of her illness, is chiefly occupied with sewing, and her first bit of work is "a fine day night-cap" into which she puts "little white puffs," of which the downright sister Ethel cannot see the sense. The embroidery on which Blanche is at work in the scene already quoted is a banner for the Volunteers—the "Home Guard" of their day. The making of slippers, especially for curates, by Victorian young ladies has become a byword; this may be partly due to Miss Yonge herself, who, for all her devotion

[1] This is Miss Yonge's way of telling us that Blanche is married.

L

to Keble, was quite aware of the ridiculous side of what one would-be learned young woman terms "curatolatry." Certainly more than one pair of slippers appears; and at least one heroine marries the recipient, though she takes him rather as a haven of refuge from the uncertainties of a governess' life than from devotion to himself or his office. But the chief and most varied efforts at production are made in answer to a demand for articles for a Fancy Fair—pincushions, watch-guards (knitted or cro-cheted), leather pen-wipers, netted purses, and the like. The making of these frivolities became a craze which entirely upset the schoolroom routine, for even the most virtuous of the May sisters preferred it (and no wonder!) to "the hemming of endless glazed calico bonnet strings" for the children of Cocksmoor. Even the governess descended so far as to countenance "paste-board boxes, beplastered with rice and sealing wax, alum baskets, dressed dolls and every conceivable trumpery" in the school-room—and, indeed, had she been among the most up-to-date teachers in a school of our own time she might well have justified herself by an appeal to the phrase "self-expression by creative work." To-day's director of children's efforts would probably have condemned most of the objects produced by her predecessor's charges as hideous, but would not disapprove of their handwork as a waste of time, as was the tendency some twenty years ago. Poor Ethel, be it noted, who is most severe in her condemnation of the crimes committed in the name of charity, is rewarded by winning in a raffle "two splendid vases" of Etruscan pattern, in poti-chomanie, the manufacture of which had so filled up the usually blank days of a hypochondriacal lady that she had found no time for her usual nervous attacks.

While the ladies of the household were busy about the works of their hands, it was almost inevitable that, in the evenings at least, they should be read to—generally by father or elder brother—though Mamma read in the schoolroom. Mrs Amy Cruse in *The Englishman and his Books in the Early Nineteenth Century* points out that it was the need of a book for family read-ing, such that it would not bring a blush to the cheek of the young person, which produced the full-length Victorian novel, its refinement being in necessary contrast to the majority of eigh-teenth-century works of fiction. Many tales, notably the novels of Dickens (as readers of *Cranford* will recall), appeared in 'numbers,' and the monthly-magazine 'improving' articles also formed an important part of the literary diet in the better-instructed families. It was customary for the male members to peruse these magazines, or the books obtained from their sub-scription library or club, before letting them loose among the household, but sometimes they would read out selected portions, or even, if suitable, the whole book. When Dr May is slipping back into family life after the first shock of his bereavement, he resumes "his old habit of skimming a club-book and imparting the cream to the listeners." (One may recall from real life that the Nightingale sisters were read to nightly by their father, and that Florence bitterly resented it, but the more placid Parthenope was able to continue with her drawing. This is not unnatural when one remembers that 'drawing' meant chiefly the copying of other people's sketches—referred to by Miss Yonge as "that dreamy work.")

Dickens, though harmless, was not considered sufficiently elevated for some cultured souls. A schoolboy, indeed, has his ears boxed for reading *Pickwick* under cover of his Latin grammar, but the stern Philip (in *The Heir of Redclyffe*) blames such "cheap rubbish" for people's general ignorance even of Shakespeare. There is a dig at Dickens' sentimentalism in the course of the conversation—or can it possibly be at Amy's?

"I made [Laura] read me the part of Dombey that hurts women's feelings most, just to see if she would go on—the part about Little Paul, and I declare, I shall think the worse of her ever after—she was so stony-hearted that to this day she does not know whether he is dead or alive."

"I can't quite say I don't know whether he lived or died," said Laura, "for I found Amy in a state that alarmed me, crying in the greenhouse, and I was very glad to find it was nothing worse than Little Paul."

By way of leading them to higher things, Philip then reads them *I Promessi Sposi* in a translation of his own. We may note, by the way, that the first speaker is an invalid, so Laura reads to him, instead of the other way about. This reversal of rôles has to occur again when *The Clever Woman of the Family* reads to her husband's blind uncle, but in the ordinary course it is almost always the man who reads to the woman. Rachel ("the Clever Woman") considers novels such as *Silas Marner* and

Framley Parsonage as "empty employments," but this is regarded
as a foolish attempt at superiority on her part, for on the whole
Miss Yonge approves of novel-reading, provided it is not exces-
sively indulged in, and she becomes more lenient as she grows
older. In one of her first books, the Waverley novels are considered
by a stern elder sister as "a sort of slow poison," because she finds
that *Guy Mannering* has taken so strong a hold on the younger
girls' imagination. When her father gave Lilias permission to
read them, "she talked of little else, she neglected her daily
occupations and was in a kind of trance for about three weeks,"
during which time she read *Woodstock* and *Waverley*, and was
half through *Peverel of the Peak*. Then Papa complained that
she had not shown him any drawings lately, and after this she
"refrained from touching one of her tempters till after five
o'clock" (can this be a reminiscence?), but, as she was a very
rapid reader, she generally contrived to devour more than a
sufficient quantity every evening. The novels made her com-
plain grievously of the dullness of Russell's *Modern Europe*,
which was being read in the schoolroom; they also led to her
writing a Romaunt in Six Cantos.

Scott's novels were considered innocuous in themselves, though
enthralling, but a really wicked book was found in the possession
of a schoolboy aged about fourteen. His stepmother had gone up
to say good-night to him and from under his pillow the corner
of a book peeped out. It was a translation of *The Three Musque-
teers*, "one of the worst and most fascinating of Dumas' romances."
"You won't tell papa!" cried Gilbert, in terror.

As he was half-way through, she kindly offered to read him
"the innocent part" when his sisters were out of the way, so as
to get the story out of his brain. It is gratifying to note that
more refined influences prevailed; at a later stage in the book
Gilbert enjoyed Longfellow's *Evangeline*, which he read to the
young woman with whom he professed to be in love. Miss
Yonge, however, does not let us take his attachment too seriously,
when she tells us that the young lover "lay about the grass in
doleful dejection, studied little but the poems of L.E.L., lost
appetite, and reproachfully fondled his cough."

L.E.L. is regarded as merely somewhat foolish, but Shelley
and Byron are positively suspect. Lucilla remarks in *Hopes and
Fears* (and this is not an early novel) that her guardian, Honora

Charlcote, would have had a fit if she had found her reading Shelley. (Honor even disapproved of Lucilla's reading *Vanity Fair*.) But Scott's poems not only are greatly beloved, but prove the highest moral stimulant, and the discussion on *Marmion* between Ethel, her brother, and Leonard Ward, sustains that unfortunate youth in his imprisonment when he is wrongly convicted of murdering his uncle.

Though Miss Yonge herself always preferred Scott to all others, she realizes the change which has taken place in the next generation. The Literary Society ("*The Mouse Trap*"—why?), in one of her last books, has adopted Browning for weekly reading and discussion. Tennyson is almost put on the same shelf, by these advanced young ladies, as Scott. But this high level of intellect is not always maintained. One is quite glad, in the same book, to hear Lear quoted—Edward, not the King. Similarly, Lance Underwood can sing *Lead, Kindly Light*, to his brother with all due feeling, yet he quotes—as if expecting the quotation to be recognized:

I wonder any man alive will ever rear a daughter,
For when she's drest with care and cost, and made all neat and gay,
As men should serve a cucumber, she throws herself away,

anticipating by some thirty years our revived familiarity with the *Beggar's Opera*.

To return from literature to other occupations—one that is often mentioned is the illuminating of texts and addresses. The nineteenth-century Gothic revival was in full swing at the time of Miss Yonge's most famous books, and several of the artistic productions she mentions, from pulpits to portfolios, bear traces of its influence. (Incidentally, it is noticeable, in reference to foreign literature, that it is the later German romantic works— *Undine* and *Sintram*—that are so frequently alluded to; Charlotte had been caught up on the backwash of German medievalism after its greatest vogue was passed.)

Averil Ward possessed an "Illuminator's Guide" and "a great deal of red, blue and gold paint, with grand designs for the ornamentation of Bankside Chapel." But illumination could also be applied to more frivolous subjects, and Mrs Pugh, a fashionable widow and Averil's pet aversion, had a book in which the Gothic letters were used for merely secular and sentimental mottoes. "Illumination," said Averil, "is desecrated by being used on such subjects," but the cynical Tom replied, "And is it not better than the subjects being desecrated by illumination?" No wonder Averil was hurt and puzzled, and she began to wonder whether it was irreverent to do illuminations. She put her trouble before Mary May, who brought back from Ethel the comforting answer

> that all depended on the spirit of the work; that it was a dangerous thing for mere fashion to make playthings of texts of Scripture, but that no-one could tell the blessing there might be in dwelling on them with loving decoration or having them placed where the eye and thought might be won by them.

Among the indubitably secular hobbies, fretwork appears in *Magnum Bonum* as the pastime of two boys, and photography in *Hopes and Fears*. The latter is regarded perhaps as rather a masculine hobby. Lucilla Sandbrook and her cousin are apt to be outrageously unconventional in their doings; moreover, Lucilla, when a governess, also helps her employer's nephew with photography, but this leads to flighty behaviour on her part which results in her losing her situation. One cannot help feeling, somehow, that it was the chemistry involved which caused the humanist in the Miss Yonge of the early days to be suspicious of so scientific a pursuit.

Among outdoor recreations walking, riding, and boating take chief place; also skating, at which many of her characters are skilful. This would indicate that the Victorian tradition of hard winters was no myth—for their dexterity could not have been gained anywhere but on natural ice.

A good deal of drawing is mentioned—and not only as a counter-weight to being read to. The productions vary from the delightful illustrations, by a little girl, to her own adventure story which include a gory railway accident (the taste of children has changed remarkably little since the days of Charlotte Yonge) to the sketches by young ladies, frequently of ruins. Geraldine Underwood, in *The Pillars of the House*, paints in watercolours, and her pictures are exhibited at the Royal Academy in the 'sixties, where they make a far better impression than do those of her professional brother, who, one gathers, was considered to pay insufficient attention to detail.

Charlotte herself cared for the graphic arts, but not much for music, and perhaps that is why her musical characters do not always carry conviction—not even Lance Underwood, who expends his first tip in buying a violin, and Geraldine, who is quite hysterically enraptured at her first cathedral service. Averil Ward, who finds her chief solace in dreaming away at her harmonium, is more natural, though (or because) rather tiresome.

Her Church music was her object in life—the dedication of the talent that had been cultivated at so much time and cost, and the greatest honour and enjoyment she could imagine.

But Miss Yonge has a good deal more real sympathy with Countess Kate (the little girl who painted the railway accident with so much crimson lake), who has "no more ear than an old pea-hen," but is compelled to learn "the accomplishments of her station," which include the piano, and to practise with her governess. Kate, alas! became a grievous torment to poor Mrs Lacy, with her patient "one, two, three—now, my dear!" The reason that Miss Yonge in all seriousness gives for learning music (which from early Victorian times has meant practising "the instrument") would not appeal to all: "It is the readiest means by which a lady can assist in Divine Service." But there are also performances, both in the home circle (Flora gave her family some music on the night that Margaret first came down from her invalid's room) and at parties. In fact, it appears almost to amount to a social solecism not to be capable of "playing one's piece." Although the unfortunate Marian Arundel had been unable to practise the piano during the last two years of her father's life, her aunt, the conventional Mrs Lyddell, will not exempt her from performing before the company on her first evening in the house, and she has to struggle through a duet with one of her cousins as best she may.

For further occupation in mixed company there was, in addition to conversation, generally historical or literary (hardly ever political), a vogue for acting—from charades to public performances—and for rather odd moral games. Not even charades were always approved, however—one severe old lady said she would never have her granddaughters standing, dressed up, speaking speeches out of Shakespeare, before a whole room full of company, "as boldly as Mrs Siddons." It is on record that in the early days of Girton College a great fuss was made because in performing some Shakespearian scenes (*not* before a mixed audience) some of the girls took men's parts, in costume. Mrs Langford's grand-daughter has to compromise on this point by a *tableau vivant* which takes place on a "stage," the bottom half of which is obscured, so that the actors are only seen as far down as their waists—and to those too near at hand Prince Hal's pink petticoat is visible at her more emphatic movements. A more obvious way of drawing attention to the lower half of the female figure could hardly have been devised.

An example of the moral game is given at a small family party. The victim is told to name an animal; its characteristic qualities and habits are then discussed, generally in uncompli-mentary fashion, and the onlookers are made to realize that they resemble the victim's own. Then a curtain is drawn back so that the victim's own face appears to him, or her, in a mirror. Paper games, such as those in which Charlotte herself excelled, could also be made to preserve a good deal of uplift—for instance, "definitions" in *The Heir of Redclyffe*. Each member of the party makes an attempt to explain the word selected ("happiness," "riches," and so on) in epigrammatic form. Here is the comment on the hero's own attempt, afterwards:

"Some were very deep, though," said Mary; "if it is not treason, I should like to make out whose that other was of happiness."

"You mean this," said Amy: "'gleams from a brighter world, too soon eclipsed or forfeited.' I thought it was Philip's, but it is Sir Guy's writing. How very sad! I should not like to think so. And he was so merry all the time! This is his, too, I see; this one about riches being the freight for which the traveller is responsible."

"There is a great deal of character in them," said Mary. "I should not have wondered at any of us, penniless people, philoso-phizing in the fox and grapes style, but for him, and at his age——"

"He has been brought up so as to make the theory of wisdom come early," said Philip.

CHAPTER IX

RELATIONSHIPS

MISS YONGE is at her best in portraying children—little girls
in particular. Her boys run more to type: the bad ones are either
weak and led away by vicious (and generally moneyed) friends
or else they are obstinate and seek ill company and low sports—
poaching or rat-hunting in town alleys. (The country rat-hunt
Charlotte approved, and was much struck by the exhilaration
and picturesqueness of such a scene in a country barn.) But it is
not in the works of Miss Yonge that we should look for the graver
temptations of Victorian lads. They do, however, bet; one gets
into debt for a dog which he keeps boarded out; and they sometimes get drunk—a misfortune that did on occasion overtake her
better boys also. Clement Underwood takes too much after a
skating party, and has dreadful conscience trouble about it,
which Miss Yonge regards somewhat ironically. She did not take
very kindly to the priggish, self-centred type of youth (evidently
not uncommon within her sphere, to judge from his frequent
occurrence in her books) who took a morbid interest in introspection and confession, though she is uncommonly skilful in
depicting him. There are excellent, and recognizably modern,
pictures also of the stupid boy who is in a continual fog about his
Euclid, and of the brilliant boy who overworks, and a good deal
of horseplay and kindly teasing of sisters, no doubt drawn from
memory of her boy cousins' visits.

Miss Yonge had an acute perception of the way in which large
families tend to fall into groups, one member in the middle being
left out. Not all her families are as ideally united as the Mays.
The division between older and younger members in one, the
Fulmorts, gives rise to a scene over a nice point of precedence.
The elder sisters are married, and after the parents' death return
to the house on a visit to their brother. They are a good deal
displeased when he insists that the young and unsophisticated
Phœbe is to be regarded as hostess and to sit at the head of the
table.

But it is Miss Yonge's little girls, and particularly the only c
solitary children, who show that Victorian children differed littl
in essentials from those of a much later age. There is Dolore
Mohun, who stays with her cousins while her father is abroad
who so much objects to being called "Dolly," and who gets th
idea from her story-books that all aunts are cruel; there is Bessie
in *The Stokesley Secret*, who won't tell the family why she doe
not contribute to their fund for buying a pig—she wants to ge
a paint-box and make little presents—and who is so delighted a
learning the governess's Christian name (Christabel Angela!)
and, above all, there is Countess Kate, with her stories, of whic
she is always the heroine, and her dreams, in which she does suc
marvellous deeds—so different from the real existence in whic
she is subject to so much restraint. She is told that she must n
longer call her former guardian "Papa," but "Uncle Wardour,"
and inwardly storms that wild horses shall not compel her t
change—but one glance from the severe eye of Aunt Barbara i
always enough to make her hang her head and mutter the require
formula. The terrors of imagination which return to Kate s
regularly with night and darkness, and the sense of strain in he
attempts to repress them, are surely reflections of Charlotte'
own childish experiences. A youthful reader once complaine
that she didn't much like this particular book of Miss Yonge's
and a discerning, if tactless, relative replied: "Little girls neve
do, because every little girl knows that she *is* Countess Kate.'
Until Miss E. M. Delafield's *Zella Sees Herself* it would be har
to find a cleverer analysis of a sensitive, imaginative child'
mind.

Two other brief examples, taken at random, may be used to
illustrate Miss Yonge's psychological insight and the 'human-
ness' of nature seventy years ago. One is when a husband who
finds his wife looking through some music is surprised, because
he had not thought she played, and she answers, "I learnt like
other people, but it was the only thing I could not do as well as
Grace [her sister] and I thought it wasted time and was a young-
ladyism"—a delightful example of rationalizing a feeling of
inferiority. The other is where brother and sister are discussing
the latter's stepchildren:

"One good thing about Sophy," said he, "is that she will never
talk her feelings to death."

"That reserve is my great pain. I don't get at the real being once in six months."

"So much the better for people living together."

"Well, I *was* thinking that you and I are a great deal more intimate and confidential when we meet now than we used to be when we were always together."

"People can't be often confidential from the innermost when they live together. It was the same before, only we concealed it by an upper surface of chatter."

This conversation brings us to the relation which lies at the centre of all family life, and perhaps particularly of Victorian life —that of parent and child. We have seen that it was the father's influence which was all-powerful in Charlotte's own life; it is therefore natural to find this so in her books, though, indeed, other evidence of fact and fiction leads us to believe that in this her families accord in the main with the Victorian habit. Perhaps for this reason, the mother, who so definitely holds the second place, is often put—one cannot say 'painlessly' but literally 'by accident'—out of the way near the beginning of the book. So it is in *The Daisy Chain* and *The Pillars of the House*. Or she may be a rather ineffective character like Lady Elizabeth Brandon, who makes the pathetic protest against the influence of an exclusive female friendship entered into by her daughter:

I never could like Theresa Marstone, and now I see that she liked to govern Emma and depreciated my judgment, very justly perhaps; but still, I was her mother and it was not kind to teach her to think doing as I wished a condescension.

The influence of the elder brother is sometimes substituted for paternal authority, as with Felix Underwood, who becomes one of the Pillars after—indeed, even before—his father, a consumptive clergyman, has finally quitted this world and his thirteen children. But though an elder brother can do much to support the family, he has to be an almost perfect being for the arrangement to work properly. The Wards, friends of the May family, are left orphaned in *The Trial*, and one of the Mays exclaims, with some justification, of Henry Ward, "Preserve us from the guardian elder brother!"

Dr May's influence, as readers will remember, is supreme in his family, and they all adore him. He can even manage the governess, who has "feelings." But except for a little trouble with some of the boys, and a complete inability to cope with the worldly Flora, he has little cause for sternness. His standard of behaviour are high; the sight of port wine, nutmeg, and a kettle, produced by his medical son to counteract the possible ill-effects of a wet walk on the delicate Aubrey, calls forth the censorious remark, "Don't teach your brother to make this place like a fast man's rooms." Felix Underwood has considerably more bother with his younger sisters, and there is a strong strain of emotion between them and himself, perhaps because he stands as a father-substitute to them. When Cherry is in a hysterical condition after their father's death, it is only Felix who can quiet her, and this although he is not her particular "pair" among the brothers. Angela, the really tiresome sister, Felix manages by such methods as getting scalded when, in a fit of temper, she upsets the kettle, and finally by dying of an injury received when her naughtiness has caused a boating accident. But parents at least could be stern; Mr Kendal's attitude in *The Young Stepmother* reminds one of the famous Mr Fairchild. His son Maurice, aged three, has nearly got himself killed by his prank:

"Maurice, I find you have been a very naughty, disobedient boy. When you rode the pony round the yard, did not I order you never to do so again?"

"I did not do it again," boldly rejoined Maurice.

"Speak the truth, sir. What do you mean by denying what you have done?" exclaimed his father angrily.

"I didn't ride the pony," indignantly cried the child; "I rode a horse, saddled and bridled!"

"Don't answer me in that way!" thundered Mr Kendal, and much incensed by the nice distinction, and not appreciating the sincerity of it, he gave the child a shake, rough enough to bring the red into his face, but not a tear. "You knew it was very wrong, and you were as near as possible breaking your neck. You have frightened your Mamma, so as to make her very ill, and I am sorry to find you most mischievous and unruly, not to be trusted out of sight. Now, listen to me! I shall punish you very severely if you act in this disobedient way again."

Yet it would seem that Miss Yonge wants to make clear how much fathers have improved in the last twenty years—since about 1830. Lucy, Mr Kendal's daughter, repeats the following bit of gossip about her grandfather:

Old nurse says a gentleman was once in love with Aunt Maria and a very handsome young gentleman too. Old Mr Pringle's nephew it was, a very fine young officer in the army. Nurse said that he wrote to make an offer for her, very handsomely, but grandpapa did not choose that both his daughters should go quite away; so he locked the letter up, and said no, and never told her, and she thought the captain had been trifling and playing her false, and pined and fretted, till she got into this nervous way. . . . And when Grandpapa died, she found the letter in his papers, and one inside for her, that had never been given to her; and by that time there was no hope, for Captain Pringle had gone out with his regiment, and married a rich young lady in the Indies!

In the next generation, a Mr Algernon Cavendish Dusautoy proposes for Lucy herself. Her father, disapproving, and with some cause, does not at first think it necessary to speak to *her*—'foolish affair—mere child—turn her head.' However, he is persuaded by the young stepmother to do so, and begins thus:

You are very young, my dear, and must trust us to take care of your happiness. This gentleman has some qualities such as may make him shine in the eyes of a young lady, but it is our duty to look further.

and ends:

There, that's right, my dear, I see you are willing to submit patiently to our judgment.

All the same, Lucy, naturally enough, goes on meeting her "Polysyllable" on the sly, and eventually marries him. Though he is a popinjay, she does not come off as badly as most of the heroines who marry contrary to the approval of their elders. Miss Yonge is particularly severe on those who marry for wealth or position—Flora May loses her baby, Bessie Keith falls over a croquet hoop and dies of a premature confinement, and Alda Underwood has a wretched life, and is to the end afraid of the effects of hereditary drunkenness.

Relations between young people supposed to be in love are not, as a rule, as satisfactorily portrayed as those within the family. The affair of Lucy, mentioned above, is enlivened by an unusual bit of comedy. The young man comes to the house one evening when the family is out, and the couple are reprehensibly sitting in the dark when the parents are heard returning. At their sudden arrival, Lucy goes into a fainting condition, and he endeavours to revive her by sprinkling, but unfortunately the bottle which he snatches up for the purpose contains, not a restorative, but ink.

There is something vaguely unconvincing about the majority of the proposals depicted, and this is perhaps partly due to the very varied and remarkable motives given for their being made —and accepted. Alick Keith tempts "the Clever Woman" to marry him on the grounds that he could then be in a position to look after her mother—on whom she has brought considerable social worry and disappointment by her own unconventional behaviour. Meta Rivers certainly cared for Norman May, and her deceased father had approved of him, but her underlying motive in accepting him was obviously that this was her only chance of sharing in the romance of the mission field. Gertrude May took Lance Underwood chiefly on the strength of his being the brother of Felix. But perhaps the most uninspiring reason to be given for a proposal is that of Louis Fitzjocelyn to his cousin Mary: "If you would have me, I would do all I could to make you happy; and it would be such a joy to my father, and—[rather like an afterthought] to me."

Louis is completely serious in this declaration, and confesses it to his aunt in much the same terms:

> I could not meet any one half so good, or whom I know so well. I look up to her, and—yes—I do love her heartily—I would not have done it otherwise. I don't care for beauty and trash, and my father has set his heart on it.

Mary, though in love with him, very properly refuses him twice, till at last he is able to convince her that he, as well as his father, has some feelings on the matter.

Not that the 'all-for-love' *motif* is absent. There is the otherwise "prudent" Tom May, who dashes off to America to bring back his Averil as soon as he has cleared her brother's name— though, to be sure, she is an Invalid by this time, and therefore belongs to a favoured class as far as devotion is concerned. There is Captain John Harewood falling in love with the penniless Wilmet Underwood for her beauty and her quiet competence in nursing her brother, and Wilmet going out without hesitation to her Captain in Egypt when he is seriously injured, and even pointing out that it would be convenient if they were to get

married on the spot—a great strain, this, on her maidenly
modesty. There is Theodora Martindale, in *Heartsease*, reject-
ing Lord St Erme because her heart is still given to the tiresome
Percy Fotheringham, who, when they were engaged before, had
insisted on exercising complete control over her social activities.
And in the same book there is an affair typical of the worst
Victorian repression and sentimentality—though mercifully over
before the beginning of the story. Helen Fotheringham and
John Martindale waited eight years for each other in vain,
because, as John's brother put it:

> First my aunt set my father against it, and when he gave in, *she*
> had a crabbed decrepit [also imbecile] old grandfather, and between
> them they were the death of her and almost of him. I never thought
> he would rally.

If we turn to the love-stories which do not end with living
happily ever after, they range from the sublime history of the
Heir of Redclyffe and his Amabel to the sad little story of the
inarticulate Sophy Kendal, who has to watch her cousin Ulick
being snapped up by an intolerable little French refugee, and
has in addition to bear the painful thought that she may have
been "unmaidenly" in believing his attentions to have been
previously directed towards herself. There is the even more
lightly sketched incident of Ethel May and Norman Ogilvie—
an affair of Commemoration Week—with Ethel's half-uncon-
scious resentment when her father turns up and distracts the
young man's attention, and her very conscious disgust with
herself when she realizes why she is annoyed.

But, as Miss Yonge travelled towards the end of the century,
her portrayals of a *grande passion* become more and more infre-
quent, and it seems as though she felt that, in girls at least,
romance existed but rarely. The last pair of lovers of any importance on her stage are Dolores Mohun and Gerald Underwood,
and, sincere as they are, Miss Yonge implies that their mutual
attraction is a good deal due to the views of social reform that
they hold in common. In the same book (*The Long Vacation*),
Gillian Merrifield's gaucheness when she is proposed to by Captain Ernley Armytage is typical and convincing. She has given
herself away by her agitation when she hears a rumour that he
has come to grief, and he takes advantage of this to tell her:

"It is the first ray of hope you have afforded me for the only jo
of my life."

"Oh don't. I never meant it. Oh dear! I never meant to b
worried about troublesome things like this till I got older an
learnt a great deal more, and now you want to upset it all. It
very—very disagreeable."

"But you need not be upset," poor Ernley Armytage pleade
"Remember, I am going away for three years. May I not tak
hope with me?"

Gillian paused. "Well," again she said. "I do like you—I mea
I don't mind you as much as most people; you have done somethin
and you have some sense."

Was this lack of romance due to *fin de siècle* materialism, o
had there always been 'modern girls'? In the 'sixties Ethel Ma
sighed over her youngest sister and wondered if she herself was t
blame because the motherless girl had grown up (to her eyes) har
and lacking in sensibility. Flora, her tactful elder sister, answere

> There is a want of softness about all young ladies of the day. .
> We have made girls sensible and clear-headed till they have grow
> hard. It is certainly not becoming . . . it is the influence of the tim
> it all tends to make girls independent.

Some thirty years later—about the time of Oscar Wilde, an
rather later than *Plain Tales from the Hills*—Miss Yonge repr
duced the conversation of two young people, Underwood descen
dants, after hearing the reminiscences of their elders abou
"the jolly old days":

> "Did you ever see Bexley?" asked Anna.
> "Yes—an awful hole," and both indulged in a merry laugh.

They talked of their Uncle Lance's "self-negation" when h
gave up music and, for the sake of the family income, set his fo
on the path of trade, which, however, has ended in his becomin
editor of the local paper.

> "All very well in that generation—*ces bons jours quand no
> étions si misérables*. . . . Prosperity means the lack of object."
> "Does it?"
> "In these days, when everything is used up."
> He strolled to the piano and began to improvise something
> yearning and melancholy that Anna was not sorry when h
> uncle returned and mentioned the tune the old cow died of.

The same dissatisfaction with the ideals of the past is shown when the subject discussed is social improvement.

"One can't live with a heart in G.F.S., like Aunt Jane, really the cleverest of any of us. Or like Mysie, not stupid but wrapped up in her classes, just scratching the surface. Now if I went in for good works, I would go down to the bottom, down to the slums."

Even this is not enough for Gerald, who wants a revolution to take place before he comes of age. *Plus ça change . . .*

Though she tends to harp on the theme of the older and the younger generation, Miss Yonge seems rather to shrink from close portrayal of the married state—or at least the state of those who have been long married. Perhaps one would be justified in imagining that any novel she might write on this subject would be a mere reiteration of the duty of wifely submission, and conquest by gentleness. This theme is embroidered in her tales from the full-length and (on this point) most unconvincing *Heartsease* to Lady Merrifield's remarks in *The Long Vacation* that she was glad none of her girls wanted to take up a career (or, in another context, skirt-dancing) because "Sir Jasper would not hear of it."

But of the intimate psychological studies of repression, jealousy, and frustration, or of the eternal triangles which form so large a proportion of the novels of to-day, Miss Yonge's ninety-nine volumes contain remarkably few. This is no doubt partly due to restraining convention, partly to Miss Yonge's happy instinct for writing chiefly about what came within her own experience, but also partly, it seems, because once her people were safely married she ceased to be interested in them as individuals, or as couples, and viewed them almost entirely as parents.

As a rule, however, the happiest pictures from Charlotte's pen are of the unemotional and unconstrained relations between brothers and sisters—their sympathy, their teasing, and their cheerfulness, with all the rubs, the catchwords, and the alliances which knit together the lives of those who have shared the same nursery, eaten at the same long table, learnt for years in the same schoolroom, and played in the same garden or neighbouring fields. These things cannot be illustrated by quotation, for, as in life, it is the gradual building up of these relationships by casual conversations and trivial incidents that makes them what they are.

M

But it is the cumulation of scenes like the game of hide-and-seek (which included Papa and Uncle John) in the Stokesley garden, the Underwoods' picnic at Penbeacon (complete with thunderstorm), the family churchgoing in *Scenes and Characters* (when Phyl is stung by the wasp), and the dinner snatched by boys rushing home from school, both at Stoneborough and Bexley, that bring home to a later and more sparsely sown generation the intensely strong effect on the Victorian character of a crowded family life. If the settlers in the great days of emigration had been only sons, rather than members of a family of a dozen, would they and their descendants have continued for nearly a century to look on this country as 'home'? Granting that in any case the numbers of the emigrants would have been far fewer, it is interesting to speculate on the influence that Victorian family life has had on the cementing of the Empire, and thus on the destiny of the world.

To turn to the more practical side, the difficulties of a poor but genteel household are brought out with a skill which anticipates the modern *Diary of a Provincial Lady*, or Wells's account of Mr Polly's Sunday dinner. Here is the home of a schoolmaster who has married the romantic daughter of a noble family. Miss Yonge is at pains to indicate that the distressing disorganization of the household occurs because the mistress is occupied in writing a Romance, and neglects her duties. She prefixes the remark:

> Of all living women, Isabel was one of the least formed by habits or education to be an economical housewife, and the mother of twins.

(The arrival of the twins, by the way, had been announced in a note from James Frost, the father, to Lord Fitzjocelyn in the following terms: "There were three of us last night; there are five this morning. Isabel and the twins are doing well; Heaven knows what is to become of us!")

On a dark, hazy November afternoon James returns with an armful of exercise books, launches them into the study, and, running up to the drawing-room, stumbles over the maid, who is at that time "scouring the stairs." His wife appears quite unperturbed about this, and continues her writing in the drawing-room. James then brings down his small daughter to the fireless study, and proceeds to his corrections with her asleep on his knee.

Louis Fitzjocelyn drops in to see them, finds Isabel, her lap too full of papers to rise, invites himself to dinner, and goes down to the study

> out of consideration that she might wish for space to attend to dinner, room and dress. The two last were scarcely in such a state as he had been used to see at No. 5—books were on the sofa, the table cover hung awry, the Dresden china shepherd's hat was grimed and his damsel's sprigged gown hemmed with dust, there were no flowers in the vases. Isabel, though she could not be otherwise than handsome and refined, had her crepe rumpled and the heavy folds of her hair looking quite ready for the evening toilette and as she sat on her low seat by the fire, the whole had an indescribable air of comfort passing into listless indulgence.

Downstairs he helps to correct Latin books and hears a "victim of an imposition" fifty lines of Virgil. On going up with the father to put the little girl to bed, Louis

> was well-nigh thrown downstairs by a dust-pan in a dark corner, and . . . entered the drawing-room which, like the lady, was in the same condition as that in which he had left it.

Dinner was announced by a maid, neat but flushed by exertions beyond her strength—the same that had been doing the stairs—and consisted of two "alarmingly small" dishes, one of haricot mutton, the other of potatoes. All that the uninvited guest got was "a chop resembling Indian rubber decorated with grease and with two balls of nearly raw carrot, and some potatoes, apparently all bruises." Unfortunately, the cook and the small girl between them had eaten the remains of yesterday's pudding, intended for the second course. The maid thereupon had hysterics, and James's comment was, not unnaturally, "Things go on in the most extraordinary manner."

> "There is no more to come," said Isabel rising, "shall we come upstairs?" James took the candles and Louis followed considerably hungry and for once provoked by Isabel's serene certainty that no-one cared whether there were anything to eat.

Dwellers in the age of the tin-opener ought not to judge Isabel harshly, but there was some excuse for the guest's comment. When he hints later that James, as a schoolmaster, ought to be more patient with the boys, he receives the reply, "After all, a schoolmaster's life does not tend to mend the temper."

"No," thought Louis, "nor does Isabel's mutton."

Domestic difficulties, however, might be due to inexperience as well as to indifference on the part of the mistress of the house. Violet Martindale, when she got away from the "palace" to which our first extract introduced her, was not without troubles in her town home.

She was very much afraid of Sarah, and never spoke to her without shrinking back into "Miss Violet" and being conscious that it was mere presumption in her to try to order one so much wiser than herself. The cook, a relation of Miss Standaloft, was much more smooth and deferential, full of resources which seemed to come from Mrs Martindale herself; and though the weekly bills always exceeded her reckonings, so many things were wanting, as Mrs Cook observed, just getting into a house. The first time of having any guests at dinner, Violet was in much anxiety, but all went off to general satisfaction until the bills came in on Monday morning. The cost was beyond her calculations, exceeded her week's portion and devoured the savings of the days when they had not dined at home. Invitations had been sent out for another party, and Violet tried to bring it within bounds, but the cook was civilly superior—"It was always so in the first families, such as she was accustomed to, but if Mrs Martindale liked to have things in a different style . . ."

She knew Arthur would consent to no external change and all she could do was to look at the price of all she ordered, reject sundry expensive delicacies, and trust to living on the relics of the feast for the rest of the week; but, behold, they scarcely served for one luncheon, and on Monday the bills had mounted up in an inexplicable manner. There were no savings left and she made up the deficiency from her own resources.

A third party was impending, and she strove more resolutely for frugality. "Well ma'am, if you choose, it must be so; but it was not what I was used to in the families such as I have lived in."

But Violet was firm, whereupon the cook harassed her with contrarieties; and late hours and London air had so far told upon her that she could not shake off her cares cheerfully. She knew all would turn out ill—tormented herself—brought on a headache, and looked unwell when the evening came. The cook sent up the dinner with just enough want of care to keep her in such continual apprehension that she could hardly attend to the conversation.

"You did not make such a good hand of it to-day," said Arthur when the guests were gone; "that soup was ditchwater . . ."

As one can see from the foregoing incidents, the domestic
staff is by no means omitted from Miss Yonge's survey of family
life. But they are drawn almost without exception from without
—that is, as seen by their mistress—and not from within. On
the one occasion when she attempts to construct a real sub-plot
of the love-affairs of the little maid (Charlotte Arnold, in *Dynevor
Terrace*), Miss Yonge only succeeds in making an unconvincing story of the penny-novelette type out of the heartbreakings
of the faithful couple, while her treatment of Mr Delaford, the
butler, not merely borders on, but oversteps the limits of caricature.

Delaford's purpose in life was, that no maiden should fail of being
smitten with his charms; and he took Charlotte's defection seriously
to heart. . . . Mr Delaford thrummed out his most doleful tunes
on the guitar that evening, but . . . Charlotte never put her head
out. He courted the muses, and walked in with a pathetic copy of
verses, which, some day or other, might serve to figure in a county
newspaper, complaining of desertion and cruelty. . . . He laid the
verses before her with a most piteous countenance. . . . "She has
transfixed my breast" was the commencement, and out poured a
speech worthy of any hero of Charlotte's imagination, but it was
not half so pleasant to hear as to dream of, and . . . at last she
mustered courage to say "I can't listen, Sir, I ought never to have
done it. I am promised now, and I can't. . . ."

He returned once more to the charge, very dolorous and ill-used;
but Charlotte had collected herself and taken counsel by that time.
"I never promised you anything, Sir," she said, "I never knew you
meant nothing."

"Ah! Miss Arnold, you cannot interpret the heart!" and he put
his hand upon it.

"Nor I don't believe you meant it, neither!" continued Charlotte
with spirit. "They tell me 'tis the way you goes on with all
young women as have the ill-luck to believe you; and 'tis all along
of your hard-heartedness that poor Miss Marianne looks so dwin-
ing. . . ."

He went on, disregarding. "My family is above my present
situation, confidential though it be; but I would at once quit my
present post—I would open an extensive establishment for refreshment at some fashionable watering place. My connexions could
not fail to make it succeed. You should merely superintend—have
a large establishment under you—and enjoy the society and
amusements for which you are eminently fitted. We would have
a library of romance and poetry—attend the theatre weekly—and "

—(finishing as if to clench the whole) "Charlotte, do you kno
what my property consists of? I have four hundred pounds an
expectations!"

If Charlotte had not been guarded, what would have been th
effect of the library of poetry and romance? But her own poetry
romance, and honest heart, all went the same way, and she crie
out: "I don't care what you have, not I. I've promised and I'
be true—get along with you!"

And so on, rather painfully. Miss Yonge had not the Wodehous
touch with butlers, nor with distressed damsels either. Perhap
the most interesting passage—and a sidelight on the taste of th
time—is when, this particular damsel refusing to be "the brid
of Delaford," he manages to make mischief between her an
her young man by producing "a crimson watered silk volume,"
on the front page of which the faithful Tom, to his horror, find
the name of Charlotte Arnold borne aloft by two doves, and i
the blank leaves several extremely flowery poems in her ow
handwriting. Of course, the complication is eventually unravelle
by Lord Fitzjocelyn (who refers Tom to *Cymbeline*!), and he late
forces a confession from Delaford on this matter as well as on
more serious crime of peculation.

This curiously eighteenth-century manner of representing
"romance in the lower orders" may be partly due to an uncon
scious reminiscence. According to Miss Coleridge, Charlott
remembered lying in bed as a child and hearing "the nurses"
(probably at Puslinch) reading romances aloud to one another
Their literature seems to have been eighteenth-century novel
of the type of *Pamela*, which might well have influenced Mis
Yonge's portrayal of the faithful servant-girl.

The most 'drawn-in-the-round' characters among the servant
are naturally those who come closest to the children, and Mis
Yonge has a regular portrait gallery of old nurses—and a few
giddy young nursemaids. Sibby, of the real old *nourrice* type
follows the fortunes of the Underwood family through adversit
and prosperity from the time they are left semi-orphaned till th
last book, in which she still insists on regarding Clem as he
nursling during his breakdown, though he is now a respecte
vicar of some fifty years. Similarly does Mrs Frost's Jane regar
the prodigal-returned-rich uncle as no more than "Maste
Oliver." On the other hand, there is more than one return t

he *motif* of the baby killed, or almost killed, by the ignorant nurse or flighty nursemaid who drugs it to keep it quiet. There is also the "kind merry Frenchwoman," the first maid of the little Countess, Kate Caergwent, who is quite untrustworthy and disobeys orders on the sly to please her charge; and Charlotte in an extraordinary vivid little passage describes the pang felt by Kate when she has given away the maid's deceptions because she herself (at eleven) has neither the wit nor the will to deceive. It is rather hard to tell whether all these are conventionally drawn because Charlotte could not write about the servants other than conventionally, or whether they are true pictures, but over-familiar to us merely because such characters, once having a genuine existence, have now become fossilized, and are only to be found in books.

But, of all aspects of domestic life, it is to the stage which follows the nursery that Miss Yonge returns again and again, and always with success. Throughout the linked sweetness of *The Daisy Chain* one is conscious of education (in the specific sense of 'book-larning') going on in the background of the schoolroom. The teacher changes, till, by the end of *The Trial*, it is the former schoolgirl, Ethel, now an experienced 'coach,' who is undertaking the lessons of her small nephew, Dickie. But the mention of lessons brings one to that additional pillar of the house —the governess.

Girls' schools are more often than not regarded by Miss Yonge as a deplorable means of upbringing, and the student of early Victorian education can hardly deny that she was right. She definitely preferred home education, of which she gives several pictures. It was usual for the schoolroom to be presided over by Mamma, or for the elder sisters to 'hear' the lessons of younger boys and girls, but when the governess was in full command, her task must have been a heavy one. Miss Fosbrook, for instance, at the age of nineteen, was in charge of a whole family ranging from a baby to a thirteen-year-old boy, and had, of course, all subjects to teach. This variety of children had to be tackled singlehanded (save when the elder boys went off to a tutor, but even then she had to explain the homework to the stupid one); in addition she took the children for walks and to church, played with them, and superintended their meals and their manners. There was an old nurse—another of the many—but, as she was, naturally, jealous of the interloping young woman, she was a hindrance rather than a help.

Even when the governess was not in complete charge, one can see how much responsibility was necessarily delegated to her. In *Hopes and Fears* there is the incomparable Miss Fennimore, whose influence, for good or ill, is second to none, as we shall see. There is also the much younger Lucilla. When seeking a post as governess to a girl who has been taught by her parents up to the age of fifteen, she is told by the mother:

> Her father brought her on in Latin and Euclid. . . . Now, at Southminster, our time is so taken up that poor Sarah gets neglected, and it is very trying to an eager, diligent girl to prepare lessons and have them continually put off, so we thought of indulging her with a governess, to bring her on in some of the modern languages and accomplishments that have grown rusty with us.

The accomplishments mentioned by Lucilla are music and sketching, and she can also give instruction in modern languages, so she gets the post (at seventy pounds a year), but is too flighty to keep it long.

It is interesting, in considering the status of the governess, to remember Lucilla's difficulty about her clothes—which are remains from better days. "Housemaids always come to be hired minus crinolines and flowers; is it the same with governesses?" But in due course Lucilla is treated almost as one of the family; so is Robina Underwood when second governess in Lady de la Poer's household (at a hundred pounds a year; but she has been particularly well educated). Miss Ogilvie, on the other hand (in *Magnum Bonum*), who was careful not to presume, "took up her line from the first as a governess, dropping her friend's Christian name."

Governesses, represented and described, vary in Miss Yonge's books about as widely as they must have done in real life. Charlotte, by implication, advises that the mother must know what is going on in the schoolroom, or the consequences will be grave in one way or another. Lady Martindale (mother-in-law of Violet in *Heartsease*) has kept up her own accomplishments after marriage, a habit which evidently was somewhat rare, but she leaves her daughter, Theodora, to a series of governesses, one of whom is an infidel German. This deplorable woman is only

brought on the scene by hearsay, but there is a full-length portrait of Miss Fennimore, drawn with a very real understanding
of the frustration that must have irked many a good teacher and
the danger to the pupil which attended it:

> As a teacher she was excellent; but her own strong conformation
> prevented her from understanding that young girls were incapable
> of such tension of intellect as an enthusiastic scholar of forty-two.
> Her very best pupil she had killed. Finding a very sharp sword, in
> a very frail scabbard, she had whetted the one and worn down the
> other, by every stimulus in her power, till a jury of physicians might
> have found her guilty of manslaughter.

At the opposite end of the scale is the governess of the fashionable household in *The Two Guardians*, described, very shock-
ingly, by her pupils as "poor, unfortunate, faithful Morley"
(after Queen Anne's nickname), and by Miss Yonge as "a little,
nicely dressed lady, who looked very little older than Caroline
and had a very good-natured face." She is completely unable to
discipline her pupils, a fact to which her reproofs are in themselves a testimony: "Clara and Lionel are sometimes sad
creatures." "How can you be so naughty, Johnny?" and—
excusing herself to her mistress in her deplorable tone:

> I am continually ordering Sir Gerald not to scribble in books, but
> he never will obey . . . boys of his age always get quite beyond
> ladies' management.

Gerald is nine, and his elder sister admonishes him with more
effect.

> "Can you say that Miss Morley has not often spoken to you about
> [drawing in] the Atlas?"
> "If you call 'O Sir Gerald' and 'O you sad boy' desiring me in a
> rational way, I don't," said Gerald imitating the tones, "laughing
> and letting me go on; I thought she liked it."
> "Now seriously, Gerald."
> "Well, I mean, she did not care. If people tell me a thing, they
> should make me mind them."

His sister succeeds in making him beg Miss Morley's pardon,
but it is, not unnaturally, deemed necessary that he and Lionel
should be sent to school.

Two contrasting governesses follow each other in the May
family—Miss Winter, who is repressive and old-fashioned in her

methods, and Miss Bracy, who is sympathetic, but over-sensitive and continually seeing affront where none was intended. On the whole, Miss Yonge does not consider the governess's a pitiable lot. She has scope and responsibility within the limits of her schoolroom, and her position is, in this author's eyes, greatly superior to that of a teacher in a school. Had Charlotte been in the place of the Brontës, on the one hand, or, on the other, among the qualified staff at Cheltenham Ladies' College (of which Miss Beale became headmistress in 1858), she might have taken a different view—and, indeed, in the later stages of her life she has somewhat reconsidered her attitude, particularly towards High Schools. But Miss Fennimore, when she is converted from her 'doubts' and no longer thinks herself worthy to stay in the Fulmort family, says she is only fit to teach in a school, and not to have the charge of young ladies. She does in fact set up a school—under the influence of Robert Fulmort's Clergy House—but it is evident that Miss Yonge takes no real interest in it, and does not allow even this rightly directed institution to have a completely good influence on its pupils. And the average schoolteacher's destiny was summed up for Miss Yonge in the words "There she will spend the best years of her life in giving a second-rate education to third-rate girls." Albinia Ferrars tells her husband she would like to rescue Genevieve, about whom these words are spoken, by introducing her as a governess to a clergyman's family.

"Happily," said Mr Ferrars, "there are worse things than being spent in one's duty. She may be doing an important work in her sphere."

But Albinia will hardly allow this, and shrewdly hits on the cause of the disparagement earned by most teachers: "She, poor child, has been but half-educated herself, and has not time to improve herself."

Miss Yonge may not have known that, some twelve years before this was written, Queen's College, in Harley Street, the training-ground of Miss Buss and Miss Beale, had been founded with the very object of giving a sound grounding to those who were themselves to be the teachers of others. In any case, she might have been put off by the Low Church views of its founders. But the time-lag was considerable before the improvement of girls' schools as a whole, and one example of such a school's products will suffice. Albinia set her stepdaughters to read the Psalms on their first morning of lessons, and suffered for it; Lucy read flippantly, and Sophy in the hoarse, dull, dogged voice of a naughty boy. Then:

> Lucy showed off her attainments with her usual self-satisfaction. They were what might be expected from a second-rate old-fashioned young ladies' school where nothing was good but the French pronunciation. She was evidently considered a great proficient, and her glib mediocrity was even more disheartening than the ungracious carelessness or dulness—there was no knowing which— that made her sister figure wretchedly in the examination.

The fashionable school at Brighton which Averil Ward attended —with a view to taking on later the governess-ship of her little sisters—was no better. Dr May complained to his daughter that Averil "cost more than the whole half-dozen of you together," and that she had learnt nothing but singing, playing the harmonium, and "dabbling in water-colours"—certainly not how to make herself useful in a sickroom. Neither did she learn there "the art of ruling her own spirit," and it would be true to say throughout that Miss Yonge's chief objection to schools for girls was on moral rather than on intellectual grounds, and that she was not blind to their improvement. In fact, by the last quarter of the century, she can view with equanimity, and only a gentle irony, the multiplying of schools as a more or less natural proceeding.

> The town of Micklethwayte was rising and thriving. . . . There were a Guild Hall and a handsome Corn Market. There was a Modern School for the boys, and a High School for the girls, and a School of Art and a School of Cookery, and National Schools and a British School and a Board School, also churches of every height.

She can even face the prospect of giving an occasional heroine a higher education. Dolores means to take up a scientific career.

> "I should like to see the world and study physical science in every place. . . . I think I shall get consent to give some elementary lectures at the High School, though Uncle Jasper does not half like it, but I must get some more training to do the thing rightly. I thought of University College. . . ."
> "You'll have to conquer the horror of the elders."

"I know. They think one must learn atheism and all sorts of things there."

"You might go in for physical science at Oxford or Cambridge."

"I expect that is all my father would allow. In spite of the Colonies, he has all the old notions about women."

But then, Dolores had always been a shade unaccountable, and, of course, her father was a scientist. Science, except botany, was not as a rule taught in the schoolroom, but a good deal of information about, for instance, shells and fossils was acquired by both boys and girls outside school hours. Only, the search for these objects and the recognition and cataloguing of natural phenomena was not in the early days regarded as work. Miss Yonge in her later books has some very shrewd remarks about the sharp distinction between occupations which are regarded as "work" and those which are regarded as "play"—a distinction from which education has suffered badly for most of the present century, and which we have only lately recognized as a grave danger.

A survey of the attainments and methods of the Victorian schoolroom—of its frequently high cultural level, balanced by its astounding lapses—would be too long to undertake here, even if it were to be illustrated from the works of Miss Yonge alone. Suffice it to say that the curriculum, from Hebrew to Mangnall's *Questions*, is fairly displayed in almost all the 'family chronicles.' During the early days boys and girls might share alike—Aubrey May was by no means the only boy either in fact or in fiction to owe his good grounding in the classics to the teaching of his governess or elder sister. Sometimes the interchange of subjects was continued even beyond the point where the boys were removed to 'school,' whither, as a rule, Miss Yonge does not follow them.

> The twins, as little children had always had the same occupations, Henrietta learning Latin, marbles and trap-ball, and Frederick playing with dolls and working cross stitch; and even now the custom was so far continued that he gave lessons in Homer and Euclid in return for those he received in Italian and Music [at sixteen].

And there is the better-known example of Ethel working neck and neck with Norman, until she is unwillingly forced to give in. When one considers the variety of her employments in the house

and in social life, with the singleness of the path open to her
brother, the potential Balliol scholar, it is hardly remarkable
that she finds she must desist. Besides, she has reached the stage
of "young-ladyhood" which in itself she finds a great trial—
and though her elder sister thought "Richard would never
succeed in making a notable or elegant woman of Ethel," this
tiresome process was about to begin.

A final example shows how, when the financial circumstances
had been eased, the idea of a career for a girl could be quietly
abandoned—or at least postponed:

> Ursula . . . after climbing up through the High School to the last
> form hoped after passing the Cambridge examination to become a
> teacher there in another year. . . . On the mention of the examina-
> tion, Mrs Egremont detected some doubt in her companion's
> manner.
>
> "I don't think she will find time to go on with the preparation.
> And to tell the truth, I don't think we are quite ripe for such
> things in this county. We are rather backward, and Ursula . . .
> might find it a disadvantage to be thought much cleverer than other
> people . . . I am sure that if my little Rose were to take it into
> her head, I should have hard work to get her father's consent,
> though no doubt the world will have progressed by the time she is
> old enough."
>
> "That settles it. . . ."

So Ursula takes to tennis, instead of to the Cambridge examination, and a general decision is not reached on the respective merits
of a career and the social life.

We have anticipated somewhat the conclusions which Miss
Yonge reached at a later stage in her life and authorship, and
must now return to the period when she was gathering experience
from the social world in which she still played her part.

BOOK FIVE

"SMALL BEER"

CHAPTER X

MISS YONGE IN SOCIETY

I<small>N</small> spite of the fact that Charlotte had reached the time of life
when the Victorian spinster was generally a confirmed old maid,
she shared with considerable zest in the outbreak of gaiety at
the end of the Crimean War. Julian Yonge had been invalided
home with an illness brought on by sunstroke early in the cam-
paign. As the ship in which he was returning became due his
mother and sister would listen anxiously of an evening, and
often imagine that they heard wheels turning in at the approach
to the house. At last, one December day, Lady Heathcote drove
over in triumph with the paper—and only such people as
Members of Parliament went to the extravagance of daily papers
in those days—announcing the safe arrival of the *British Queen*
at Falmouth. It was perhaps a little flat to receive a young soldier
invalided home by sunstroke rather than by wounds received in
the heat of battle, but Julian's return was a sufficient event to be
marked by a special thanksgiving in church, and he himself
looked pale and languid enough to allow his mother and sister
the delight of cosseting him. After weeks of anxiety it was
pleasant to sit quietly talking and writing letters by the fireside,
with Rover, Mr Yonge's spaniel, stretched at Julian's feet, happy
to see a man in the family again.

As soon as Julian's health had been set up by a visit to Norway
and the first year of mourning for Mr Yonge was over, Charlotte
and her brother spent many pleasant hours dining out and
paying calls together. In 1856 Charlotte paid a visit to the
Coleridges in London, which she particularly enjoyed because
Julian at that time had chambers in Lincoln's Inn and was able

to go about with her. Besides entering into the peace celebrations, they drove in a hansom cab, which they found "great fun,
so smooth and quick," and paid a visit to the Zoo, which expedition ended by their walking home arm in arm in the rain, as
they were too wet for a cab.

The provinces too had their share of gaiety, and Charlotte
enjoyed with relish the great Naval Review at Southampton.
She was no more *blasée* than was the much younger cousin,
Charlotte Pode, who shared in the expedition. They cheerfully
put up with the discomforts of being jammed in the close-packed
waiting-room at Winchester from 7 to 8.30 A.M., after a night
spent at the Warden's house, and then travelling thirteen in a
carriage to Southampton. Here their troubles ended. Once they
were on the steam-yacht of Admiral Martin, their host, the day
was all happiness: sunlight on dancing waves, flags, music, and,
above all, the Queen. Charlotte's patriotic heart was thrilled by
a really close view of the majestic little lady. When they finally
returned to Otterbourne at nine at night, she was full of the
wonders of the day, and ready to live them over again for her
mother's benefit.

Charlotte's most exciting experience during these years was,
however, the journey to Ireland with Anne under the care of
"Uncle Edmund," who had survived the cowhouse cure of
Hyères to become a hale and hearty old gentleman. The two
young ladies were invited to be bridesmaids at the wedding of a
favourite cousin, Jane Colborne, the youngest daughter of Lord
Seaton, who was at this time Governor of the Royal Hospital at
Dublin. The fortnight there was quite a whirl of gaiety after
the more sober social round of their homes—grand military
reviews, formal dinner-parties, listening to Grisi at the Opera,
and a long day's expedition to the Devil's Glen and Glendalough.
Here Charlotte made good use of her time, and stored up her
impressions of the crags, waterfalls, bright green grass, and
gloomy lakes, as well as of the facetious guide and godforsaken
inn with its brackish tea, which "Ne'er saw Hyson nor Bohea,"
for use in the circumstantial account of Lucilla and Rashe's
Irish adventures in *Hopes and Fears*, one of the books on hand
at the moment. The expedition ended with the most lovely
picture of all in the twenty-mile drive to Bray station, of
"the moon shining on the waste heath and a great purple

A Naval Review in the Eighteen-fifties

By courtesy of "The Illustrated London News"

CHARLOTTE M. YONGE WITH HER MOTHER
By courtesy of John Yonge, Esq.

hill rising up against the sky as if it would never come any nearer."

As to the wedding itself, Charlotte entered into it all with the greatest zest, and, from the description of every minute detail which she wrote to her mother, one would guess her to be a girl in her first season rather than a staid and intellectual woman just turned thirty-four. She gave herself up entirely to the duties of a bridesmaid, in which were included arranging the flowers and the wedding presents, dosing the bride with sal volatile, till she was "quite composed and like herself," pinning the wedding favours on to the guests and helping the best man to make the first incision in the gigantic wedding-cake. Charlotte, with her novelist's eye for the *mise en scène*, was tremendously impressed with the wedding procession moving through a long vista of rooms to the chapel, through lines of old pensioners in their red coats and cockèd hats, drawn up to form a bodyguard on either side of the hall. "Jane's bending, shrinking towards him [the bridegroom] was the prettiest bride-like thing" she ever saw. Jane was clearly the ideal bride of the period. Charlotte goes on to paint for her mother more cameos of the ceremony:

> The picture was perfect, the bright-painted window above the dark, almost black oak carvings—Corinthian columns with festoons, in the Grinling Gibbons style—the wide chancel, Graham looking so tall and well in his surplice and scarf; Jane's slim bending figure, Captain Moore upright and soldierly in his scarlet staff uniform, and his best man in dark cavalry blue; Lord S. of course most beautiful, white-haired and upright, and then the half-circle of bridesmaids, all white picked out with blue, as pretty a dress as could be.

If Charlotte had realized that the authoress of *The Heir of Redclyffe* was as much a sight to Dublin society as the bridal splendours of Lord Seaton's daughter, she would hardly have got through the wedding breakfast. A hundred and sixteen people sat round a great horseshoe table, and the formidable ceremony of the giving of favours fell to Charlotte, who breathed a sigh of relief when she chanced on people she knew. Her worst moment was when the Lord Lieutenant came up and spoke to her. ("Aunt Seaton had introduced me before, and I had made a curtsey as well as nature or art would permit, and thought of Miss Brontë.") She was thankful that no one who knew her was

N

near to mark her flounderings, as he talked graciously to her of scenery, Miss Austen, and *Barchester Towers*. It was obviously a relief to her when she made her escape. The nine bridesmaids ended their day by carrying up to bed their piece of wedding-cake, that had duly been passed through the bride's ring; but Charlotte confessed to her mother, "I did not dream at all, being much too sleepy."

In spite of the presence of many guests, there was a sufficient background of Colbornes and Yonges to set Charlotte at her ease and to enable her to abandon herself entirely to that favourite amusement, the playing of paper games, and to pleasant discussion with Delia Colborne and another intellectual member of the party on historical subjects. Talking history was all very well, but Charlotte felt she lived it as she hung on every word from Lord Seaton's lips. Mrs Yonge had taught her daughter the same hero-worship of the gallant general as she had felt herself from her own childhood, and both loved to dwell romantically on all the incidents of his career in the Peninsula, and later as Governor-General of Canada. In appearance Lord Seaton was all that a military hero should be—very tall and upright, with bright blue eyes, curly white hair and fresh complexion, and features strangely reminiscent of the Duke of Wellington. His character matched his appearance, so he was worthy to be admitted into the Valhalla of Charlotte's admiration, and she vowed that she would always remember him and Mr Keble as the two most humble men she ever knew. Lord Seaton too was very fond of the clever daughter of his little stepsister, Fanny, and, in spite of all the wedding bustle, he was ready enough to devote his time to her entertainment.

Though the society of Lord Seaton did not pall on Charlotte, the general excitement did, and her letters to Mrs Yonge during the last few days in Dublin betray a fret and worry at the constant chopping and changing of the day of return by her escort. (Really nice young ladies, even though turned thirty-four, did not cross St George's Channel without one.) She was not sorry in the end to get back to her parochial and literary pursuits.

The Young Stepmother, whose slow unfolding in the numbers of *The Monthly Packet* during the years 1856–60 must have sorely tried the patience even of a generation rich in that virtue, was already begun. This story was dated by the introduction of the Crimean War. One wonders whether the heroic deeds of Gilbert Kendal at Balaclava were the compensation that Charlotte's dreams allowed her for the somewhat ignominious return of Julian after a mere sunstroke. The character of Albinia herself, who bursts on the provincial conventionalities of the little country town as Mr Kendal's second wife, is drawn at full length, while as a background Miss Yonge depicts with considerable satiric power the society of Bayford. Albinia's relations with her stepchildren and with the first wife's family are convincing enough, though the story when it appeared in novel form was shorn of some of its social humours. This book is probably the "one of Miss Yonge's deservedly popular tales" to which Professor F. T. Palgrave refers when he tells how he watched Tennyson lying in bed "reading hard the book which on this trip he had taken for his novel-companion." The poet read on by candlelight till Palgrave heard him cry with satisfaction, "I see land! Mr — is just going to be confirmed." Then he put out the light.[1]

As far back as 1853 Charlotte was discussing in her letters with Marianne Dyson the plot of the story that was later to be called *Hopes and Fears, or Passages in the Life of a Spinster*. It had obviously arisen from their interchange of ideas on 'Bild-worship,' a subject on which Charlotte says she cannot go as far as her friend in theory; she is well aware of its peril. But it was not until 1860 that Honora Charlecote was sent out to warn unattached ladies of the dangers of 'live *Bilds*.' The matter of her story is strangely modern, and shows Miss Yonge dealing with a psychological problem of which she has an intuitive rather than a reasoning grasp.

Honora spends her youth waiting until she is free to marry Owen Sandbrook, who goes out as a missionary to Canada, but he, soon tiring of this life, takes a fashionable wife and an easy country living. When his two children are left orphans, Honora magnanimously adopts them and transfers her affections to his son, Owen, who is the image of his father. Lucilla, the girl, is exactly like her mother, and, in spite of excellent intentions to be "justice and mercy combined," Honora metes out stern justice to her, while Owen gets all the mercy, as Lucilla

[1] This version of the incident is based on the account given by Mrs Cruse in *The Victorians and their Books*.

penetratingly remarks. Honora, a sentimental and charming spinster; Lucilla—both as a child and later as a Society beauty; Humfrey Charlecote, the old-fashioned country squire; and Mr Prendergast, the curate—all are convincing portraits. The last two were probably to some extent taken from life, for Charlotte said of "Uncle Yonge" of Puslinch: "He has some elements of Humfrey in him, chiefly the kindly common sense, and the sense of duty which is indeed a good heritage." Mr Prendergast, whether as the shy young curate who was the playmate of Owen and Lucy or as the rather untidy and quaint man he became later, is reminiscent of Mr Bigg-Wither, who had always been so good-natured to Charlotte and Julian in their childhood, and before whose visits Mrs Yonge was apt to remove the new chair-cover, for fear he should crumple it.

The sub-plot concerned the doings of the Fulmort family, and might be entitled: "Phœbe, or How a Young Girl kept her Innocence in the midst of Worldly Surroundings, and how she converted her Rationalistic Governess and her Reprobate Brother." Characters from this part of the book appear in Miss Yonge's later works, so she was evidently fond of them. But, as a whole, the story contains rather too much material to be well constructed, and one can well believe that she had struggled with it on and off for several years. For over both *Hopes and Fears* and the latter part of *The Young Stepmother*, there broods a certain sense of depression. The rest of her output for the years 1858 to 1860 consists chiefly of works written earlier but not previously published, such as two of the little plays written for the Moberly children and the *Conversations on the Catechism*, which, having run through years of *Monthly Packets*, now appeared in three volumes, weighty with erudition.

It is obvious that Charlotte's creative faculty was for the moment at a low ebb, but it is impossible to assign any positive reason for this. The fact that both these novels contain unhappy love-affairs might lead us to wonder whether Charlotte herself was suffering from a like trouble, but there is no evidence at all in support of such a theory. In any case, one who, like Miss Yonge, was always reserved where her innermost feelings were concerned was hardly likely to provide it consciously. Whether because of her devotion to her father or for any more obscure reason, there are simply no traces of a love-affair—on her side, at least—to be found in the life of this prolific creator of romance. People, of course, speculated. Some thought that Mr Bigg-Wither remained a bachelor for her sake, but there is no proof that he ever entertained for her a more tender passion than he did in the days when as a shy young curate he enjoyed the chatter of the intelligent little girl of eleven. There is, however, a type of character, reserved and considerably older than the object of his affections, sometimes portrayed as a clergy-man, whose appearances in her books are distinguishable enough to hint at a living model.

Other inquirers would stress Charlotte's obvious liking for her cousin John Yonge of Puslinch, and there is a family tradition that one of the Puslinch cousins wished to marry her. But even if her affection for him was of a different nature from that which she felt for his sister Anne, it would have come to nothing. Years later she told one of her nieces, who asked point-blank whether she had been in love with him, that she certainly had not, nor would she have dared to be, so strong were her father's views on the subject of marriages between first cousins, to which (very understandably) he considered his family much too prone.

Again, from the purely subjective point of view, as suggested above in connexion with the depressed tone of her work at this period, we might speculate on the possibility of a late develop-ment in one who had in many respects remained emotionally a child until she was past thirty, and who was busy creating imaginary—to the exclusion of personal—romance. One remark, made years later to Miss Wordsworth, might possibly refer to an unrequited passion: "I have had a great deal of affection in my life, but not from the people I cared for most."

All this, however, is mere speculation, and, as to her change in tone, there may well be another cause. Perhaps it is safest to assume that Charlotte's work was thrown slightly out of gear by the domestic reorganization entailed by her brother's marriage, in 1858, to Miss Frances Walter. Although she dwelt much in her letters to Anne Yonge and Miss Dyson on the new sister-in-law's beauty and charm, and the village people told her that she seemed quite proud of having a sister, it was bound to upset the ordered existence of Charlotte and her mother to have Julian and a bride of nineteen breaking into the midst of it, when the couple returned from their honeymoon to take up permanent quarters at Otterbourne House. It was thought no more necessary for Charlotte to have a room to herself for her writing than for Miss Austen in her day, though by the late 'fifties Miss Yonge had so well established herself that her authorship did not, as with her predecessor, involve a speedy hiding away of manuscripts at the approach of strangers.

It is not surprising that the year 1859 was a lean one from the literary point of view, for in it Charlotte's first little nephew was born and died. During the few months of his life she was a most devoted aunt, her letters are filled with chat about his baby doings and descriptions of his large dark, soft eyes, his merry smile, and his unusual intelligence. But, somewhat morbidly, she supposed that by his excessive beauty and charm he was "as if marked from the first for a brighter home," and could even write: "Somehow I am half glad, though grieved, that my father's name and Mr Keble's godson should be safe from any stain or dimming."

It was not long before the nursery at Otterbourne House was again occupied, so Mrs and Miss Yonge amiably decided to leave the house to the rising generation. At the beginning of 1862 they betook themselves to Elderfield, in those days a pretty cottage set in a large, old-fashioned garden. This had a private path into the adjoining grounds of Otterbourne House, so Charlotte was not cut off from her old dreamy rambles there and in the daffodil copse, nor from pleasant intercourse with her brother and his family. The new house was made homelike by Mr Yonge's portrait by Richmond, which looked down on his widow and daughter from among their many favourite pictures, including, of course, the Dürer of Paris fame. Where there were no pictures there were bookshelves filled with many of the acquisitions of Charlotte and her father. Books and periodicals lay about on the round table, and a photograph shows the room well lined with bric-à-brac. Their three windows looked out on to the life of the main Southampton road and of the school and church opposite. Red Rover and Hirondelle no longer dashed with gay blasts of the postilion's horn down the hill, but there was life enough on the road even during the happy seventy years' lull between coach and charabanc.

The new environment was propitious to Charlotte, and, to the delight of all lovers of the May family, she continued to follow their fortunes in *The Trial*, which came out in *The Monthly Packet* from 1862 to 1864. The main theme of the book—Leonard Ward's trial for a murder he had not committed—was the fruit of an interest in the law that dated from the childish beginnings of Miss Yonge's lifelong friendship with Mary Coleridge, and her sight of the latter's father, the Judge, on circuit at Winchester. While Charlotte was working up the plot of *The Trial* she was actually thorough enough to get Sir John Coleridge to take her on a tour of inspection of Portland prison, so it is no wonder that this, as well as the trial, is vividly and accurately described.

The law-court appears to have had a great fascination for Miss Yonge, and a trial scene plays an important part in *The Clever Woman of the Family*, which appeared in 1865. It is one of the few novels she wrote for an entirely grown-up public, and contains a shrewdly critical portrait of a nineteenth-century "intellectual woman." Rachel Curtis, who lives in a stodgy and conventional set of county and ecclesiastical families, is left to satisfy her leanings towards bookishness and philanthropy from periodicals, where she picks up all the catch-phrases of the moment and thinks herself far in advance of her neighbours. After she has been humbled by the utter failure of her schemes and duped by a common sharper, she is allowed to repent into normality, a transformation completed by her marriage with Alick Keith and her association with his uncle, Mr Clare. (This clergyman, of all Miss Yonge's characters, is the most reminiscent of Keble.) It is strange that this novel has not enjoyed a wider popularity. But by the feminists growing up during the latter half of the century Rachel was condemned as a piece of propaganda on the opposite side, though Miss Yonge does not allow one to forget one's sympathy for her in laughter at her foibles, and an unprejudiced reader of our day sees in her a tale of failure in practice rather than in ideals.

To this same productive season belong those two delightful children's stories *The Stokesley Secret* and *Countess Kate*, of which the latter, at any rate, may well claim to be a classic of the schoolroom. In *The Stokesley Secret*, a country house and the turbulent schoolroom of a hearty naval captain's family are preserved in unfading outlines. The kitchen garden, where the Merrifield children roast potatoes in the bonfire and play hide-

and-seek; the schoolroom, with its view of the chestnut-tree and the backyard, where they watch the activities of Purday, the farm man—these places and their inhabitants are substantial. Good though this is, however, the story does not attain the perfection of character-drawing to be found in *Countess Kate*. In Kate we are shown the crystallization of a child's dream of the attainment of rank and riches, and her sad disillusionment when, on becoming a countess, she meets with tiresome proprieties instead of grandeur. Disguised by circumstances, however, the imaginative Kate, with her shrill voice, long words, and terror of the dark, can be none but Charlotte herself.

These two tales were the first stories of contemporary life that Miss Yonge had written for children of her own class, though she had already produced for them many historical tales. Even though Guardsmen and professors might no longer seize on her books with eagerness, the admiration of her schoolroom public was quite unabated. Through *The Monthly Packet* she had become the oracle of many a young lady in her 'teens, and from among these was formed during the eighteen-sixties an inner circle over which Miss Yonge exercised an influence typical of that which she wielded in lesser degree over her wider and unknown youthful public. The idea came from Mary Coleridge, who had growing up round her various young nieces and cousins, for whose lively young intellects she felt that schoolroom routine was not a sufficient outlet. Accordingly, "Cousin Charlotte" was set up as a "Mother Goose" to a society of "Goslings," who submitted monthly sets of questions and answers to her on all subjects in science and art. (Even the omniscient Miss Yonge, however, had to veto such promising subjects as "Who was the man in the iron mask?" or "What is the secret of Freemasonry?") Christabel Coleridge, who afterwards became Miss Yonge's biographer, was one of the original "Goslings," and Mrs Henry Wood, as well as others who later became writers of some reputation in their day, was in her childhood a member of the society, and enjoyed the stimulus of Miss Yonge's leadership in these intellectual pleasures.

The "Goslings" were keyed up to a great pitch of expectation when they received invitations to meet their "Mother Goose" one afternoon in January 1861 at Sir John Duke Coleridge's London house. But when they had been ranged in a circle ound her, flanked by their mothers, they were perhaps a little disappointed to find that the wonderful person who had created the May family was less ready with her tongue than with her pen. Christabel Coleridge even can only admit, "I remember hardly anything that passed. She was then tall and rather thin, with dark hair touched with grey, worn in a net, and very bright dark eyes." What poor Charlotte felt at being confronted with a room full of admiring mothers and daughters is not recorded.

It was another story if any "Gosling" was privileged to catch her in less formidable surroundings. When, in the spring a year later, Christabel was invited to spend the day at Elderfield, she carried away a very different impression of the stiff and frozen figure she had met on the previous occasion. When Cousin Charlotte discovered that the little Londoner had never made a cowslip ball, all her shyness melted away. She impetuously took off the narrow velvet on which she wore a locket, and used it to make one for the girl's delight. Later in the day Miss Yonge even unbent so far as to tell Christabel the plot on which she was working. This she loved to do, when she found a sympathetic listener with whom she could forget her shyness. Miss Coleridge could always remember her pouring out every detail of her stories in dramatic manner, sometimes stopping in the midst of a walk to emphasize a point, or sitting on the floor in front of the fire, lost to all but her eager narration; and it was thus, not as the centre of an admiring group, that the "distinguished authoress" was most happy.

CHAPTER XI

SORROWS

AFTER about 1860 Charlotte's life seems to eddy along apart from the main currents of thought, and in 1865 she wrote to Miss Dyson, "I have just seen that Miss Yonge has lived her day . . . it is odd to stand for a generation gone by." She had settled down in her country cottage to watch the last years of her mother and of the Kebles. Charlotte had always loved the couple at Hursley as well as her own kith and kin, and she grieved as she saw their grip of life loosening. There were still happy flashes, however, of the peaceful gaiety natural to that household, as when, in August 1865, Queen Emma of Honolulu made a four days' visit to Hursley. Miss Yonge came in for her share of the festivities. If Mr Keble was the saint towards whom Queen Emma's pilgrimage was directed, she realized that to the authoress of Otterbourne also homage was due. The Queen and her tales of her native land were bathed in the glamour that Charlotte's imaginative sympathy had always cast for her over the mission field. She was left with the happy memory of this last occasion of the "light and peace" round her friends, and she was spared the watching of their last weeks. They died at Bournemouth in the following spring, Mrs Keble surviving her husband only forty days.

Charlotte Yonge was a prominent figure in the vast concourse which assembled at Hursley for Mr Keble's funeral. Always sensitive to atmosphere, she was upborne at the burial by many happy chances. It was a beautiful spring day, and bright sunlight lit up a butterfly flitting through the church, and the glistening celandines round the grave. In the midst of her sorrow she was able to enjoy the gathering of her prophet's friends and admirers, which one enthusiastic onlooker likened to Paradise, so many were the meetings there! The outward token of her love and admiration for the greatest saint produced by the Oxford Movement was the cross she put up in Otterbourne churchyard to his memory; but her true monument to im was piled by her many volumes, which, during the remaining thirty-five years of her life, never ceased to bear the impress of his spiritual teaching.

There were two years between the deaths of the Kebles and of Mrs Yonge. The first part of the time was a fairly happy interlude for Charlotte. It was then that she grew intimate with the family of Canon Butler, the Vicar of Wantage, who later became Dean of Lincoln. Shortly after Keble's death Miss Yonge had the solace of a visit to Wantage, with the especial delight of a drive through the downland country to Fairford, the place of Keble's birth, where she wished to collect impressions for her introduction to *Musings over the "Christian Year."* The whole atmosphere of the place and the great beauty of the glass in the church made a deep impression on her, and Canon Butler was a thoroughly congenial guide, being imbued with an admiration for Keble that rivalled her own.

Canon Butler, who was of the second generation of the Oxford Movement, excelled in the practical exposition of its ideas, and was the driving force that kept alive and prosperous the undertakings of the Sisterhood at Wantage. Miss Yonge enjoyed her glimpses of his lessons to pupil-teachers and his guidance of the manifold activities of the place, both parochial and conventual, that followed each other throughout the day at a speed that almost took her breath away. She compared the atmosphere of the place to a brisk, frosty morning, because of the dislike shown there for any kind of unreal sentiment—of which she highly approved. Her prevailing impression was that "everything was done with full activity by day, and at night there were conversations lasting into the small hours, and then the doves cooed and the clock chimed."

The autumn of 1867 saw Mrs Yonge and her daughter setting forth on a round of most congenial visits. That year Dr Moberly had retired from his headmastership and taken the living of Brightstone, in the Isle of Wight. Their departure left a great blank in Charlotte's life, for, since Mr Yonge's death, she and her mother had fallen into the habit of spending their Sunday evenings with the Moberly family when they were at Fieldhouse, their Hursley farm. Charlotte was delighted to find herself again in the pleasant circle at Brightstone. She entered with zest into the decorations for the Harvest Festival, and undertook a double triangle of grapes and corn. The other helpers were much entertained at seeing the famous Miss Yonge, with dress tucked up, vigorously sweeping out the chancel with a long-handled broom.

Later came a visit to her distant cousins the Miss Pattesons, sisters of the Bishop of Melanesia, for the consecration of All Saints' Church at Babbacombe, which they had built. The chief attraction was Bishop Selwyn, "as vigorous as ever," and his wife, looking "very bright and joyous." Miss Yonge writes to Marianne Dyson:

> The only difficulty is to choose between bishops, sermons, and meetings, but we stick fast to our Primate whenever we can, and our meals and walks to and fro are specially delightful.

When Charlotte was not drinking in the words of her missionary Bishop, she was enjoying the conversation of Samuel Wilberforce of Oxford, or of the lesser ecclesiastical luminaries of congenial views with whom Torquay was thronged. Altogether, she writes, "It is all so free and easy and merry that I don't know how to enjoy it enough." Charlotte herself, handsome in middle age, her grey hair contrasting with dark eyebrows and still youthful face, her wit evoked by a sympathetic *milieu*, was no small ingredient in the pleasure of the other guests at the consecration. Mrs Yonge was able to enjoy her daughter's social success. Her maternal pride overflows in a postscript to the long letter to Marianne:

> To see Charlotte so well and happy is delightful. . . . To see her doing the honours of the place and people . . . is charming.

This is almost the last evidence we have of the happy relations between Charlotte and her mother. Only a short time after the visit to Torquay Mrs Yonge developed softening of the brain, and the last few months of her life were probably the most trying period her daughter ever went through. Charlotte Yonge's nervous temperament instinctively shrank from the sight of physical suffering. If this was so even in an indifferent case, we can well imagine the grief she experienced at the sight of the gradual failing of a mother with whom her relationship had been little short of perfect. They had always been such good companions, viewing everything in the same way, even to seeing the same absurd likenesses in people, comparing them to objects animate and inanimate like the game in *The Pillars of the House*, which they appear really to have played. Mrs Yonge had not only been the most sympathetic listener to all her daughter's plans and visions, but she had constantly warded off from her those worries of a practical nature with which Charlotte was temperamentally unfitted to cope. (It was only by exercising her strong will and resolute principle that she could wind herself up to the accomplishment of trivial matters.) When Mrs Yonge began to fail, her middle-aged and famous daughter experienced the sensations of a fledgling turned out for solitary flight. By strength of purpose alone she nerved herself to take the chief burden of the nursing of her mother, although it was shared by Mrs Yonge's faithful maid, Harriet Spratt, and many friends, of whom the most constant was Alice Moberly, always a great favourite both with mother and daughter.

All through the spring and summer of 1868 Charlotte Yonge had to watch with a heavy heart the increased enfeebling of mind and body: how, from needing one arm to lean on, her mother had to be supported by two, and, worst of all, the gradual loss of the power of speech. As these symptoms developed, the woman who had on principle curbed too free an outward expression of affection in her children displayed a craving for lavish caresses. She could hardly bear to let Charlotte out of her sight, and was never so happy as when her daughter sat by her side, fondling her hand. When the end came, it was but natural that quiet sadness should be mingled with relief. Just after her mother's funeral Charlotte writes to Marianne Dyson:

> Things have gone on well and quietly; I only wonder that I seem to have no breakdown in me, but I cannot help feeling for ever that the "Ephphatha is sung" when I think of the frowning look with which she would try to make us understand her, and that struggle to say words of praise. . . . It is so very gentle and as she wished, and I really did miss her much more four months ago, when the real response failed me, and I saw her in the state I knew she hoped not to be in, than now that the habit of leaning on her has been so long broken. It is as if the threefold cord of my life had had one strand snapped suddenly fourteen years ago, but slowly gently untwisted now.

All but the most insensitive have their place of escape from reality, when it presses on them too heavily. Charlotte Yonge's

refuge was undoubtedly history. In her old age she writes
"History never failed to have great power over my imagina
tion." It was natural that she should have turned early to
historical stories. During the ten years after the publication of
The Lances of Lynwood, however, Miss Yonge had written no
long historical tales. But, as we have already seen, she made
various playlets on historical subjects for the Moberly children
and had produced text-books for Marianne Dyson's school. The
Landmarks of History were to the Dogmersfield children as the
Cameos to the readers of *The Monthly Packet*.

To these years belongs also a work philological rather than
historical, to which, however, Miss Yonge was chiefly stirred by
her love of history. *A History of Christian Names* would in
these days of specialization be attempted by none but a philo
logist.[1] We must not expect in Miss Yonge's book perfect accuracy
but her method of working out the reasons for the popularity of
a name in a certain country or period is most entertaining. There
are interesting references to the great figures in history who have
acquired so many namesakes, and to the racial psychology that
tends to special types of nomenclature. From one example we
can see the knowledge (wide, perhaps, rather than deep) and
the cultural interest that Miss Yonge put into her work. She is
speaking of "Tabitha."

> As the charitable disciple raised by St Peter, her names were
> endeared to the Puritans; Dorcas has become a term for such alms
> deeds as hers; and Tabitha must, I am much afraid, have been an
> unpleasant strait-laced aunt before she turned into a generic term
> for an old maid, or black and grey cat. However, this may be
> a libel upon the Tabithas, for it appears that *tabi* was originally an
> Italian word for a species of watered silk, the taby waistcoat worn
> by Pepys, the tabby and tabinet dress of our grandmothers. Further
> Herrick called barred clouds "counter changed tabbies in the ayre,"
> so that it would seem likely that the barred and brindled colour
> of the cats was the cause of likening them to the stuff. Yet Gray's
> pensive Selima, though "demurest of the Tabby kind," had "a
> coat that with the tortoise vied." On the whole it is likely, however
> that the cat was called from the stuff, and that the lady must divide

[1] Since this passage was written, E. G. Withycombe has brought out
The Oxford Dictionary of English Christian Names, and, while not
blind to Miss Yonge's shortcomings, pays handsome tribute to her
book as "the standard work on the subject in English."

the uncomplimentary soubriquet with puss and some grim Aunt
Tabitha—it may be with Smollett's *Tabitha Bramble.*

(Miss Yonge has got slightly mixed, as the proper name
Tabitha was the Hebrew word for a gazelle. The real derivation
of 'tabby' as applied to both silk and cats is from the name
Attabiya, a quarter in Baghdad, where a certain variety of
watered silk was first made. No doubt the word did reach us
through the Italian traders.)

Here is another example where Miss Yonge makes use of
more common knowledge:

> St Æthelthyrh was a queen who must have been a very uncom-
> fortable wife, and who, finally, retired into a monastery, getting
> canonized as St Etheldreda, and revered as St Audry. From the
> gewgaws sold at her fairs some derive the word *tawdry*; and at
> any rate Awdry has never been extinct as a name among the
> peasantry, and has of late been revived, though with less popularity
> than the other more modern contraction, Ethel, which is sometimes
> in modern times set to stand alone as an independent name.

When she turned again to historical tales, Miss Yonge set
forth her object in the preface of *The Prince and the Page*,
which appeared in 1865:

> The author is well aware that this tale has all the incorrectness
> and inconsistencies that are sure to attend a historical tale; but the
> dream that has been pleasant to dream may be pleasant to listen
> to; and there can be no doubt that, in spite of all inevitable faults,
> this style of composition does tend to fix young people's interest
> and attention on the scenes it treats of, and to vivify the characters
> it describes, and if this sketch at all tends to prepare young people's
> minds to look with sympathy and appreciation on any of the great
> characters of our early annals, it will have done at least one work.

Thus far Charlotte Yonge had only written historical stories
for children. Since *The Little Duke* had appeared, there had
been a new flowering of the historical novel, and during the
eighteen-fifties had appeared *Henry Esmond, Hypatia, West-
ward Ho!*, and, in 1861, *The Cloister and the Hearth*. In 1866
Miss Yonge followed suit with a tale written for an older public,
though it can be enjoyed from twelve years old upwards. *The
Dove in the Eagle's Nest* had a strange beginning. While staying
at her aunt's house in Torquay, which was named "Sorel,"

Charlotte had a vivid dream of the return after a fight of two young wounded knights to a castle on a steep rock. Hence the tale of Christina *Sorel* and the scene of the return of Ebbo and Friedel to Schloss Adlerstein. It is a romance of the days of Kaiser Maximilian, whose portrait is vividly drawn there, with a background of Dürer-like pictures showing the cultured life of the burghers of Ulm, contrasted with the barbarous ways of the last of the robber barons.

Many people have thought *The Dove in the Eagle's Nest* is Charlotte Yonge's best historical novel. Looking back, however, at her tales from our present angle, we find *The Chaplet of Pearls* less marked by the faults of her period. The worst that can be said of it applies equally to all writers who followed in Scott's footsteps and imitated his "Gramercys," "Forsooths," and other mock archaisms. But, apart from this defect and Miss Yonge's natural tendency to view the ecclesiastical history of Elizabethan times through nineteenth-century eyes, *The Chaplet of Pearls* is an admirable tale, and has been approved by such eminent historians as Dr Stubbs and Dr Bright. The plot which hinges on the Massacre of St Bartholomew and details the wanderings of Beranger and Eustacie de Ribaumont, is exciting and better constructed than some of Miss Yonge's, and the hero and heroine themselves more living than those in most historical tales.

It is impossible to speak of all the historical novels of Miss Yonge. Suffice it to say that she wrote more than thirty, of which at least half were produced during the last fifteen years of her life. She also wrote a number of short historical stories and there is hardly a period of European history that is not covered by one or another of her tales. She also made excursions, late in life, into Biblical and early Christian history. To some extent she tried to adapt the family-chronicle principle to her historical tales. With great ingenuity she follows the fortunes of the famous Chaplet of Pearls and various descendants of the Ribaumont family through the Fronde in *Stray Pearls*, down to the French Revolution in *The Release*. There are also connecting links between *Grisly Grisell*, a tale of the Wars of the Roses, and *Two Penniless Princesses*, which in its turn follows after *The Caged Lion*, the central character of which is James of Scotland. The Stuarts, indeed, exercised over Charlotte Yonge the same fascination as they did over most of the Trac

FACSIMILE OF A LETTER FROM CHARLOTTE M. YONGE
By courtesy of Miss Alethea Yonge

FASHION PLATES, *circa* 1848

arians. She is constantly harking back to their history. As we should expect, her romantic side was stirred by Mary Queen of Scots, whose story forms the background of *Unknown to History*. Here, a quite fictitious daughter of Mary and Bothwell is brought up as a child of honest English parents. It has thrilled generations of schoolgirls, even if historical purists shake their heads over it. Canon Butler, indeed, was so much disgusted at this lapse on the part of his learned friend that his wife and daughter were compelled to read the book out of his sight!

A Reputed Changeling, published in 1889, is perhaps the most successful of all the Stuart tales. Its chief merit lies in her insight into old wives' superstitions in the days of Charles II and their effect on the childhood of Peregrine Oakshott, the "reputed changeling." His later career is somewhat melodramatic, and none but Miss Yonge could have conceived his repentant death-bed in the bosom of the Anglican Church after a Puritan upbringing and an early manhood as a zealous Roman Catholic convert! It is also highly characteristic of the authoress that the heroine should be a rocker to the baby Prince of Wales and follow James II into exile, while her uncle, as a Non-juror, resigns his living.

Even if Charlotte Yonge had never written a novel, she should be remembered as a competent writer of historical text-books. Altogether she produced some twenty-five of them, as well as the *Cameos from History* that came out in *The Monthly Packet* during the years from 1851 to 1898. It was a tribute to the excellence of her work that in 1872 she was asked by E. A. Freeman to undertake the volume in his Historical Course for Schools dealing with the history of France. Again in 1879 she was honoured by a request from J. R. Green to deal with France in the series of history primers he was editing. The standard of Green was extremely high, and there could be no greater compliment to Miss Yonge than that the work should have been given to her rather than to some University man. The *Cameos* were, however, her most considerable work. Her object was to supplement dull schoolroom histories by taking characters and events such as "might form an individual Cameo, or gem in full relief." It was of course impossible to hold firmly to this idea throughout the long years when the *Cameos* were appearing, especially since it was soon discovered that it was preferred that the monthly instalments should form a consecutive history.

o

It is naturally easy enough to pick out slight inaccuracies in work which had to be done in season and out of season. These are only serious when Miss Yonge, or her authority, chooses to improve on original documents. Charles I's last words to Herbert, for instance, were, according to Herbert's memoirs:

> Let me have a shirt more than ordinary, by reason the season is so sharp as probably may make me shake, which some will imagine proceeds from fear. I would have no such imputation; I fear not death.

Miss Yonge, however, turns the end into, "I would not have such a supposition possible." When we consider that she wrote purely by the light of nature and home training, and that she had no great library for reference, we can only feel amazement that such lapses are not more frequent, especially since the wealth of detail is excessive.

Miss Yonge's worst defects were her sketchy treatment of affairs economic and financial. The contempt she pours on monarchs base enough to concern themselves with such matters is most characteristic. Poor Henry VII, who made so many mercantile treaties, "could neither by shrewdness nor display adequately represent the real grandeur that had passed away"; but there was "a golden age coming" with his spectacular son. Again, in dealing with the eighteenth century, which, as a period of unbelief and slackness in religion, obviously did not appeal to her, she represents the prevalent degeneracy as showing itself in "a fierce lust for gain." Money speculation was an entirely "new feature in civilized life," every one being occupied with "those financial complications hitherto left to Jews, Venetians, and Genoese." Thus Miss Yonge contrives to jump straight from the Middle Ages, as if the 'new rich' English of Tudor times and the Fuggers had never existed. Like most historians of her period, she was not interested in social developments of the mass of ordinary people. She vouchsafes little more than such sweeping generalizations as that in the fifteenth century "every one ate beef and drank ale . . . and flew into a passion on the least provocation." Yet when she comes to draw the individual peasants of, for instance, her National Society stories they are alive, and their surroundings accurately drawn.

Few works date sooner than historical text-books. Only a

Gibbon or a Macaulay may triumph over oblivion. The angle from which we view the past is changing perpetually, and each generation must interpret the facts anew. Miss Yonge's attitude towards her facts was like that of the Victorian Churchman or the Hebrew prophet, in that she saw everywhere the hand of God. She could write:

> It is certainly remarkable that the tide of victory should have turned in favour of the English when Anne was doing her best to heal the wounds of the Church; and against the French when the zeal of Louis was the most blind and cruel.

As a serious historian Miss Yonge may be forgotten, though she provides very entertaining reading. It should, however, be noted that, while nearly all of her novels of contemporary life, which are the delight of those who would savour the quaintness of Victorian days, are out of print, fresh editions of the chief historical tales have never ceased to appear. The same may be said of *The Book of Golden Deeds*, though this tends to be associated with prize-givings—and the giving of 'good conduct' prizes at that.

CHAPTER XII

FRESH SCENES AND ACQUAINTANCE

AFTER her mother's death Charlotte Yonge set about refashioning her life. For one moment she even wondered whether she might find satisfaction for her craving for guidance and submission in a conventual life. But Julian, Mr Bigg-Wither, and Canon Butler protested with one voice against the idea, and she was satisfied with becoming merely an Exterior Sister of Wantage. She still lived on at Elderfield, her circumstances in some ways unchanged. She kept an open carriage, which she used in turns with the closed one belonging to her brother at Otterbourne House, and was thus able to look in on any of the numerous friends within driving distance. Nearer home she had the great resource of the little nephews and nieces, now ranging from eight downwards. They were constantly in and out of "Aunt Char's" house and garden, and her letters to her friends were full of their sayings and doings.

To recover from the long strain of nursing she paid a visit to Puslinch, where it was always a great relief to be just "Charlotte" and not the famous authoress, and even to be rather teased about this. Moreover, she and Anne were as close friends in middle age as they had been when little girls playing together on the shore. It was Anne who helped to tide Charlotte over the first homecoming, with no one to welcome her. She stayed until she had seen her cousin tranquilly settled into her routine of mornings spent in writing, teaching, and churchgoing, and afternoons in visits and walks.

It was not long before she was offered the best of all antidotes to depression. Miss Yonge, who had depicted French, Swiss, and German scenes so vividly that one might have imagined her a constant traveller, did at last, at the age of forty-five, set out for her first journey on the Continent. Madame de Witt, the daughter of the great Guizot, wished to translate some of Miss Yonge's works into French, and got into touch with her through Macmillan's, her publishers. The result was an invitation to

Miss Yonge, her brother, and sister-in-law to spend a week at Val Richer, the Norman estate of Monsieur Guizot.

Charlotte's impressions of the fresh scene were chronicled in almost daily letters for Miss Dyson. Although she had not, like her sister-in-law, succumbed on the crossing, Charlotte's first glimpse of France was not auspicious, for she saw Calais through clouds of misty rain. But she was determined to enjoy herself, and found even French electric wires a novelty, not making "the weird Æolian harp sound that ours do," but going "tinkle, tinkle, like little bells." All was strange and charming—the masters of a priestly seminary, on Amiens station, sending off their pupils for the holidays with "great kissing on both cheeks"; the blue-clad woman at each station, with a high-glazed hat over her white cap, holding up a staff perpendicularly as a signal; Rouen Cathedral, which she thought like getting into the middle of a picture of Prout, wooded crags and valleys with meadows or ripe cornfields sloping down to a stream; cottages with high-pitched roofs; linen bleaching on the lower slopes of the wooded hills. At last came the drive through a delightful country of streams and low but steep hills to Val Richer, where even the feeling of shyness that had been growing on the Yonges throughout the journey could not mar their impression of the long house of old whitish stone with a huge high-pitched roof of dark old red tiles, the walls quite covered with creepers of all sorts. As they drove in at the great white gates the whole family was on the doorstep to welcome them, and Charlotte, by the end of the first evening, found them very kind.

Monsieur Guizot was in 1869 an old gentleman of eighty-two, small, wiry, active, and alert, with bright eyes and courteous, eager manner, a great politician and historian—Anglophil—a Protestant in sympathy with the more liberal group in the Catholic Church—a personality, indeed, on whom Charlotte could exercise to the full her instinct for veneration. In spite of his great age, his intellect was still keen, and he was at work on the fourth volume of his *Meditations*, and on a history of England for his granddaughters. The hardy old man was out in the garden at 6.30 every morning, and always insisted on ceremoniously giving his arm to Miss Yonge when they were walking uphill, a proceeding which she considered quite unnecessary. His evening's recreation after the day's hard work was an

English novel or a French book, which he read aloud (beautifully, thought Charlotte) to the whole family. He and Miss Yonge were never at a loss for conversation, though Charlotte laments that she never could remember the gender of a word till she had said it wrong, and when she wanted to say anything she cared about her French forsook her altogether. Monsieur Guizot's English was fortunately more fluent, so they could talk to their hearts' content about history, art, and a hundred other topics. There was, strangely enough, very little political talk. It was the only sign of his great age that Monsieur Guizot's thoughts were absorbed in the past, and instinctively turned away from the politics of the Second Empire, where there was no more place for him. The Yonges elicited few facts from the rich store of his past experiences. The best tale was, perhaps, about Madame Adelaide, the sister of Louis-Philippe. She always had a set of bonbons placed beside the seat of each member of her brother's Cabinet whenever they met, and they were of a superior quality or not according to whether she liked the Ministry or not. Monsieur Guizot said he had had experience of both, for at first she was very fond of him, and then they were very good, but when she liked him less the bonbons deteriorated.

Miss Yonge's books, apparently, had a similar effect on the French as on the English public, for the de Witts were able to report the tears shed by a gentleman of their acquaintance over Guy. They themselves approved thoroughly of *The Chaplet of Pearls*, and soon the children were sufficiently intimate with Miss Yonge to "set upon" her about her stories "in a very comical way." The whole de Witt family were obviously ready to appreciate Miss Yonge, and not only had they many tastes in common with her, but—what was to her the most important of all—they were "good to the backbone," addicted to family prayers and Sunday sermon-reading. Besides this they sympathized so well with her pedagogic tastes that they drove her to see the only school in the district that had not broken up for the holidays. She inspected it with the eye of a connoisseur, and reported on it at great length to Miss Dyson. She was thankful, for the honour of her native land, to be able to produce an exquisite bit of marking on her handkerchief when questioned by the teachers about English embroidery.

The French visit ended with a stay in Paris, where Miss

Yonge admired Notre Dame a good deal more than she had expected, though "the grand St Michael at the Louvre, and Marie-Antoinette's cell at the Conciergerie" were the two things she cared for most. Versailles oppressed her "like a great terrible tragedy, between the guilt there and the doom upon it." And, even in the intellectual Miss Yonge, femininity was strong enough to make her turn aside from a survey of the historical sights to enjoy the shops in the Palais-Royal.

But on her return to England Charlotte was plunged straight from keen enjoyment into deep sorrow. She was met by the news of the sudden death of her cousin Anne. She writes to Mary Yonge, Anne's sister:

> I believe it was a more than commonly close link that united our dear Anne and me . . . and I was wont to turn to the knowledge of her feeling and opinion many a time when nothing passed between us, being sure that one day I should be with her and talk. . . . How much the recollection of those ways and thoughts of hers should be with me, and guide me still, having lived with them for more than half a lifetime, and written to one another since baby-hood.

The French journey remained Charlotte's only experience of foreign travel—a fact which no one has succeeded in explaining. Some people have argued that the news of Anne's death meeting her when she was still knocked up, not having quite recovered from the effects of hot journeys and strange food, fixed in her a distaste for tours abroad. This supposition appears rather far-fetched. Miss Coleridge tells us that

> partly from habit, partly from the vividness of her village interests, and partly, I think, from the weakness of the heart of which she often speaks, which made bustle and anything like hurry-scurry distasteful to her, she did not like travelling, and never seemed to feel the need of change.

When, two years after the French visit, the Heathcotes asked Charlotte Yonge to winter in Rome with them, she declined on the grounds that "There seems so much to do here; and, with an old mind like mine [she was not yet fifty], it is difficult to take in fresh impressions." Perhaps these last two words may give a clue to Charlotte's unconscious shrinking from new experiences. To a person who had spent a lifetime in romantic reconstruction of other times and lands, the "fresh impression" of historical scenes might bring a painful disillusionment.

Whatever may have been the true reason for her shrinking from foreign travel, it seems a pity that Charlotte never again indulged in this stimulus, for the French visit was obviously beneficial to her work. On her return home she immediately set to work on *The Pillars of the House*, her longest and, as many think, her best family chronicle. The very fact that it is more mature work than *The Daisy Chain*, however, robs it of the freshness and quaintness of Stoneborough and the May family; and the England of 1870 is in any case a less romantic spectacle to us than that of 1850. Yet Charlotte Yonge had always possessed a gift for casting a halo of romance over commonplace incidents and scenes, and this is nowhere more apparent than in *The Pillars of the House*. One of the favourite dreams of the young is a communal existence with no grown persons set in authority over them. The Underwoods, who, at their father's death, must fend for themselves under the care of Felix, aged sixteen, and Wilmet, aged fifteen, have for the young reader the attraction of such a dream. It was a great feat of characterization to invent this family of thirteen, of whom each has a distinct individuality. Miss Yonge follows their fortunes over a period of nineteen years, and successfully links up their fate with hosts of old friends—Sister Constance of the *Castle Builders*, Robert Fulmort of *Hopes and Fears*, Countess Kate, and the May family; this at the request of countless admirers. The range of the story is tremendous. We are taken from the dingy pottery town of Bexley to the quiet dignity of Minsterham, and as far afield as the Pyrenees and an oasis town in Egypt. Best of all is Vale Leston. So clearly did Miss Yonge see the church and Priory, with its green lawns and bright flowerbeds sloping down to the river, that she must needs draw plans of them so that her readers may have a vision as clear as her own of the Paradise Regained whither the Underwood family are transported in the day of prosperity.

At the same time as she was at work on *The Pillars of the House* another congenial task fell to Miss Yonge. In September 1871 Bishop Coleridge Patteson of Melanesia had been killed by natives, who mistook him for a trader. Charlotte was full of sympathy for his sisters, but was none the less proud to be con-

nected with a genuine martyr of modern times when they asked
her to be his biographer. "What a mixture of crush and triumph
the thought of dear Coley is!" she wrote at the news of his
murder. Miss Yonge had given vent to her missionary enthusiasms in small tales or articles, but this much longer work was
their culminating expression. It involved her in the pleasant
occupation of reading all Patteson's letters to his sisters, and in a
week's stay at the Palace at Lichfield, collecting the impressions
of the Selwyn family.

Some people had murmured that this was no woman's task,
but Charlotte Yonge showed herself a most competent biographer.
The sympathy and enjoyment with which she wrote the life
of her missionary hero is obvious, and particularly good is the
vivid background of his Eton and Oxford days. Miss Yonge's
skill as a biographer was evidently not soon forgotten, for in
1890 she was commissioned to write a life of the Prince Con-
sort for the "Statesmen" series. Even though Albert the
Good was no Tractarian, he was a fit subject for Miss Yonge's
pen.

That Charlotte could have on hand at the same moment two
such works as the life of Patteson and *The Pillars of the House*
gives no small proof of her mental energy. In spite of the slight
weakness of the heart that made bustle distasteful to her, she
must have been a remarkably healthy woman, and she had
nothing of the so-called 'artistic temperament.' Her muse was
as little capricious as that of Trollope. On most days she would
break off her work to give a lesson at the village school and to
attend both Matins and Evensong. Yet, in spite of the many
hours spent in the fulfilment of her duty towards God and her
neighbour, Miss Yonge usually had on hand a story, a 'Cameo,'
and some writing on Scripture-teaching. (In her earlier days she
abstained from writing stories in Lent, until forced to give in
to the necessities of the trade.) She pursued the original method
of having all three manuscripts on her desk, writing a page of
each in turn, leaving it to dry and going on to the next. Few
authors could boast of such a morning's work as Miss Yonge,
when she came in to lunch remarking, "I have had a dreadful
day; I have killed the Bishop and Felix."

There were many pleasant interludes in Charlotte Yonge's
life during the years that followed her visit to France. It is not

difficult to imagine the pleasure she took in the foundation of Keble College. In April 1868 she had been in Oxford for the laying of the foundation stone. She was made very happy by a speech of Bishop Selwyn's, in which he mentioned *The Daisy Chain* and the ship for the Melanesian Mission. Two years later she was again in Oxford for the opening of Keble College, and had the pleasure of helping to decorate the temporary chapel for the ceremony. This was her only sight of Dr Pusey, and she tells how she shook hands with him "in his red doctor's gown." There followed another visit to the Wantage Sisterhood, where she again comments on the "eager life . . . so much the sparkling, hurrying stream."

It was under the congenial guidance of the Butlers that Miss Yonge paid her first visit to Cambridge some time in the early 'seventies. (Canon Butler was a Cambridge man.) To her great surprise she was mobbed by enthusiastic crowds of young dons and undergraduates. She was no longer the fashion among Guardsmen, but in academic circles she obviously still had her male public. It was apparently a fashionable pastime among her admirers to set examination papers on her novels at their parties. Miss Coleridge reports a dinner party given by Lady Frederick Cavendish where this was the evening's diversion. She also gives a set of questions set by Dr Bright, Regius Professor of Ecclesiastical History, in an unofficial moment. Cambridge was not to be outdone by Oxford, and Miss Yonge was highly gratified by the correct textual knowledge displayed by several members of both Universities in their answers.

Charlotte made a new friend in these years—Miss Elizabeth Wordsworth, who was to become the first Principal of Lady Margaret Hall. This friendship shows that Miss Yonge could have sympathy with at least one very 'modern' development. It is true, as she wrote many years later, that she had tried to impress on some of the promoters of Lady Margaret Hall that the old colleges began by regarding training for the Church as the first object, and the secular work as a sort of appendage, but she realized that "times are too strong, and Elizabeth Wordsworth and Anne Moberly at St Hugh's do make their Colleges in many respects training for the Church." Miss Yonge has allowed herself to go a little astray over the foundation both of men's colleges and of women's, but, at any rate, Miss Words-worth got an invitation to spend a few days in May 1872 with Miss Yonge at Otterbourne.

On the drive from the station they both talked hard to cover their shyness, and Miss Wordsworth confessed afterwards to thinking: "What *shall* I do if she goes on in that voice for the next three or four days?" After a stroll in the woods, however, they thawed, and by the evening were on excellent terms. When they were settled down in the drawing-room to the tea that followed the dinner of those days, Miss Wordsworth thought her hostess "looking more like an old French *Marquise* than ever, in a red and black Dolly Varden dress, with pink skirt . . . and showing a very pretty pair of feet in white open-work stockings." The ball of talk was set briskly rolling when Charlotte began to read out loud Keble's review of the life of Walter Scott in an old *British Critic*. They read at the rate of a page an hour, as they "went off into interminable discussions about everything, and, of course, a great deal of laughing and nonsense." When they got on to the subject of *The Antiquary* they took it out and read "that fine passage . . . about a stormy sunset and a fallen monarch (early in Chapter vii)." Miss Wordsworth "never knew a face that it was a greater pleasure to watch, and certainly never saw any woman (or many men) who seemed so perfectly *un-tireable*."

On the next evening of the visit they passed from Walter Scott to Jane Austen, Miss Yonge's other great literary affection —a remarkable evidence of good taste in one who grew up at a time when the immortal Jane was little thought of. The two ladies thoroughly enjoyed themselves "capping Miss Austen *con amore*."

Miss Wordsworth ventured, after she had been some time in the house, to ask Miss Yonge about her own work. Charlotte then told her the plot of *The Pillars of the House*, "exactly as if she was explaining the involutions of some *real* piece of history, and she was quite as much in earnest." Like Christabel Cole-ridge, Miss Wordsworth observed that, as soon as Miss Yonge's shyness wore off, she liked to talk about her characters. She was highly entertained by the request for a comic song from the unmusical Miss Yonge. She obligingly provided the song that Angela sang on the river, and the two sober ladies sat down to a solemn transcription of

> Six o'clock is striking;
> Mother, may I go out?

The portrait of Charlotte that emerges from Miss Wordsworth's reminiscences is a very complete one. Contrasted with the evening magnificence of the Dolly Varden dress, we see her in her careless working attire. She was not in the habit of giving much time to studying her personal appearance, so that one morning on coming out of church she amused Miss Wordsworth by asking, "Do tell me, *is* my hat on hind side before? I have had such horrid misgivings about it." Luckily her fears were unfounded. Miss Wordsworth's account of Charlotte's attitude towards dress tallies with that of most people who remember her. She alternated between handsome, dignified garments on public occasions and extreme untidiness when at home. She had a taste for bright colours, so that she appeared in a bonnet trimmed with orange at a time when this colour was out of fashion. When a young lady of the æsthetic 'eighties startled the conventional world of Otterbourne by her jaunty appearance with a hat perched picturesquely on her curly head Miss Yonge was ready to champion her, though her sister-in-law remarked disapprovingly, "Surely you can't admire her, Charlotte. She's all on one side and *so* untidy."

By her last evening at Elderfield, Miss Wordsworth had grown so intimate with Miss Yonge that they exchanged confidences on their family histories and relatives, and Charlotte confessed that one of the things that had first drawn her to her new friend was seeing how much she looked up to her father. So congenial were they that they parted with mutual confession of never having got to love anyone so much in four days, and at Whitsun next year Miss Wordsworth was back for another visit, spent in decorating the church, seeing friends, and in more delightful talks.

It seemed as if these pleasant visits were to become a yearly institution, but fate and Miss Yonge's instinct for self-immolation willed otherwise. In September 1873 Mrs Julian Yonge's sister, Miss Gertrude Walter, moved from Otterbourne House to Elderfield. She came for an indefinite period, and she stayed there until her death in 1897. Miss Walter suffered from a severe form of rheumatism, and had to lead an invalid life, which meant that the house was filled with all the paraphernalia of sickness, and that Miss Yonge had no room to put up her friends. Moreover, Charlotte, who had a constitutional shrinking from illness, was often involved in a share of the nursing. It is, indeed, quite beyond the comprehension of the twentieth century that Charlotte Yonge, an author of considerable repute, should thus have had planted on her such duties as the custom of her day assigned to the superfluous spinster.

CHAPTER XIII

TRANQUIL SUNSET

To some extent the latter part of Charlotte's life is a withdrawal from her friends and from the new interests of the times. Miss Gertrude Walter's establishment at Elderfield was indubitably one of the factors in this. Not only was Miss Yonge deprived of the visits of stimulating friends, but she often refused invitations to stay with interesting people for the sake of dancing attendance on her invalid. Miss Coleridge tries to make the best of the case by telling us that Gertrude Walter was clever, sympathetic, and had kindred tastes to Charlotte:

> She called herself playfully "Char's wife" . . . and . . . for many years gave her friend all the companionship which so genial and sympathetic a person required.

This may have been true, but the price Miss Yonge paid for the companionship was quite disproportionate. It is impossible not to deplore the well-trained unselfishness that allowed her to saddle herself with such a burden.

The other reason for Charlotte Yonge's narrower existence was the failure in 1875 of a company into which her brother had put a large part both of his money and of her own. The immediate effect of this catastrophe on Miss Yonge was the realization of the proverb that charity begins at home. Instead of giving a large sum of money towards the endowment of Otterbourne as a separate parish, she turned over this act of piety to a friend, and devoted her savings to family claims, depriving herself also of small luxuries which she might well have come to regard as her due. One of the most trying effects of her economy was that the giving up of her carriage left her dependent on trains and hired vehicles, thereby considerably shortening the length of her tether.

For ten years the Julian Yonges lingered on at Otterbourne House, but in 1885 they sold it and moved to London. Charlotte bore in silence the grief of seeing strangers in the home of her

childhood, but it went deep. She was left by herself at Otterbourne with the old dog, Graf, who was apparently unsuited to
town life. Finally he too went, and was buried with all honours
by the parish clerk, Miss Yonge walking "in a solemn procession
of one" all down the path behind.

But the barriers set up between Charlotte and the world were
raised as much by her prejudices as by her circumstances. Most
of the Tractarians were characterized by an inability to see
anything good in views divergent from their own. In none of
them was this more marked than in John Keble, full of charm
and saintliness as he was. By the age of fifteen Charlotte Yonge's
standards in matters of belief had been fixed by him where they
were to remain, with slight and immaterial changes, for life.
People with views differing from her own she constantly branded
as "those whose foundations are not safe." It is characteristic
of her that she was much disgusted at a paper by Dean Stanley
in *Macmillan* on Keble, where "he constantly finds his own
latitudinarianisms all through the poetry. It is much worse than
any real enemy—open enemy, I mean." Similarly, Miss Yonge
saw the Enemy at work in many of the arguments of *Lux Mundi*,
of which Dean Inge has said that its publication "gave the High
Church party a new lease of life when it seemed in danger of
losing itself in sterile mediævalism." Not that Miss Yonge had
any great sympathy either for the "sterile mediævalism" that
had developed from what Newman had called "the gilt ginger-
bread school" of Tractarianism. But on questions of ritual she
kept an open mind, thinking that the outward trappings of
religion could not shake the "safe" foundations laid in the
heroic age of the Movement. When, after thirty-seven years at
Otterbourne, Mr Bigg-Wither retired, and a new Vicar took his
place, Charlotte watched without a murmur the removal of the
cushions from the altar, the pew doors, and the gallery that had
been put up by Mr Yonge. She even built a side-aisle to take
its place, at her own expense, and presented an organ. When
the new clergyman introduced a surpliced choir and choral
services she used her prestige with the village to silence the
"No Popery" cry evoked by these startling innovations.

The secluding influence of the Church guided also her
choice of reading. In her latter years she wrote to Miss Annie
Moberly, who had apparently been indulging in "doubtful

books," that she thought it a questionable thing for women to do:

> I do not mean if one was asked distinctly to read and give an opinion on any one book seriously; then I suppose one must do so, but to read popular undesirable books for the chance of discussion seems to me not good for one's own mind, and very doubtful for others' sake. Clergymen may and must do it. They have greater safety than a woman can have, being trained in theology, the history of opinions, and in logic.

Charlotte Yonge was clearly no feminist. Even her most ardent admirers smile at the views set forth in *Womankind*, a series of papers that appeared for the guidance of the young readers of *The Monthly Packet* during the eighteen-seventies. Here we find sensible ideas on education and quite advanced views on examinations for women interspersed by such announcements as: "I have no hesitation in declaring my full belief in the inferiority of woman, nor that she brought it upon herself [that is, at the time of the Fall!]."

As with the Church so with the State. The Tory principles implanted by Mr Yonge, like the cast-iron religious views of Mr Keble, were too firmly embedded in Charlotte to be moved one fraction of an inch by later political developments. To her the enlightened educational measures of the eighteen-seventies were so many nails in the coffin of a great cause. The Irish Church Disestablishment was a betrayal, and the opening of college fellowships to men of all religious opinions a pandering to infidelity. Making all Civil Service appointments competitive and abolishing purchase in the Army might, in comparison, be borne with, as not striking at the roots of religion. The villains in the political piece to Miss Yonge the Liberals. It is an amusing paradox that the converted Jew, doing lip-service to the Church of England, should have been the leader of the political party to which Charlotte owed allegiance, while the politics of Gladstone could not be condoned, in spite of his Churchmanship. Even Marianne Dyson had to avoid the subject of Mr Gladstone, while in her later years Miss Yonge had many skirmishes with her younger friends of Liberal views. So much was she depressed by the political outlook of the 'eighties, with Disestablishment as her chief bugbear, that she writes at the time of an election: "Next time I have to set down 'Likes

and Dislikes,' I shall put a General Election as my chief antipathy."

With the Church threatened on all sides by modern developments, Charlotte was ready to seize on every means of strengthening its position. In the Girls' Friendly Society and the Mothers'
Union she saw new ways of spreading old truths, and accordingly
gave both movements her enthusiastic support. Her G.F.S.
interests are reflected in many of her later books, notably in the
character of Jane Mohun, that indefatigable worker for the cause.
They led her also into many pleasant expeditions to join in the
discussion of G.F.S. affairs in the Winchester diocese. Sometimes
Miss Yonge went as far afield as London for a G.F.S. week. She
was in London, too, for the Jubilee of 1887, and here, at least, she
met a person so far removed from her limited sphere as the
Italian Ambassador. The next year she writes, "I have been
meeting Edna Lyall, among other adventures."

A very pleasant friendship arose through Miss Yonge's work
for the Mothers' Union. Mrs Sumner, the Bishop's wife, had for
many years been acquainted with her, but, on account of the
shyness which made Charlotte appear cold and unapproachable,
she had been "content to admire her from a distance." In 1890
she plucked up courage to ask Miss Yonge to become the editor
of *Mothers in Council*—a remarkable task, one would think, for
a spinster lady. The suggestion, however, was immediately
accepted, and no sooner had the two ladies got a common object
to work for than Charlotte's shyness melted away, and Mrs
Sumner was admitted into the charmed circle of intimacy.

On the platform at meetings Miss Yonge was disappoint-
ing, for she always read her speeches, and never seemed to
know them or to be able to decipher her own handwriting.
It was only when interested unawares at some point in an informal discussion that she was able to get up and speak with
any eloquence. A fellow-member of her G.F.S. committees
wrote:

> She often said a thing on the spur of the moment that she would
> have been shy of saying with premeditation, and she never was cut
> and dried. You could never tell how she would view a thing, and
> to the very end her advice was always wise.

However, even at a public meeting Miss Yonge's presence was

P

most gratifying to the audience, for in the Winchester diocese she was a popular and important figure.

In spite of the London excursions and these moments of escape from her humdrum existence, Charlotte lived, as the years went by, increasingly in "the world that the post brings round one." Anne Yonge was gone, and Miss Dyson died in 1878. There was, however, a younger generation growing up, with whom Charlotte delighted to keep in touch. Besides Christabel Coleridge, there were many yet newer authoresses of children's tales, with whom she shared her literary schemes. Occasionally she even collaborated with them, as she did in *Strolling Players* written with Christabel Coleridge. This seems to have been a mistake. Miss Yonge was still more than capable of writing her own books.

Miss Yonge also spent hours in answering those letters which in these days would be consigned to a secretary and a typewriter. Unknown admirers wrote to her from every corner of the world. She even enjoyed the glory of being considered a classic by Indian universities in her lifetime. In 1890 she mentions with some amusement having received two letters from a Hindu professor,

> asking elucidations of some bits of slip-slop in *Golden Deeds*, which it seems is a class-book at Bombay and posed the poor professors. To have one's bad grammar come round in that way is a caution!

Miss Yonge was even more gratified when she was told by a lady missionary that a Hindu student "had been so much impressed with *The Pillars of the House* as to accept Christianity, and that he was going to be baptized."

On the Continent Miss Yonge was regarded as 'safe' reading for young girls, a reputation shared with certain other English authors. She received countless letters from foreign admirers. A seventeen-year-old German princess writes of *The Heir of Redclyffe* and *The Daisy Chain*:

> I cannot tell how much these books are to us [herself and her sister]; it is not enough to say that they are our favourite ones, because they are far more than that, and cannot be compared to other books.

On another occasion came a long letter from the German governess of Princess (later Queen) Margherita of Savoy, telling how it was *The Daisy Chain* that spurred on the young princess to take pains with her English and how she had arrived at the point of translating *The Lances of Lynwood* into French for the benefit of her brother. The worthy governess considered that Miss Yonge's works should have a good influence in Italy, "where education is on the *lowest scale,* notwithstanding the *brightness* and *intellectual* gifts of the nation," and where the inhabitants "are so entirely devoid of *moral sense* particularly, and of education in general."

So well known on the Continent were Miss Yonge's works, either in Tauchnitz editions or in translations, that she became a legend there, of whom mythical anecdotes were related. Miss Coleridge was told in Ulm Cathedral that Miss Yonge had been married there to a German officer, and no contradictions on her part produced the least effect on the guide who was showing her round. At Christmas 1882 Dean Church sent Charlotte for her amusement the following extract from an Italian newspaper:

> E morta la celebre scrittrice Inglese, Era di Ratcliffe. Suo nome era Jong, ma in recognizione di suoi talenti, la Regina Vittoria l'ha fatto Viscontessa.
> Sposò l'ambasciatore Inglese a Costantinopole, ma non lasciò di scrivere bellissimi romanzi fin a poco tempo fa.[1]

The letters from English admirers were, of course, legion. Miss Yonge was constantly reading such outpourings of enthusiasm as:

> You don't know what an element you have been in the life of thousands; how we have laughed with you, and how your little wise sayings have helped in many a difficulty.

During the last twenty years of the nineteenth century Miss Yonge was no longer fashionable with grown persons, excepting those old enough to remember the heyday of her vogue, but she was still most popular in the schoolroom. In these years the rise

---

[1] This may be translated: "The famous English authoress Era di Ratcliffe has died. Her name was Jong, but in recognition of her talents she was created a viscountess by Queen Victoria.

"She married the English ambassador at Constantinople, but did not cease, until recently, to write very beautiful romances."

Some of the confusion in this is doubtless due to the fact that the well-known English Ambassador in Constantinople, Sir Stratford Canning, bore the title of Stratford *de Redcliffe.*

of elementary education introduced her to a fresh public, and
she became a great favourite with intelligent pupil teachers and
G.F.S. girls. For this public she wrote the series of tales, mostly
historical, that she brought out every year from 1887 onwards
for the National Society.

In America too Miss Yonge was increasingly popular. In
1898 she believed that the Americans were the chief readers of
her books, "to judge by the gushing letters" she received. It
was no small tribute to be so well liked in a country where the
children's story was enjoying a period of great fertility. Miss
Yonge was writing all through the years that saw the appearance
of the works of Miss Alcott, the 'Katie' books, and such a
favourite as *Helen's Babies*. An American who had seen Miss
Yonge 'unwitting' was, of course, the first enterprising journa-
list to make up an interview with her, since she utterly refused
to submit to such a penance. She was highly entertained by
American lion-hunting proclivities. She writes:

> Have you heard the last variety of American Lion hunting—
> writing to ask for a bit of one's dress to put into a literary quilt?
> I actually had such a request, and while I was laughing at it I
> came on a book of Miss Alcott's where the dear Jo—after she had
> become a noted authoress—has the same entreaty made to her.

At the height of Miss Yonge's popularity Dr Moberly laugh-
ingly said that the College and Cathedral at Winchester were
"being treated as mere stepping-stones for pilgrims to the
villages of Hursley and Otterbourne for the sake of Mr Keble and
Miss Yonge." Those days were over, though in Miss Yonge's
latter years 'pilgrims' were not lacking. Those from America
were, in fact, so numerous that, at the sight of Dr Bright, whose
name the parlourmaid had not repeated distinctly, Miss Yonge
remarked with some relief: "I thought you were the first drop-
pings of the American storm." In spite of her shyness, Charlotte
often derived much amusement from these unknown visitors.
In 1867 she reports:

> We had a wonderful visit yesterday from an utterly unknown
> little American girl of fourteen or fifteen, who bobbed into the
> room, rushed up to me, shook hands, "Miss Yonge, I've come to
> thank you for your books, I'm an American." . . . And presently,
> "I came to thank you for writing so much for the Church. We

value that so in America." . . . It was odd to be thanked by a little bolt upright mite, as if in the name of all the American Republic, for writing for the Church!

Yet many of the admirers who took so much trouble to gain a sight of Miss Yonge must have met with great disappointment at their reception. Invariably the presence of strangers acted as a sudden check on her spontaneity: it might render her speechless, or reduce her to a nervous giggle. No wonder that she steadily declined the urgent invitations which she received "to be the lioness of a London season, and to take her place as one of the popular authors of the day."

During her latter years not only did Miss Yonge live withdrawn from the world, but, like all ageing people, she dwelt with increasing frequency on the past. If we look carefully at the works produced during the last quarter of the nineteenth century, we shall see that she is most successful where she looks backwards. The coming of Miss Walter to Elderfield undoubtedly did affect Miss Young's creative powers. She never again rose to the heights of *The Pillars of the House*, the last novel written before Miss Walter's advent. This book was followed in *The Monthly Packet* by *The Three Brides* and *Magnum Bonum*, another family chronicle. In the latter Miss Yonge recaptures some of her old brightness in describing the youthful freaks of the Brownlows and in giving a detailed picture of their schoolroom life, which takes us a stage further in the development of education since the *Daisy Chain* era; but as they grow older the story degenerates into melodrama and is overweighted with morality. Charlotte herself had no delusions about her capacity for describing the modern world. After writing *Nuttie's Father* in 1885, she says, "I don't care much for Nuttie myself. I am getting too old to write of the swing of modern life: I don't see enough of it."

Yet, at the same time as she was working on this somewhat unsuccessful book, she was publishing (in *The Monthly Packet*) *The Two Sides of the Shield*. This admirable children's tale was written in answer to "many a letter in youthful handwriting" begging "for further information on the fate of the beings that had become favourites of the schoolroom."

During the later years of her life Charlotte Yonge's "lifelong companions," the characters of her earliest books, came thronging round her. She writes to an old admirer of her tales:

> I am glad you like Jane [Mohun]; somehow she has erected herself to me into the heroine. [This is of *Beechcroft at Rockstone.*] I find myself living in sympathy with my old people rather than the young. But I really do shrink from bringing Dr May and Ethel on the stage again, he must be grown so old.

In *The Long Vacation* the Underwoods fill the centre of the stage, though well supported by Mohuns and Merrifields. It is remarkable how naturally even the younger generation talk here. Charlotte Yonge did not often come into contact with girls and boys just grown up, but, when she did meet them, she must have kept her eyes and ears open. The most improved by time of all the older characters is the former ritualist Clement Underwood. Like Soames Forsyte, he needed several volumes to mellow.

These old friends survived with Charlotte right into the twentieth century. In 1900 appeared *Modern Broods, or Developments Unlooked for*. The memory and ingenuity displayed by the old lady of seventy-seven in marshalling before us, without any great strain on probability, nearly the whole of the Mohun, May, Underwood, and both branches of the Merrifield family is amazing. The newer characters whose fortunes she entwines with theirs are of little account. There are persons to-day who, at the sight of the names "May" or "Underwood" in a newspaper, instinctively wonder to which descendant of those prolific clans they refer. It was for such admirers that Miss Yonge wrote these later novels, which she called "family news for those who wanted to know how their old friends had got on."

It was in 1881 that Charlotte returned to "Langley," the scene of one of her earliest literary efforts. Her enthusiasm for Sunday schools had found a vent in *Langley School*, which appeared in *The Magazine for the Young* at the end of the eighteen-forties. *Langley School* preserves for us a world long since passed away. Demure little girls in pink and white print frocks and white tippets trot about the village, from the Lees' timbered smallholding with its own orchard to the cottage of Mr Gray, the keeper, in a clearing of the wood. All the children are alive—wild Clemmy; nervous Amy Lee with her journey through the wood past the dead snakes and wild dogs; Jane

Anstey, who was caught greedily drinking her delicate little sister's milk.

Miss Yonge wrote altogether some thirty stories of this kind, and they were produced at intervals during a space of fifty years. They cover a period of swift and great changes in the life of the village. The growth of sophistication is nowhere shown so clearly as in the last two books of this kind—*The Carbonels*, published in 1895, and its sequel, *Founded on Paper*. These cover all the period remembered by Charlotte Yonge herself, and draw on the recollections of early days at Otterbourne handed down to her by her parents. The Carbonel family come to Uphill Priors shortly after the Napoleonic wars. They find the village lawless and poverty-stricken. The story is of their attempts to civilize the wild working women and their ragged, shock-headed children, but all their benevolent efforts do not prevent some rick-burning in the "Jack Swing" riots, which form the climax of the tale. Yet they persist, and the result is seen in later days. For in *Founded on Paper* Miss Yonge comes back, in the Jubilee year of 1887, to a changed Uphill, and shows us the highly sophisticated descendants of the villagers of the earlier story, a few of whom are still surviving. Between the two Jubilees, the modern world gains yearly on the old order. Products of the "godless education" so odious to Miss Yonge disturb the tranquility of the village with their slovenly existence, which in one case comes to a sensational end by suicide. But, in spite of these dire results of modern civilization, the solid backbone of village life, nurtured by the teaching of the Carbonels and their like, remains firm, and it is on such folk that the curtain falls at the time of the Diamond Jubilee.

As one would imagine, the villagers of Miss Yonge's tales are generally seen through the eyes of the Sunday-school teacher, though her shrewd intuition often penetrated into the cottage interior where parental embargo and her own timidity made her personally almost a stranger. The full-length portraits found in her stories are, of course, drawn only from the village folk that came under the influence of the good squire's families, the clergy, or the schoolmasters, who hover benignly over them. The evildoers are only slightly sketched in, as sinister forms that beset the path of the unwary boy and girl to lead them into temptation. But, granted these limits, we can only regret that Miss

Yonge did not crystallize her knowledge of village life into a more abiding form than tales written as rewards for good Sunday scholars.

Yet Miss Yonge herself would not have admitted this regret. On her seventieth birthday she received a present from three hundred old scholars of Otterbourne School, ranging from five years old to seventy-two. This she probably felt to be nearly as important a tribute to the work, which she so constantly describes as being *Pro Ecclesia Dei*, as the thousands of signatures of her more cultivated admirers which enriched another handsome gift received on the same day.

This latter scheme had arisen from a conversation between Miss Moberly and Mrs Romanes, who later wrote an appreciation of Miss Yonge's works. They agreed that many other people would like to join them in sending birthday greetings, but were resolved that the signatures should be those of real enthusiasts, and not "sent broadcast." They took care that those selected should include distinguished people whose autographs were valuable, and over five thousand signatures were collected in a charmingly bound book, its back tastefully ornamented with daisies. As an afterthought it was suggested that those who signed should pay a shilling, and in this way a sum of two hundred pounds was presented to Miss Yonge. This she spent in putting up a lych-gate at Otterbourne Church, and, when all protested that she must have something for herself, in buying a little table and tea equipage, which she used every day for the rest of her life.

Rumours of the intended presentation had gone as far afield as Spain and Italy, and the Queens of these countries sent signed photographs to be presented with the daisy-covered book. After the presentation had been made, it was discovered that several members of the Spanish and Italian Courts would much have liked to add their signatures. Charlotte Yonge was highly gratified at this tangible proof that she was not forgotten. With her usual humility, however, she shared her triumph with the departed saints of her calendar. She wrote to the Dean of Salisbury:

> I do feel that Mr Keble's blessing, "Prosper Thou the work of her hands upon her," has been most marvellously fulfilled, and this has brought me to think that the peculiar care and training that were given me by my father, Mr Keble and [Miss Dyson]

seem to have been appointed to make me a sort of instrument for popularizing Church views that might not have been otherwise taken in.

Yet, in spite of this satisfaction and the tributes to her fame, old age was bringing its inevitable sorrows on Charlotte. One by one her friends were departing. She had seen little of Canon Butler since he had become Dean of Lincoln, but had always kept up a lively correspondence with him. It was only six months after she had, on that memorable seventieth birthday, received a warm letter from the Dean, expressing his deep affection and reverence, that Charlotte heard the news of his death, which was shortly followed by that of Mrs Butler. Miss Yonge writes: "To me it is another of my lamps gone to be a star, and, at seventy, one has hardly any left on earth."

The last of the circle who had known her as a child was Mr Bigg-Wither. Every Sunday since he had left Otterbourne, Charlotte had written him a letter. She kept up this habit until he died, at a great age, when she herself was already an old lady of seventy-five.

One of the saddest moments of Miss Yonge's old age was when she was asked at the end of 1893 to resign her editorship of *The Monthly Packet*. For the last few years Christabel Coleridge had been associated with her as co-editor, in the hope that she might infuse a more modern tone into it. They worked together in outward harmony, but in this way neither could have a free hand, and Miss Coleridge admits that their ideals clashed. Inevitable though this was, Miss Yonge felt it bitterly when she was turned out of the editorship of the magazine she had made and worked at for over forty years. She wrote to one of her cousins:

The old friends [of *The Packet*] are nearly gone, and the young ones call it goody-goody. So the old coachman who has driven it for forty years is called on to retire! They are very civil about it, and want to call me Consulting Editor, but that is nonsense, for they don't consult me. . . . Don't speak of my withdrawal as ill-usage, but only as Anno Domini, which it may be more than is in the nature of things I should understand, for I think I am as much to the fore as ever. Only most of my old friends have passed, and it is not the same.

In the spring of 1897 Charlotte Yonge was released from her

years of patient care by the death of Gertrude Walter. At last her house was her own again, and she was free to receive the visits of friends. Most of her contemporaries were either dead or reluctant to undertake journeys, so her visitors were chiefly of the next generation. She was rarely left to solitude, for when her niece Helen Yonge could not be with her, Christabel Coleridge or a cousin would make long visits. The last ten years of Miss Yonge's life were brightened by the presence at the vicarage of another of her nieces, Alethea, whose husband, Mr Bowles, had been given the living of Otterbourne. Charlotte was just as fond a great-aunt as she had been an aunt, and the Bowles children were in and out of Elderfield as much as the earlier generation had been.

In this serene and happy old age came one day of radiant brightness. Eighteen hundred pounds had been collected from her admirers all over the world, and this was to be presented to her, so that a scholarship to one of the Oxford or Cambridge colleges from the Winchester High School for Girls might be founded in her honour. On a perfect July day in 1899 Charlotte Yonge betook herself to Winchester for the great ceremony. Characteristically she would not allow this to interfere with the diocesan gathering of Sunday-school teachers. She sat in a corner of the Guildhall listening to all the speeches addressed to them, and then got up to say that "she regarded herself even more in the light of a veteran Sunday-school teacher than in that of an author." The doughty old lady even wanted to go on to the service at the Cathedral, but she was borne off by friends for a quiet tea in the Close, to nerve her for the function at the High School.

The great schoolroom had been decorated with daisy-chains and heartsease. Thither Charlotte was conducted by the Bishop of Winchester, with two of her old "Goslings" walking hand in hand behind her. Many speeches were made, vying with one another in extolling the usefulness, as well as the charm, of Miss Yonge's books. One lady said:

> She has taught us History; she has taught us to use our eyes and our minds; it was she who laid the foundations of those ideas which have led the women of our own day into so many paths of activity and self-denial.

The Bishop made the great presentation; he handed her the

scholarship money and an illuminated address. Miss Yonge was also given a basket of flowers emblematic of some of her books —daisies and heartsease, tied with violet ribbons. The Victorian era was not yet over, and people still dared to make a delicate gesture of sentimental allusion.

The ceremony ended with an entertainment. Some High School girls, dressed in thin white frocks, did a daisy-chain dance, while others presented tableaux from some of Miss Yonge's historical tales. She was entirely delighted, and later referred to it as "one of the prettiest and pleasantest recollections of a lifetime." For once enjoyment had vanquished her shyness. She was only disconcerted to find that the speech of thanks she had written out beforehand did not fit, and said:

> I could not help, when they said I had made clergy and good men seem real, almost murmuring that my good men were not ideals, but I had really known their equals (and superiors) in reality.

(So delighted was one of the Cathedral clergy at this optimistic view of humanity that he sent after the reporter to have it added to Miss Yonge's speech.) As the central figure of the ceremony Charlotte Yonge played her part nobly—"as a white-haired, bright-eyed handsome Victorian lady." At the end of this memorable day she drove back to Otterbourne with the basket of flowers on her lap and a smile of intense happiness on her face.

BOOK SIX

VICTORIAN RETROSPECT

CHAPTER XIV

TRAVEL, TIMES, AND TASTE

As an old woman Charlotte Yonge could look back on three-quarters of a century of perhaps most radical change till then achieved in our whole civilization. Yet in her books we are primarily conscious, not of the difference, but of the similarity of outlook between her earlier and later works. The underlying stability of ideas, of standards, and of economic security in the society portrayed from *Abbeychurch* to *Modern Broods* is what strikes the present-day reader at first sight. It was otherwise with the author herself. She is at pains to stress the progress, for good or ill as she conceived it, that is represented even in the lives of the limited circle she depicts. If, then, we look closely at a few details in the everyday social life she represents, we can see that the Victorians were in no sense so static as we might at first glance believe.

Take, for example, the question of travel. From the days of Horace Walpole and Lord Chesterfield, the Grand Tour had been a part of the life and education of the young nobleman, while Thackeray's Victorian novels accustom us to the Continental travels of his artistic and aristocratic characters. But it is a little unexpected to hear Tom May, a mere medical student, suggesting that he should take his younger brother "for a run on the continent," and to find the two of them going off to the Tyrol for Aubrey's holidays. True, Tom is really making this proposal in the attempt to get over an unsuccessful love-affair, and he annoys his father a good deal by the apparently casual way in which he affirms that "a run now and then is a duty, not a pleasure," but Tom must evidently be considered more representative than his father, of the eighteen-sixties. Holidays abroad seem to have been quite the accepted thing even for a girl. Robina Underwood at sixteen joins her sister and brother-in-law in the Pyrenees, escorted by her cousin's lady's maid and young Bill Harewood, not much older than herself, who shows her about Paris.

When they went abroad for pleasure, it would seem that Miss Yonge's characters preferred out-of-the-way, or at least not ultra-fashionable, places. The Fulmort family eschew Nice and Monte Carlo and settle down at Hyères to effect Bertha's complete recovery. As late as 1892 (in *That Stick*) Lord and Lady Northmoor go to a village in the Dolomites so remote that the last part of the journey has to be done by mules or *chaise à porteur*. The place has been recommended by a fearless and unconventional cousin, Mrs Bury, and the hotel where they stay is of the simple kind which persisted up to recent times in Tyrolese villages, with the *Speisesaal* and the bedrooms in separate buildings. One gathers that in the 'nineties the English public was beginning to 'discover' the Dolomites; if so Tom's selection of the Tyrol for his trip abroad was thirty years ahead of the fashion.

In cases of illness or emergency the Victorians, young and old, middle or upper class, appear as mobile as one could wish. Wilmet Underwood's betrothed, an engineer, is injured in an accident on the half-completed Suez railway, and the news is telegraphed to his father. The girl herself shows no hesitation in going off at a moment's notice, accompanied by old Mr Harewood, to nurse her lover, whom, incidentally, she marries as soon as he is sufficiently recovered, in order that she may with propriety stay out in Egypt and let the old clergyman return to his cathedral duties at home.

Again, when Gilbert Kendal, a hero of the Crimea, is invalided back to Malta, his stepmother insists on accompanying his father, who is to set off immediately. "I am going to Malta, Maurice, to-morrow evening . . . you must not prevent me from travelling day and night." Fortunately "there were few detentions to overthrow her equanimity on the way to Marseilles," and Miss Yonge's readers must have been gratified that the pair arrived in time for a most edifying death scene.

When arrangements could be determined in advance, it was

quite possible to fit the journey to a time-table. Dr Spencer (in *The Daisy Chain*) goes off to Vienna to obtain from a friend the necessary permit to proceed with the building of Cocksmoor Church. He says that he will have four days to spare there, and will return on the last of the month. This he does—and brings back the permit—saying he has travelled comfortably.

That experienced traveller Tom May, whose views on Continental trips have already been mentioned, makes a double journey from Paris with even more admirable consequences. He interrupts his medical studies to return for the funeral of Dr Spencer, his father's friend, and forthwith goes back to collect his possessions. While still in Paris, he has the good fortune to light on the piece of evidence that has so long been missing, which enables him to force a confession from a murderer and to clear his friend's name.

It is hardly surprising that a young man of Tom's determination should think little of crossing the Atlantic in pursuit of his bride. No sooner has Leonard Ward's innocence been proved, owing to Tom's efforts, than Tom himself professes a great desire to have a medical work of Dr Spencer's published in America— this being, as his shrewd sister Ethel perceives, merely a pretext for finding Averil Ward and giving her the news of her brother's release. He has to follow Averil and her sister to the miasmic swamp where they have been deposited by their elder brother, Henry. Henry Ward had put his money (and Averil's) into a company, the object of which was to build homes for pioneers in newly cleared forest. Unfortunately, a singularly unhealthy site had been selected for this outpost of civilization, and Henry eventually went off to join the Northern Army (in the Civil War) as a doctor. Tom, making his way to Indiana, finds the two girls in desperate straits, brings them back to England, and eventually secures his reward.

Even farther afield go the characters in *Dynevor Terrace*. The journey to and from Peru is undertaken no less than eight times during the story by the various principal persons, and that though the voyage must have been made as a rule by Cape Horn. At least, this is the implication about the earlier voyages, for Louis Fitzjocelyn remarks, "It would not take long going by the Isthmus," and the comment is, that this route "had recently become practicable for adventurous travellers." This is in 1853

—sixty years before the opening of the Panama Canal. The double journey, which, indeed, was not without adventure, was made by Louis in about five months.

When it came to seeing one's own country first, Miss Yonge rather emphasizes the ease of travel in her day compared with earlier times. However, to most of the characters a journey is still something of an adventure—for instance, to Ethel May: "once beyond Whitford, the whole world was new to her"; her father, on the other hand, was "hankering to run up to Oxford for the day." Later on Ethel is to take her brother and the convalescent Leonard to the seaside, and is told it is "a very easy journey—only four hours' railway and a ten-mile drive"—sufficient, one would think, for an invalid. It is of interest to note that her father looks up the route in the already familiar Bradshaw, and, as he rather oddly puts it, "There are places in Wales nearer by the map, but without railway privilege."

Curiously enough, "the Clever Woman of the Family" is no great traveller, though in her usual headstrong fashion she proposes to go to London alone. This procedure her husband strongly opposes, and she is forced to confess that she has only been twice before, once when her father took her to the Great Exhibition, and the second time passing through with her husband. A compromise with the conventions is reached when she agrees that the housekeeper shall accompany her on the journey, though she finally sets off not with her, but with Mr Clare, her husband's uncle.

Certainly, railways play an important part in the lives of the ordinary families in Miss Yonge's later works. The Underwood family forgather at a junction before making their descent *en masse* on Vale Leston, when they appear there as rightful owners. Dolores Mohun goes by train to meet her disreputable uncle, an adventure which the foolish Constance (who loses fifteen pounds to this sharper) regards as quite romantic. There is also a vivid description of another train journey undertaken by Dolores, on the occasion of the trial of this same fraudulent uncle, and Miss Yonge uses the weather, the surroundings, and the stern attitude of Dolores' guardian to enhance the feeling of dumb, sullen misery from which the girl is suffering. Yet another traveller is the young Countess Kate, who at twelve years old runs away

A Fashion Plate, *circa* 1860

THE OPENING OF KEBLE COLLEGE, OXFORD, 1870
See p. 218.
By courtesy of the Bodleian Library

241

from her London aunts to her former home. A young lady in her position did not travel unescorted, but

Nobody remarked her; she was a tall girl for her age, and in her sober dark dress, with her little bag, might be taken for a tradesman's daughter going to school. . . . Trembling she saw a cabman make a sign to her and stood waiting for him, jumped in as he opened his door, and felt as if she had found a refuge for the time upon the dirty red plush cushions and the straw. "To the Waterloo Station," said she, with as much indifference and self-possession as she could manage.

Not only the railway, but the railway refreshment room was among the accepted conveniences of life in the second half of the century. It is said—with what truth one does not know—that a certain firm of caterers, having lent the Great Western Railway large sums, insisted that when an important connexion was to be caught at Swindon there should always be a wait of twenty minutes. Experience would seem to bear this out, and so would a reference in *The Daisy Chain*: George fed the Oxford-bound party with everything that he could make them eat at Swindon Station, whisking his wife into the carriage with her last sandwich in her hand. Miss Yonge evidently thought highly of the sandwich; when Bertha Fulmort makes her abortive attempt at an elopement, is fetched back by her brother, tries to starve herself, and develops brain-fever, the doctor severely remarks that if Robert had given her a sandwich at Paddington Station her illness would never have occurred.

Of course, for short distances riding or driving were the normal means of travel, and sometimes a carriage was taken by train, as a car might be to-day. Amy (in *The Heir of Redclyffe*) takes hers to the remote part of England in which Redclyffe is situated, and drives the last thirty miles. It is interesting to speculate on how many horses Dr May kept: his practice, of course, required a gig (until Flora forced him into a brougham, for the sake of respectability), but Norman seems to find no difficulty in obtaining a horse whenever he wishes to ride over to Meta's house, though, to be sure, when "four of the young gentlemen" are invited to dinner, they go on foot. So does Guy Morville when, while staying at a farm for vacation reading, he walks over to a dinner-party five miles off.

In the earlier works Miss Yonge sometimes stresses the

Q

newness of "modern inventions." Sir Francis Willoughby on his return from India towards the middle of the century, after an absence of thirty-five years, is bewildered at the giddy pace of a world that travels by train where he only remembers coaches, and by the alacrity with which journeys are undertaken. He is amazed at the speed with which his eighteen-year-old son, not seen since the age of three, has come up to town to greet him. And in *Henrietta's Wish* "the electric telegraph and the railroad brought the surgeon" to Frederick's bedside even before his mother had seriously begun to expect him. The same book opens with Frederick's return from school to where his sister is in "an open carriage waiting in front of a painted toy looking building which served as the railway station of Teignmouth."

The introduction of machinery on the farm and the country people's prejudices against newfangled *inventions* has already been described. The "brilliant blue wheat drill" of Henrietta's uncle occasions some comment—though, one may imagine, not so much as would have been evoked by a contraption envisaged by another cousin: "a scare-crow full of gun-powder which fires off every ten minutes." "Inventions," however, should be devised by scientists, not by farmers—a principle found by implication in Miss Yonge's works, but applied also in modern times.

Henrietta's Wish gives a pleasant picture of life in the household of a country gentleman, and of his son, who lives on one of the farms, managing the estate, and whose small income and large family preclude many social pretensions. The hours of meals may be taken as typical of the mid-century, and day begins with the bell for prayers, before breakfast. Luncheon was presumably a light meal, for when the church clock strikes one, the young people who are putting up the decorations, "instead of going back late to luncheon," buy six penn'orth of ginger-bread at the village shop, which they eat walking up and down the churchyard. On the other hand, when they walk over to the farm, and stay till about one o'clock, the hospitable "Aunt Roger" begs the party (four in number!) to stay, and they find themselves partaking of "the family dinner." Even for this meal some of the boys did not arrive till nearly three, and one's admiration for Aunt Roger's powers of housekeeping is mixed with envy of her obliviousness of domestic difficulties.

The Langfords' own dinner is an evening meal, and on Henrietta's arrival (in the winter) she found "The half-hour bell rang, . . . dinner would be ready at half-past five." Mrs Langford, suffering from the effects of the journey, did not come down to the dinner, but when her daughter, Henrietta, went up to see her afterwards, she was told, "It will never do to have you staying up here all the evening," so she went down again for the ceremony of tea-drinking.

In the more fashionable household of Marian Arundel's guardian dinner was, apparently, later, for the young ladies went to bed at 9.30, and Marian, who particularly wanted to see her cousin Edmund, was in agony lest the gentlemen should not by that time have appeared from the dining-room.

Tea-drinking after dinner was a well-established custom, as we remember from Jane Austen's books, but Violet, in *Hearts-ease*, was surprised at meeting it earlier in the day. "Lady Martindale asked me to have some tea. I never heard of such a thing before dinner"—and wonders whether she should have accepted. Her husband only laughs and tells her how his strong-minded sister, Theodora, "despises women who drink tea in the middle of the day."

Customs have changed with regard to the details of everyday life, but in nothing so much, perhaps, as in people's outlook on what might roughly be called culture. In Miss Yonge's progress of stories we can watch taste changing—especially as it affected the social life of the class on whom she concentrated. A few references show the trend.

Mention has already been made of the architectural developments of the period. These were the province of men, but women, having the 'feminine touch,' were supreme in church decoration, then still a new idea. In *Henrietta's Wish* we hear of "festoons round those two columns of the chancel arch" and evergreens that "cover the Dutch cherubs at the head of the tables of commandments." Henrietta also makes a cross and monogram in holly. The Mays, too, were great church decorators. The decking of the Minster for Christmas was obviously a festive occasion for them, for it put them into such high spirits that they were emboldened to attempt the ascent of the tower, which nearly led to a fatal accident. The Easter decorations were done, however, in the solemn mood of Holy Week. In

The Pillars of the House we see Gertrude wrangling at Cocksmoor with Rupert Cheviot as to whether the festoons should
hang "loose and natural" or "follow the architectural lines."
Even the invalid Averil takes her share in decorating the church,
though it is too cold for her to venture into it, and she drives
over in a donkey-chair, bringing "her choice manufacture of
crosses and devices." It would appear that not an inch of the
church could have been left uncovered, for the very candlesticks
were carried into the parsonage to be adorned by Averil. The
interest of all this lies in the setting of the fashion, church decoration being, like illumination, all part of the Tractarian revival,
with its resulting craze for the Gothic.

The following is perhaps less a reflection of the taste of the
times (which is more truly mirrored in the *Wreath of Beauty*, a
book in which various aristocratic ladies appear in classical
costume) than a tribute to the unsophisticated taste of school-
boys, but the incident merits quotation. Marian, aged fourteen,
has a younger brother and cousin who want to give her a present,
and they go out under the care of an elder brother to find something:

> Marian might have been grateful to him, had she known all that
> he averted from her, a stuffed fox, an immense pebble brooch, a
> pair of slippers covered with sportive demons. At every shop which
> furnished knives or fishing tackle they stopped and lamented that
> she was not a boy, for there was nothing in the world fit for girls;
> they tried a bazaar and pronounced everything trumpery and
> Walter was beginning to despair, when at last Lionel came to a
> stop before a print shop containing a picture of Raphael's St
> Margaret.

Walter rejoices "that their choice was likely to fall on anything
which a young lady might be so glad to possess," and effects the
purchases without more ado; Marian is, of course, delighted.

In the 'fifties we meet the full force of the Pre-Raphaelites,
for Theresa Marstone, author of those high-flown allegories
Folded Lambs and *Pearls of the Deep*, is herself a "walking
Pre-Raphaelitism," her conversation being full of "symbols and
emblems." A man seeing her for the first time most appro-
priately asked, "What crypt did they dig her out of?" Miss
Yonge approved just as little of the imitators of the great Pre-
Raphaelites as she did of Miss Marstone's appearance, and she

acquiesces in the universal condemnation of Edgar's painting of Brunhild in *The Pillars of the House*:

> [Geraldine's] feeling had been that the Pre-Rafaelitism of the hauberk was too like worsted stockings, and not in keeping with the Turneresque whirl of flame and smoke around the sleeping Valkyr.

She was even more disgusted with the pictures of Edgar's Bohemian friend:

> They are Scripture subjects—Ruth and Rachael—made coarse and vulgar by being treated with vile reality—looking like Jewish women out of fruit-shops.

These were painted in the 'sixties, but we are reminded of the uproar made when *The Carpenter's Shop* had been exhibited by Millais some fifteen years earlier. Dickens himself had swelled the chorus of vituperation by an article in *Household Words*, in which he wrote:

> You will have the goodness to discharge from your minds all Post-Raphael ideas, all religious aspirations, all elevating thoughts; all tender, awful, sorrowful, ennobling, sacred, graceful, or beautiful associations; and to prepare yourselves, as befits such a subject —Pre-Raphaelly considered—for the lowest depths of what is mean, odious, repulsive, and revolting.

Miss Marstone was by no means alone in insisting on a moral, for symbolic representation was perhaps the outstanding characteristic of the middle of the century. Even when the artist had no intention of painting a picture which 'told a story' the English public was quite capable of supplying its own moral. Percy Fotheringham reads into an Academy picture the story of his attempt to tame Theodora:

> It was a fine one by Landseer of a tiger submitting to the hand of the keeper, with cat-like complacency, but the glare of the eye and curl of the tail manifesting that its gentleness was temporary.
> "It may be the grander animal," muttered he; "but less satisfactory for domestic purposes. . . . That is a presumptuous man," he said, pointing to the keeper. "If he trusts in the creature's affection, some day he will find his mistake."

The next day Percy stands contemplating a picture of Paul Potter's,

> where the Pollard Willows stand up against the sunset sky, the evening sunshine gleaming on their trunks, upon the grass, and

gilding the backs of the cows, while the placid old couple look on at the milking.

Wounded at his break with Theodora and wishing to marry a more biddable girl, he remarks, "There's my notion of felicity."

This taste for allegory is even more strongly developed in Geraldine Underwood, who in her youthful days, before she had become a professional artist, drew a picture entitled *The Waves of this Troublesome World*. This showed thirteen boats, representing the thirteen Underwoods, sailing through "the sea of life . . . all making for the golden light of Heaven, and the star of faith guiding them." She is still painting allegorical pictures some thirty years later, for we hear of one dealing with a similar subject in *The Long Vacation*. It was no doubt this element in her which attracted her to Mr Grinstead, a famous sculptor, who dealt in such subjects as *Mercy at the Wicket Gate* and *Una and the Lion*—"grave and graceful creations—more from the world of Christian than of classic poetry, and if less æsthetically beautiful, more solemn and more real." Geraldine undoubtedly loved a story, for she was fond of doing illustrations such as "a water-colour of the scene in The Lord of the Isles when Ronald's betrothal ring falls at the feet of Isabel Bruce in the convent," and, when saving money by the sale of her pictures to pay off Edgar's debts, she painted a "Maiden spinning for her lover's ransom." It should be noted, however, that Geraldine is most successful when doing less pretentious work. She excels at portraits, in both watercolours and crayons, which sound delightfully natural. In her appreciation of this fact Miss Yonge shows an instinctive feeling for the kind of Victorian art, free of transitory fashions, which was most likely to live.

In Miss Yonge's later books we meet references to the æsthetic movement of the last quarter of the century, generally to its more frivolous aspects. There is one lady who wears a terra-cotta dress and a chain of watch-cocks, and another who does very 'greenery-yallery' embroidery. In *Nuttie's Father* we are told that "after having seen *Patience* at the Prince's, it was not easy to avoid criticizing a provincial 'Lady Jane.'"

But the objects used by ordinary people and the ways in which *their* taste displayed itself is what strikes us most in Miss Yonge's stories. Most of her characters go along happily with contemporary taste, and it is only exceptions like the artistic Geraldine

Underwood who look beyond it. The strictures passed by her and Edgar on Mrs Froggatt's wallpaper and the lament for the softened tints of their old faded one might have come from the modern æsthete. Here is Geraldine engaged in choosing a coal-scuttle with the help of her two young sisters:

> Is it not a curious study to see invention expended on making an intrinsically hideous thing beautiful by force of japan, gilding, and painting? You see the only original design nature provided for a coal-scuttle is the nautilus shell, and unluckily that is grotesquely inappropriate! Just look at the row of ungainly things craning out their chins like overdressed dwarfs. I am decidedly for the simplest and least disguised, though Robin is for the snail, and Angel, I believe, for that highly suitable Watteau scene.

And yet Geraldine is as eager as countless other women of her time to adorn herself with lockets, containing the hair of her nearest and dearest. This habit appears in Miss Yonge's stories to have been ubiquitous. Robina Underwood even went so far as to have an engagement ring of the fiery red locks of Bill Harewood, her betrothed, made up on a foundation of the hair of a chestnut horse!

It may be contended that by the end of the century there had been some reaction against the worst of the fashionable knick-nacks with which mid-Victorian life was cumbered. But Charlotte herself had not entirely passed out of that phase, and right at the end of the century the otherwise modern Dolores, for instance, mentions without dismay or malice old Miss Smith's feather screens—circles of pheasants' feathers and peacocks' eyes outside a border of drakes' curls, while among the more acceptable gifts sent to a bazaar are some "very graceful and beautiful articles of sculpture and Italian bijouterie," which had been spared from Mr White's marble works.

It is not entirely fair to judge the taste of any age by its shows and pageants, but Miss Yonge in almost her last book (*The Long Vacation*) devotes a great deal of time to the description of a *fête* and bazaar (held, of course, with the laudable object of raising money for Church schools). Perhaps she meant to contrast this grand function with the Fancy Fair of the much earlier *Daisy Chain*, which, we have seen, was almost entirely a 'home-made' affair. At any rate, she comments on the enhanced social importance of such shows.

They had so advanced since their early days from being simple sales to the grand period of ornaments, costumes and anything to attract.

The climax was a performance of an operetta based on *The Tempest*. The side-shows included an interpreter of handwriting and an amateur photographer, who "was zealously photographing group after group, handing his performances over to his assistant to print off." The sellers were in fancy costume, those of one of the stalls being an anticipation of a 'period piece' in an Ideal Home Exhibition:

> The charity stall was quaintly dressed in the likeness of an old-fashioned school, with big alphabet and samplers, flourished copies and a stuffed figure of a "contrary" naughty boy with a magnificent fool's cap. [Jane] herself sat behind it, the very image of the Shenstone school-mistress, with wide white cap, black poke-bonnet, crossed kerchief and red cloak and formidable rod, and her myrmidons were in costume to match.

As to the objects for sale in the bazaar itself, they included cushions ("a fat red cushion like brick-dust, enlivened by a half-boiled cauliflower"), shawls, bags, drawings, screens, scrap-books, photographs, and a statue, half as large as life, of the Dirty Boy. Each stall was "in a sort of cave," and it needed Geraldine's "wonderful touch" to make out of a miscellaneous collection of dolls and "a bevy of figures in Indian costumes" a truly artistic setting, "transforming the draperies from the aspect of a rag and bone shop . . . to a wonderful, quaint and pretty fairy bower backed by Indian scenes."

But best of all is the procession which opens the *fête* and which is fully described by Charlotte, with all her old zest and skill in bringing out the pictorial effect of the whole, while not omitting the touches of individual character. The Pageant has not succeeded in detaching itself (as it did in this century) from the sale—it has not yet become the corporate expression of civic pride or a mere method of presenting history to the general public. There is a glorious and inconsequent mixture of styles, plenty of scope for individuality, and a generosity in the matter of costumes that recalls the wide range of the author's own books.

> The procession started from the garden entrance of the hotel, headed by the town band in uniform, and the fire-brigade likewise, very proud of themselves, especially the little terrier whom nothing

would detach from one of the firemen. Then came the four seasons belonging to the flower stall, appropriately decked with flowers, the Italian peasants with flat veils, bright aprons and white sleeves, Maura White's beauty conspicuous in the midst, but with unnecessary nods and becks. Then came the "Medieval" (quotation marks very necessary!) damsels in ruffs and high hats, the Highland maidens, with Valetta and Primrose giggling unmanageably: and Aunt Jane's troop of the various costumes of charity children from the green frocks, long mittens and tall white caps and the Jemima Placid flat hats and long waists, down to the red cloaks, poke straw bonnets and blue frocks of the Lady Bountiful age. These were followed by the merry fairies and elves; then by buccaneers and the captive prisoners: and the rear was brought up by "Mac Prospero" [the latter being characters from the Masque].

One has the feeling that *The Long Vacation*, though not actually the last of Miss Yonge's books, is the climax of her story-telling. It is well conceived that the majority of her own created figures should be last seen sweeping past in a grand and typical Victorian pageant.

CHAPTER XV

CLOTHES AND CONVENTIONS

THE whole history of nineteenth-century costume could be brought before the eye by a well-illustrated edition of Miss Yonge's works. The early fashions, of which she must have been told by her mother, are described in the retrospective and, by 1895, almost "historical" stories of *The Carbonels* and *Chantry House*. We have already seen how the arrival of Mr and Mrs Yonge at Otterbourne was probably reproduced in the former tale. A younger sister arrives later, and, though Miss Yonge is not often specific about waistlines and 'figures,' one must imagine the girl in a short-waisted frock, probably of muslin, or perhaps of transparent net over a satin slip.

> Sophy . . . was a damsel of thirteen, in a white frock and cape, a pink sash, pink kerchief round her neck, pink satin ribbons tying down her broad Leghorn hat over her ears in what was called gipsy fashion. She had rosy cheeks, blue, good-natured eyes, and shining, light-brown curls all round her head. Her appearance in the school was quite memorable . . . and the little ones were so engaged in looking at her that they quite forgot to be naughty, except that Billy Mole, in curiosity to know what anything so glossy and shining could be, pinched the end of her sash, and left the grimy mark of his little hot hands on it.

Sophy—even so early as this—was teaching in the Sunday school, but here is the description of the regular schoolmistress (who had, before her appointment, been a maid in a neighbouring large house) and of her children:

> Mrs Thorpe arrived with her two little girls, the neatest of creatures, still wearing her weeds, as indeed widows engaged in any business used to do for life, as a sort of protection. Under her crape borders showed the smoothest of hair and her apron was spotlessly white. The two little girls were patterns, with short cut hair, spotted blue frocks and checkered pinafores in the week, lilac frocks on Sundays; white capes on that same day, and bonnets of coarse straw, tied down with green ribbon, over little bonnet caps with

plain net frilling, the only attempt at luxury apparent in their dress.

One of the incidents, founded on fact, turns on the forcible cutting of the village children's hair by the outraged amateur teachers from the Manor, and the following is an explanatory note on the difficulties of keeping hair tidy in the days before the permanent wave:

It was a time when it was the fashion for young ladies up to their teens to have their hair curled in ringlets round their heads or on their shoulders. Sophy's hair curled naturally, and had been "turned up" ever since she had come to live at home in the dignity of fourteen, but she and both her sisters wore falls of drooping ringlets in front, and in Mary's case these had been used to be curled in paper at night, though she would as soon have been seen thus decorated by day as in her night-cap. But there was scarcely another matron in the parish who did not think a fringe of curl-papers the proper mode of disposing of her locks when in morning *deshabille*, unless she were elderly and wore a front—which could be taken off and put on with the best cap.

Maid-servants wore short curls or smooth folds round side-combs under net caps, and this was the usual trim of the superior kind of women. The working women wore thick muslin white caps, under which, it was to be hoped, their hair was cut short, though often it straggled out in unseemly elf-locks. Married women did not go bareheaded, not even the younger ladies, except in the evening, when, like their maiden sisters, they wore coils of their back hair round huge upright ornamental combs on the summit of their heads.

Here is a description of the heroine of *Chantry House* (the date supposed to be about 1830) "in her white worked cambric dress, silk scarf, huge Tuscan bonnet, and the little curls beyond the lace quilling round her bright face." The outstanding feature of all the descriptions of dress in the earlier part of this book is headgear. Besides the "Tuscan bonnet" we hear of a "sweet cottage bonnet," while elderly ladies wore in the house "the cap of the period, one of the most disfiguring articles of headgear ever devised." No less startling was the *coiffure* of the fast Lady Peacock, who wore her hair "in a most astonishing erection of bows and bands, on the very crown of her head, raising her height at least four inches."

The forbidding of curls in Sunday schools, indeed, seems to

have been general until far into the century, for there are constant references to the zeal of Sunday-school teachers in forbidding both curls and the wearing of jewellery.

Scenes and Characters, almost the earliest of Miss Yonge's published works, is still in the first half of the century. Here are "young ladies" again. The Mohun sisters appear at the service which precedes the Whit Monday Club Walking in *Scenes and Characters* clad in fresh muslins and new bonnets, while the villagers wear striped and spotted prints and clean smocks.

Another early work is *Henrietta's Wish,* and a delightful account is given of Beatrice Langford, prepared for a morning's skating. She wears "a small plain black velvet bonnet, a tight black velvet 'jacket' as she called it" (the word as evidently as new as the style), a brown silk dress with narrow yellow stripes —this had been chosen as a kind of joke, because it was like her namesake, the bee—"not a bit of superfluous shawl, boa or ribbon about her, but all close and compact," most suitable for the exercise she was going to take.

How much there might have been of the "superfluous" we see from the account of her cousin, the dawdling Henrietta, who, being helped to dress in a hurry, "let her cousin heap on shawls, fur cuffs and boas in a far less leisurely and discriminating way than was usual with her." The girls also took their gloves, though they were only going to decorate (or "dress") the church. But this may, of course, have been as much due to the weather as to convention, although the latter was no doubt insistent, and much later on Ethel May, while agreeing that "sea-places have no manners and customs," finds it necessary to "toss on" a hat before she walks down from the lodgings to the beach. The Langford girls are provided with clogs against the mud of country roads, but they also have boots, as do Miss Yonge's later heroines for such occasions.

The eighteen-forties were the age of shawls and mantles— that is why Beatrice's lack of anything flowing is remarkable; for on a more conventional occasion she says to Henrietta, "Now, here is your shawl ready folded, and now I will trust you to put on your boots and bonnet by yourself"—but five minutes later she finds her cousin still measuring the length of her bonnet strings before the glass. It is bonnets, bonnets all the way— and if we are brought up against a somewhat unfamiliar phrase, "taking off their bonnets," we have only to remember that the early twentieth-century "taking off their hats" may sound as strange to a future generation whose habit is to go bareheaded.

Bee's "short jacket" was remarkable in its trimness, and by the middle of the century shawls, jackets, or mantillas of muslin or some light material are mentioned as part of almost every outfit, even those of little girls. Countess Kate's simple "delicate blue and white muslin, worked white jacket and white-ribboned and feathered hat" is evidently in the best of taste, and a contrast to a small cousin of hers who appears in "a little turban hat" and a flounced frock. Even more fully described are the clothes of a little girl of nine in another story, who is the daughter of rich and indulgent parents.

> Her hat was black chip, edged and tied with rose-coloured ribbon and adorned with a real bird, with glass eyes, black plumage except the red crest and wings. She wore a neatly-fitting little fringed black polka, beneath which spread out in fan-like folds her flounced pink muslin, coming a little below her knees, and showing her worked drawers, which soon gave place to her neat stockings and dainty little boots. She held a small white parasol, bordered with pink, and deeply fringed over head, and held a gold-clasped Prayer-book in her hand.

Certainly the chances given by the mantle for a display of contrasting colour could be sadly misused. Albinia Kendal came down on her first Sunday in her new home (herself clad in a quiet dark silk Cashmere shawl and plain straw bonnet) to find her stepdaughters in the hall, "in sea-green mantillas and pink bonnets over the lilac silks, all evidently put on for the first time in her honour." She refrained from disparaging comment, but when, a little later on, this display was repeated on the occasion of their going to call on a neighbour, Albinia "requested that they might be changed for the straw-bonnet and large black tippet"—not considering sea-green appropriate for the dirty lanes—to the girls' great disgust. Later still a setting forth for a *fête* gives Miss Yonge an opportunity of the kind she really enjoys for describing pretty clothes:

> With every advantage of pretty features, good complexion and nice figure, the English Lucy in her blue and white checked silk, worked muslin mantle and white chip bonnet, with blue ribbons, was eclipsed by the small swarthy French girl in that very old black

silk dress and white-trimmed coarse bonnet, just enlivened by little pink bows at the neck and wrists . . . redolent of all her own fresh and sprightly archness and refinement. Albinia herself was the best representative of English good looks and never had she been more brilliant, her rich chestnut hair waving so prettily on the rounded contour of her happy face, her fair cheek tinted with such a healthy fresh bloom, her grey eyes laughing with a merry softness, her whole person so alert and elastic with exuberant life and enjoyment that Grandmamma was as happy in watching her as if she had been her own daughter and stroked down the broad flounces of her changeable silk and admired her black lace, as if she felt the whole family exalted by Mrs Kendal's appearance.

Here, during the next decade (the 'sixties), is another smart guest arriving at a party:

> Up came Lady Keith with her two brisk little Shetlands. She was a mass of pretty, fresh, fluttering blue and white muslin, ribbons and lace, and looked particularly well and brilliant.

Yet Miss Yonge takes almost as much care in describing the characteristic attire of her less well-dressed people as the party frocks. Rachel Curtis is introduced in

> a thick dress of blue and black tartan, still looped up over the dark petticoat and hose and stout high-heeled boots that like the grey cloak and felt hat bore witness to the early walk.

When she first meets the young man she is destined to marry, she wears on her head a "black lace pall or curtain"—later referred to as "a cap set *against* instead of *at* him." However, she improves on marriage, and he thus describes her to the blind uncle:

> "A long white feather in a shady hat trimmed with dark green velvet; she is fresh and rosy, you know, Sir, and looks well in green; and then—is it Grace's taste, Rachel? for it is the prettiest thing you have worn—a pale buff sort of silky thing embroidered all over in the same colour."
>
> "Indian, surely," said Mr Clare feeling the pattern, "it is too intricate and graceful for the West."

The delicate shade, the intricate design, and the use of the then fashionable velvet go to show that Rachel had abandoned her pose of superiority to feminine vanities and her flouting of the mode and convention.

Rachel was worth dressing, but Miss Yonge knows well enough

the kind of person whom no amount of fashionable clothes will succeed in rendering smart.

Emma left insufficient time for her maid to try to set out her soft scanty hair, to make her satin and gauze look anything but limp and flabby, and to put on her jewels in the vain hope of their making her seem well-dressed. Whatever was ordained for her to wear, Emma always looked exactly the same.

Emma's dress on the occasion of this party (*Heartsease*, 1854) is not fully described, but Violet wears bridal lace, a wreath of roses, a new "serpent" bracelet, and carries a posy of brilliant flowers. Her sister-in-law, Theodora, sweeps past in black lace, her coronal of hair wreathed with the strings of pearls then so fashionable, and looking, at nineteen—no wonder!—like the Tragic Muse.

So elaborate was hairdressing in the days before the net and *chignon*, that it is perhaps not surprising that Theodora Martindale, independent-minded as she is, cannot do her own hair for a party until she is taught by the more humbly brought-up Violet. Violet herself, when she went home for a visit, came out in "pretty plaits and braids"—a welcome sight to her husband—and omitted to put on her cap. But this was not really for his benefit; she explains that she would not look more old than she could help for fear of disturbing her mother. Violet was then about twenty-two. Amabel, the twenty-year-old widow of Guy Morville, however, was not going to let her ringlets appear again; "she put on such a dress as would be hers for life—black silk and lace cap over her still plain hair."

We have mentioned the long reign of the bonnet, but gradually during the 'sixties these became smaller, were worn farther back on the head, and eventually gave place altogether to the small feather-trimmed hat and the "pork-pie." Ethel, when a bridesmaid at Flora May's wedding, in the middle of winter, pleaded for "dark silks and straw bonnets," and even the frivolous Flora conceded that "the ordinary muslin garb" was unsuitable. The compromise (blue merino trimmed with swansdown) eventually satisfied Ethel, and she was allowed

a bonnet of a reasonable size, for Mr Rivers' good taste could endure, as little as Dr May's sense of propriety, the sight of a daughter without shade to her face.

And, from other remarks on "exposed" faces, one gathers that Miss Yonge agreed with these gentlemen.

Nothing is so subject to change of fashion and to suitability of occasion as headgear. Lucilla Sandbrook and her cousin had the misfortune to lose their luggage during their ill-advised journey to Ireland. They felt quite uncomfortable at going about Dublin in their travelling hats. Poor Lucilla was equally in trouble when she appeared looking startlingly stylish, while seeking a post as a governess. The chief unsuitability lay in

> an exquisite white rose, once worn in her hair and now enlivening the white ribbon and black lace of the cheap straw bonnet, far back upon the rippling hair turned back from her temples and falling in profuse ringlets.

We have seen how the hat (or bonnet) could never be dispensed with, but one might not otherwise have thought Lucilla's small black hat trimmed with mallards' tails the most suitable thing (on another occasion) for the river.

While the fashionable and frivolous Lucilla wears a hat, and her profuse flaxen tresses are "arranged in a cunning wilderness of plaits and natural ringlets," the more sober Phœbe Fulmort is choosing an outfit which consists of white muslin worked mantle, white bonnet with a tuft of lady-grass, white evening dress, and wreath of lilies of the valley. She had also insisted on a green *glacé* silk—"the true delicate pale tint of ocean, one that few complexions could have borne," but in virtue of her "fresh cheek" it is owned, even by the fastidious young gentleman who accompanies the shopping expedition, that she is right in her selection, and also in refusing a garniture of lilac. Presumably Phœbe's difficulty in finding the correct shade was partly due to the prevailing taste in the 'fifties for more violent colours, though Honora Charlecote at the same time succeeds in getting "a delicate lavender." Lucilla and her cousin are found following to the uttermost the masculine fashion of "tightly fitting black coats, plain linen collars and shirt-like under-sleeves, with black ties round the neck." To enliven this Lucilla's skirt is of a rich deep gentianella-coloured silk, and the buttons of her white vest of beautiful coral—a modish decoration, sometimes worn as bracelets to terminate the sleeves. This rather hard style does not suit the cousin, but enhances Lucilla's femininity, her

A Victorian Ball (1867)

By courtesy of "The Illustrated London News"

CHARLOTTE M. YONGE AT SEVENTY-FIVE
Reproduced, by courtesy of Messrs Macmillan and Co., Ltd., from
"Charlotte Mary Yonge," by Christabel Coleridge

fairness, and her taper waist. Lucilla, however, could go into flounces when she chose, and went to the length of having a ball dress entirely trimmed with fishing-flies, and hooks; this was done as a bet, and was a piece of gross extravagance for which she later had to pay dearly. She appeared on another occasion with "an azure gossamer-like texture surrounding her like a cloud, turquoises on her arms and blue and silver ribbons mingled with her blonde tresses." The "cloud" effect continued to be admired, and many years later we find Alda Underwood fashionably dressed in pink tulle, with earrings. But by this time there was evidently a choice between wearing drapery and having the neck and shoulders completely bare. The extreme *décolletage* to be found in pictures and illustrated papers during the middle of the century is rather remarkable in an age of prudery. One can only assume that it was not worn in Miss Yonge's own circle—as, indeed, a reference in *The Three Brides* would indicate. Rosamond Charnock comes from a noble Irish family, but evokes considerable censure by "an innocent following of what she has been brought up to," which, however, according to her mother-in-law, is "not a style of dress I could ever have worn nor have let my daughters have worn, if I had any." Rose is converted to decency by the admiration of a woman she particularly dislikes and "the repetition of some insolent praise." It may be noted that Rosamond in her ordinary day-dress is apt to be untidy, almost slovenly. Another heroine to whom dress is nothing but a trial is, of course, Ethel May, whose sartorial adventures are a worry to her from the first page, on which the gathers of her frock are torn out by her twelve-year-old brother. (Incidentally, nothing is said to *him*—Ethel merely has to mend "the unlucky frock.") Even in *The Trial* Blanche's wedding is made the occasion for putting Ethel "into a hoop" (and her father into a brougham) in the interests of respectability. The bitterest occasion is early in *The Daisy Chain*, when, full of anxiety to help her father, she meets him on the way home from a muddy walk, during which her brother has already shown his disapproval of her "draggle-tail petticoats and unfortunate skirt, its crape trimmings greatly bespattered with red mud." Dr May's rebuke is, for him, really fierce:

those muddy ankles and petticoats are not fit to be seen—there, now you are sweeping the pavement. Have you no medium?

R

One would think you had never worn a gown in your life before.

Flora was continually trying to mend Ethel's taste, and succeeded, at least, in turning her out properly for the visit to Oxford, even though Ethel had

> really got a new gown on purpose—a good useful silk, that papa chose at Whitford—just the colour of a copper tea-kettle where it turns purple.

But Flora had brought back from Paris (already by the 'fifties the the capital of fashion) mantles, ribbons, collars, bonnets, "all glistening with the French air of freshness and grace," and tastefully chosen with a view to the wearer. Before she knew where she was, Ethel found "that instrument of torture, a half-made body was being tried on her"—but she could not deny that the result was an improvement on her "white muslin, made high, black silk mantle and brown hat," which had "a scanty schoolgirl effect."

Hoops must have distressed Ethel, but they are well 'in' by the days of *The Trial*, which ends in the midst of the American Civil War. Averil Ward on her return from the fashionable school had "her petticoats reaching half across the room," and looked to Dr May "like a milliner's doll." He might, however, have been imbued with the prejudices of his profession, for there was no doubt that in illness, such as overtook the Ward family, the crinoline made one practically useless in the sick-room. Averil is continually knocking things over, and is eventually sent away "to rest." Helpless as she was by nature and training, her costume was likely to render her a positive hindrance.

> Her hair, still in its elaborate arrangement, hung loose, untidy, untouched; her collar and sleeves were soiled and tumbled; her dress, with its inconvenient machinery of inflation, looked wretched from its incongruity, and the stains on the huge hanging sleeves.

The "machinery" was subsequently unfastened from its hooks, "a mountain of mohair and scarlet petticoat remained on the floor, upborne by an over-grown steel mouse-trap," and poor Averil, relieved of her heavy, tight costume, was made comfortable in a dressing-gown—itself "quite a dress."

The hoop could be a danger as well as an inconvenience. Gertrude May is wearing one when they ascend the church tower, and though she compresses it sufficiently to get through the door, her small nephew's prophecy—"Aunt Daisy will sail away like a balloon"—is not far from being fulfilled, and frightful disaster almost occurs.

It is perhaps hardly surprising that the young ladies of the 'greenery-yallery' period revolted against these excesses of apparel, and turned to the arty costumes ridiculed in *Patience*. But Miss Yonge has scant sympathy with eccentricity in that direction either. Here is Janet Brownlow in a dress that she has "studied" from an old Italian costume:

> Janet was arrayed in a close fitting pale-blue dress, cut in semblance of an ancient kirtle, and with a huge chatelaine, from which massive chains dangled, not to say clattered—not merely the ordinary appendages of a young lady, but a pair of compasses, a safety inkstand and a microscope. Her dark hair was strained back from a face not calculated to bear exposure, and was wound round a silver arrow.

It is no wonder that she is greeted by her brother with: "Marry come up, mistress mine, good lack, nothing is lacking to thee save a pointed hood graceless!" and by other members of the family with equally uncomplimentary expressions.

It would seem that during the last twenty years of her life Miss Yonge somewhat outgrew her own interest in clothes—or perhaps she thought the styles less attractive. At any rate, full descriptions are less frequent. The last book in which dress seems to play a really important part is *The Pillars of the House*. Here not only the women's clothes, but the men's and even boys' garments, are often mentioned as part of the picture—and small wonder when we consider Edgar in his Bohemian days, "studying the picturesque in his own person." Even his brother was startled when he marched into the shop

> in Tyrolese hat, green knickerbockers, belt, knapsack, loose velvet coat, and fair moustache, and while the customers gazed in doubt between gamekeepers and stage banditti, holding out a hand too fair and dainty for either character. . . .

By contrast, the eldest brother, Felix, has something slightly clerical about his garb, though it is Clement, the priest, who is described (seated, rather incongruously, in the Old Squire's sporting-looking dog-cart of varnished wood) as "a long, black figure."

Not that the subject of men's dress was ignored in previous books, though there are not many long descriptions. They are clad, if anything, rather more typically than are their womenfolk, but even in those days, they could hardly compete in attractiveness. There is Humfrey Charlecote in his country clothes, "looking homely, though perfectly gentlemanlike" in his "mighty nailed shoes and long untanned buskins," his hands comfortably thrust into the pockets of his coat, and Arthur Martindale, "no unpicturesque figure in his loose brown coat." There is the chemist's nephew, Mr Augustus Mills, who gives a lecture at the Mechanics' Institute, wearing "a plaid velvet waistcoat in which scarlet was the predominant colour." And there is young Gilbert Kendal, whom his stepmother finds

> touching up his toilette at each glass and seriously consulting her and Sophy upon the choice between lilac and lemon-coloured gloves and upon the bows of his fringed neck-tie.

And, younger still, there is the schoolboy, Bernard, who makes such a fuss about wearing his brother's outgrown suits, even though his elder sister has been kind enough to remove for him the frill that had been obligatory for the former chorister.

Miss Yonge has a few general theories and prejudices—violent colours, for instance, are generally associated in her mind with vulgarity, and excesses of any kind are to be avoided: but, for the most part, the descriptions are of the individual "in habit as he lived"—and the garments are highly characteristic of their wearers. Indeed, sometimes they characterize the phases through which the wearers are passing—Angela Underwood wears an outrageous Tyrolean hat, with long feather, when she is at her most temperamental, and Wilmet's outfit—the pale fawn-coloured skirt, loose open jacket, and white vest—has been enlivened with "dainty fresh knots of rose-coloured ribbon at the throat and down the front" when she is being courted. There is also the problem of clothes and convention, for some of the most formidable of Victorian conventions were connected, as such conventions have been in every age, with dress.

We have seen how the exposed countenance and the bared shoulders were looked at askance in Miss Yonge's circle; also how, as was true to a much later date, a lady leaving her house must always be fully equipped with hat and gloves, even for a walk

hrough the fields at 6.30 A.M. A parasol was also a desirable
sset. (But she should not be burdened with anything that could
be of *use*: says Lucy to her stepmother, "It looks *so* to carry a
basket.") The age of decorum for young ladies began very
arly, and Felix is scandalized at the thirteen-year-old Gertrude
May's having taken off her shoes and stockings to walk over the
ocks, and averts his eyes from her ankles. As for the outline of
he human figure, which so generally forms a part of the descrip-
ion in a modern novel, it is simply ignored by Miss Yonge. There
s hardly a mention of words and phrases such as 'curves,'
boyish slimness,' so commonly used by writers a few years ago.
She does, however, describe some one as having "a dove-like
orm," while another has a figure of the "plump partridge
order."

The suitability of a garb to its proper occasion is touched on by
Charlotte Yonge with delicate irony—it is at overdressing rather
than at genteel poverty that she gently points a finger, though
she does not admire a frump or a sloven. Selina (Lady Marchmont) belongs to a circle far more *élite* than that of Marian's
guardians, Mr Lyddell (a county member) and his wife. Yet she
always dresses with great taste, and her clothes can be quite
simple on suitable occasions. She dislikes the ultra-fashionable
clothes of Caroline Lyddell, the daughter, and she laughs at
Mrs Lyddell for having insisted that Marian must buy a new
bonnet to go with Selina to a flower-show.

But, in whatever grade of society, there was one convention
with regard to clothes which was always observed—mourning.
A funeral was an occasion for a sea of black. When Mrs May
died, the two Margarets (the baby and the invalid) were "the
only white things in the house," and months later Meta Rivers
recognizes the family when she meets "four girls and their
governess" in deep mourning when they are out walking. Even
little Kate Caergwent has to wear black braid for the relative
(never seen) through whose death she becomes a countess, and,
as we have shown, Amy Morville intends to wear mourning for
Guy all her life, though she removes her weeds (veil?) at her
cousin's wedding.

Miss Yonge's characters sometimes illustrate the convention
that women left the actual attendance at funerals to their male
relatives. As a rule, however, they make rather a point of going.

Dr May particularly says, "I should wish you all to be there," and Henrietta Langford goes to her mother's, while her brother is still too ill to attend. Marilda Underwood rides to her father's funeral in the foremost carriage, supported by her adopted sister and brother, and a point of precedence arises when a less intimate relative tries to forestall Felix Underwood, whom she desires to accompany her. The widow, however, is not present on this occasion, and the implication is that Marilda is here taking the place of a son, as she does in other respects. (Marilda even took to going daily to the City and carrying on her father's business years before such a career for women was thought of.) Much has been made of the respect paid to funerals in Victorian times, and there is certainly plenty of opportunity in Miss Yonge's books for display of emotion, but there is little sentimentality (except perhaps over the "backward"—that is, "deficient"—Theodore) and not a disproportionate amount of gloom on these important occasions.

Illness, as well as death, played a vastly important part in the lives of Victorian families, and is described by Miss Yonge as accompanied by a quite incredible series of symptoms. Perhaps this was because, until the last illness of her mother, Charlotte had had practically nothing to do with nursing. If so, she certainly made up in imagination for what she lacked in knowledge. The most frequent signs are "spasms"—first displayed in the person of Mrs Frederick Langford, mother of Frederick and Henrietta. This lady suffered from a serious complaint, which could not be *reached*, but which produced "uncomfortable fits of palpitations," thinness, and "a beautiful pink bloom," and which came on in increasingly violent attacks. Her son's symptoms, after he has been thrown out of a carriage, are even more remarkable. There was no fracture, we are told, so presumably he was suffering from concussion or merely shock, but he felt considerable pain, and he suffered from a relapse when he succumbed to eating, at his grandmother's suggestion (but contrary to the doctor's orders), "a tempting glass of amber-coloured jelly." It caused the inflammation to return and his pulse to quicken prodigiously, so that leeches had to be applied, and these saved his life, though he was left prostrate for weeks. To the end of her days, Charlotte seems to have been uncertain of her ground in describing illness: Clement, after overworking for years in a city parish, suffered from a breakdown during which "a long low lingering fever had attacked every organ in turn," until he was removed to his sister's "pretty home at Brompton."

Most of Charlotte's books can boast at least one permanent invalid; indeed, invalidism might quite be considered as one of the professions. It was open to both sexes, but as a rule the candidate was feminine. It is remarkable how often, and how cheerfully, a female member of the family may be said to enjoy ill-health all her life. She lies on a sofa, and this couch becomes a centre of family life, in a way more heavily emphasized by the American author of *What Katy Did*. One can, of course, compare the historical existence of Elizabeth Barrett. Margaret May is early incapacitated by a carriage accident, from the effects of which she eventually dies, but an interesting point is that by the end of the chronicle her sofa has been, as it were, bequeathed to Averil, wife of the doctor son, Tom. Averil was worth studying as a patient, for when Tom went to fetch her home from America, producing her as "the veiled muffled figure of his bride," in hat, cloak, muff, and respirator, she had been suffering from a variety of diseases. Her little sister had died of fever, and since that time she herself had been subject to

> distressing attacks of gasping and rigidity, often passing into faintness; and though at the moment of emotion she often showed composure and self-command, yet nature always thus revenged herself.

In addition, she had ague and pleurisy, and she had only recovered from this "to a certain point, but there had stopped short, often suffering pain in the side and never without panting breath and recurring cough." In moments of agitation she was still liable to utter a hoarse, hysterical cry and to become a "stiffened figure on a couch—the eyes wide open, the limbs straight and rigid" and suffering from "a terrible access, of that most distressing kind that stimulates convulsion."

Yet on Averil's return to England Dr May was happy to find that there were indications that the organic disease was in the way of being arrested, and sofa life, with a good deal of nursing, became her portion—for Miss Yonge's invalids, unlike Mrs Browning, did not as a rule recover beyond a certain stage. Other examples include Ermine Williams, who writes articles under a pseudonym and is really a "clever woman," her modestly concealed knowledge being opposed to Rachel's shallow display of learning. She has met with an accident by fire some years before the beginning of the story and suffers patiently without recovering very far, even by the end of the book. But by this time her mental superiority has been recognized, and she has, not without some hesitation, become the wife of her early admirer.

For, by way of compensation, a female invalid *always* has a faithful admirer. There are, besides Ermine and Colin Keith, Margaret May and her sailor, Alan Earnescliffe, Averil and Tom, and even Geraldine Underwood and her elderly sculptor, Mr Grinstead. Cherry, however, is only half an invalid, for though she begins by lying on a sofa, and is unduly sensitive and gives way to hysterical fits, yet, after a stay at the convent has emboldened her to have her foot amputated, she walks about very gallantly with a stick, and she survives to the end of the saga, apparently in the best of health. Perhaps illness became less attractive as Miss Yonge, and the century, grew older.

It was pretty generally established—as a literary convention, at any rate—that weak health and timidity in women were attractive to the Victorian male. These afflictions, however, probably grew up out of the emptiness of the lives of girls and women among the newly well-to-do classes. They had been deprived of most of their normal occupations by the conventions which delegated to servants the tasks about which they themselves and their mothers used to be busy, and they had become a prey to imaginary fears about their own health and the outer world, concerning both of which they were extremely ignorant. But the majority of Miss Yonge's characters are well occupied both mentally and physically, and (apart from accidents, mortality among mothers of families, and occasional bouts of "brain-fever") there is not an undue proportion of ill-health among her people. They faint or become hysterical more frequently than is the case in these days, though generally (in the later books at least) not without fairly reasonable cause. Mary May is overcome by the heat of the unventilated room in which she is teaching; Kate Caergwent even when grown up is completely upset by a thunderstorm; Norman May cannot make himself go past the scene of his mother's accident; and Gerald Underwood, who as a child has nearly been scalped by Indians, dies of overwork on a newspaper in America. Much of the feminine ill-health was certainly due

the unreasonable clothing, which Miss Yonge and her contemporaries took as a matter of course. Up to the end of the
century it was, for instance, common at school for girls to faint
during a singing-class because of their tight stays. But as a rule
their ways of life were so peaceful and the pursuits of Victorian
womanhood so moderated that it was perhaps natural that an
unaccustomed exertion or mental strain should bring on some
physical reaction.

Something has been said of the Victorian family pursuits as
far as these included literature and the arts, but, even in the lives
of "the ladies," sport had also its part. As a rule, Miss Yonge does
not permit her more admirable heroines to share in any pastime
which involved the taking of life, though, of course, this does not
apply to heroes. Shooting parties are taken as a matter of course
in the country houses, and Charlotte perfectly enters into,
though she does not share, the feelings of George Rivers when
Norman answers that he does not shoot, and of young Bernard
Underwood when his brother Clement is hesitating about accepting the family living: "O Clem, you'd never be so viciously spiteful as not to come. Think of the rabbits and salmon and a licence
by and by!"

She realizes, too, the controversy over preserving, though one
can see with which side she sympathizes. The following is from
Magnum Bonum:

Like other ladies, she could never understand exaggerated
preserving, nor why men who loved sport should care to have
game multiplied and farmed so as apparently to spoil all the zest
of the chase; but she had let Allen and his uncle do whatever they
told her was right by the preserves, except shutting up the park
and all the footpaths. Colonel Brownlow, whose sporting instincts
were those of a former generation, was quite satisfied; Allen never
would be so, and it was one of the few bones of contention in the
family.

One must not forget the fishing episode which takes Lucilla
and her cousin Horatia to Ireland. But it is the fact that they go
unprotected which causes the journey to be frowned on, not the
sport itself, though Miss Yonge makes us feel that in some subtle
way the two are connected. In the same way she does not really
approve of women hunting, though they may ride to the meet:

The ladies mustered strong on the smooth turf of the chalk down bordering the copse which was being drawn . . . the field were well away over the down, the carriages driving off, the mounted maiden following the chase as far as the path was fair and ladylike.

Of riding as exercise she is in favour. Guy Morville display considerable skill in horsemanship, and the virtuous, not to say priggish, Marian is introduced for the first time on horseback wearing, incidentally,

a long black and white plaid riding skirt, over a pink gingham frock and her dark hair hidden beneath a little cap furnished with a long green veil, which was allowed to stream behind her in the wind instead of affording the intended shelter to a complexion already a shade or two darkened by the summer sun.

Her cousin Edmund, who is also her guardian, insists that, even when she is being turned into a young lady, she shall be allowed to ride, "guessing that her want of spirits might very probably arise from want of the air and freedom to which she had always been accustomed."

Another pursuit to which Miss Yonge raises no objection is skating, which takes place in several books. But in the middle of the century it is still viewed askance by old Mrs Langford, who could not bear to hear of anything so boyish, and had long ago entreated Beatrice to be more like a young lady. It is rather curious that her granddaughters, Beatrice and Henrietta, who enjoy skating, do not hold such liberal views about dancing, and are a bit shocked when another (not so ladylike) cousin responds to the invitation of a sailor home on leave: "I'll show you how we waltz with the Brazilian ladies."

If the practice of waltzing was not to be admired, there was something which was very nice in the perfect good humour with which Jessie answered her cousin's summons without the slightest sign of annoyance at his evident preference of Henrietta's newer face.

"If I can't waltz, I can play for you," said Henrietta, but she was "perfectly shocked and amazed" all the same. It is perhaps unnecessary to add that Grandmamma will have no waltzes or polkas at her party, and says the young must be content with country dances and quadrilles. Evidently to Miss Yonge it is on the type and circumstances of the dance that her approval depends. We have already seen that by the end of the century it is "skirt dancing"—not allowed even at a charity bazaar—that meets with censure. It is not the pursuit of dancing itself. One may fancy, however, a touch of Charlotte in Emma Brandon (*Heartsease*), who hated dancing—"above all, there was the nuisance of dressing"—though she was prepared to accept Violet's defence—that she liked it, and "my mother does not think it foolish."

It seems as if the middle of the century must have marked the turning-point at which round dances became acceptable even to the more circumspect. In *The Castle Builders*, which deals with the eighteen-forties, it is one of the signs of Emmeline's unsatisfactory state of mind that, though she went to her first dance as "resolute against waltzes and polkas" as her sister Kate, she is carried away by excitement and succumbs. This leads to a conversation on the merits of round dances with Lady Frances Somerville, who tells how her dead sister Anne had loved to waltz madly round the room at home with her brother Herbert, but would not have dreamed of indulging in such a pastime in public. By the time we come to the early 'sixties the propriety of polkas appears to be no longer in doubt. Ethel May enjoys a breathless dance with Harry, though the younger brother, Aubrey, is not so successful at steering her round, and even the serious-minded Rachel Curtis looks on indulgently at Bessie Keith's success in the ballroom, though when asked by Alick to dance, she confesses that polkas are against, not her "theory," but her "practice." By the eighteen-eighties waltzing is not taboo even at a G.F.S. party, where "Cousin Rotherwood" tries to cheer up his young cousin Dolores by dancing with her.

Among the prettiest of social sports must have been archery. Right up to the end of the century (if we are to trust Kipling) it held its sway among the fashionable, and even now it survives as a rather self-consciously old-time pursuit. But when Arthur Martindale brought home his unsophisticated bride, one of the first things he did was to ask his sister Theodora for "the light bow you used to shoot with." (Another was to give Violet riding lessons on the old pony.) One of the fullest descriptions of this sport is also in an early book, *The Two Guardians*. At the *fête* given by the fashionable Mrs Faulkener at High Down there was to be archery in the morning and a ball in the evening, and much trouble and expense went to the making of the costumes for both.

It was to be a Kenilworth fête; eight young ladies of Lady Julia's especial party were to appear in the morning in a pretty uniform dress, a little subdued from the days of the ruff and farthingale [that is, "a white skirt and green polka . . . and a little ruff"]; and in the evening there was to be a regular Kenilworth quadrille, in which each lady or gentleman was to assume the dress of some character of Queen Elizabeth's court.

Sport, then, contributed to a large extent to the lives of people in Miss Yonge's stratum of society, young and old, male and female. Grandfather Langford says, "I have hunted rats once or twice a year now these seventy years or more and I can't say I am tired yet," and his granddaughter complains that town people can never understand "that hunting spirit of mankind," and hates above all things to hear it cried down, and "the nonsense that is talked about it." Miss Yonge does not exclude even her heroines from simple games. Marian joins in a game of cricket with her younger brother and the other little boys as soon as she has ascertained that none of the big ones are playing, while at the end of the century, tennis has found its place in Miss Yonge's books, as well as in Cheltenham Ladies' College. Even croquet—evidently regarded as a 'fast' form of sport in the 'sixties—is not really disapproved, but Miss Yonge is suspicious of it because it lends itself (one can hardly imagine how!) to the evils of flirtation. One would think that mere walking was even more liable to this disadvantage, and certainly the mention of this pastime brings us to the most complex of all conventions of female respectability—the question of the escort.

It is no exaggeration to say that Society up to the end of the nineteenth century seriously took it for granted that no young woman could go out either alone or with a man (unless in special circumstances) without some harm coming of it. The position is put by Miss Yonge when she is moralizing on the situation into which Lucilla has placed herself when she is being followed by an ill-bred admirer:

> She had proved the truth of Honora's warning, that beyond the pale of ordinary *convenances*, a woman is exposed to insult, and however sufficient she may be for her own protection, the very fact of having to defend herself is well-nigh degrading.

To prevent a woman from falling into this degradation the most thorough precautionary measures were necessary. Margaret

May, aged eighteen, withdraws from the family walk when her sister Ethel (aged fifteen, and therefore still in the schoolroom) tactlessly asks their young male visitor to accompany them, and this even though the governess is to be present. At this display of modesty, her mother is compelled to admit that "Margaret has behaved very well," and it is no wonder that Margaret herself murmurs to her infant sister, "Oh! lucky baby to have so many years to come before you are plagued with tiresome propriety!"

"Tiresome propriety" is discovered at an even earlier age in Mrs Lyddell's household. Clara and Marian are asked why they are staying in the garden, instead of going for a walk, and explain that they are waiting for Mr Arundel, Marian's cousin and guardian. "I think," said Mrs Lyddell, "that as I am going out, it is not quite *the thing* for you young ladies to wait to receive a gentleman in my absence." Marian thinks Mrs Lyddell's interference "a needless piece of unkindness" towards herself, for "at home she would have thought it strange not to hasten to greet cousin Edmund," but she acknowledges that, as far as Clara is concerned, Mrs Lyddell is right.

The elderly continued to respect the convention right up to the 'nineties:

> Miss Hackett would not be persuaded not to see [Dolores] to the door of Miss Vincent's lodgings, though lengthening her own walk alone, a thing more terrible to her old-fashioned mind than to that of her companion.

So well established was the rule of escort that one has to assume it even where it is to be observed only by implication. Theodora goes in a carriage to call on her friend, Mrs Finch, and prefers to walk back. This must have entailed the services of a maid. (We know that one of the objections to afternoon school at a Ladies' College was that parents could not afford to send their servants on *four* journeys a day, nor spare time for these themselves.) It is incredible that she should have walked alone, for even when she goes *with* Mrs Finch to a lecture on Mesmerism, and subsequently to another on electricity, unaccompanied by her brother, these adventures incur her father's censure as being "independent proceedings." Marriage, however, completely changed the situation, for her sister-in-law, though younger than Theodora herself, is considered a sufficient chaperon to escort her to an evening party, and when Violet is not well enough to go Theodora arranges to be called for by Mrs Finch.

The exceptions to the rules for chaperonage seem almost as unreasonable as the regulations themselves. Once married, for instance, a man, unaccountably, ceased to be in the least dangerous. For example, Henry Ward insisted that he would not have his sister going to choir practice after dark,

> but she was fortified by the curate's promise to escort her safely. . . . The existence of that meek little helpless Mrs Scudamour, always shut up in a warm room with her delicate baby, cut off Henry from any other possible objection, and he was obliged to submit.

Moreover (as in the East, with girls under marriageable age) the conventions did not hold until the young lady was 'out.' We have seen that Ethel May was not hampered by Alan Earnscliffe's presence on the walk, as was her sister, being three years older—"and it is no matter for the others," was the mother's comment. Ethel could even spend an hour with him at "amateur navigation" (which included logarithms), and, though her choice of occupation was regarded as odd and not very ladylike, no one made any objection on grounds of propriety. (The family only objected to her wearing spectacles, on the theory that it would make her even more short-sighted and ungainly than she already was.) However, to be on the safe side, Phœbe Fulmort tries to keep herself and her sisters in the schoolroom wing of the house, and they do not come down to dinner when their brother's friends are staying, so they are uncontaminated by pernicious influences, until Bertha, at fifteen, decides she is grown up, and starts a clandestine correspondence with a young man, which almost immediately leads to an attempt at elopement.

As a compensation for such an early arrival at years of indiscretion it was possible to pass out of the dangerous period at what we should consider a remarkably early age. Rachel Curtis at twenty-five considers that she may dispense with a chaperon both within doors and without. "Rachel's age was quite past the need of troubling herself at being left alone *tête à tête* with a mere lad like this."

But this is irony, for the "lad" turns out to be really her senior by a year. She is likewise deceived by the embezzling sharper, who first poses as an artist, and is sketching within full view of the windows, and she tells her mother that she is going to ask the price of his sketch.

"Perhaps, but I don't know, my dear. Won't it be odd? Had you not better wait till Grace comes in or till I can come down with you?"

"No need at all, mother, I can do it much better alone, and at my age . . ."

Of course, brotherhood, and, in Miss Yonge's eyes, cousinhood as a rule, set matters on a completely different footing. So much is allowed to members of the same family that the Mays are continually going in and out of one another's rooms, and Harry goes in to see his sister in bed without the slightest hint of lack of decorum. So, as we have seen, Honor and Humfrey Charlecote, being cousins, take long walks together which are not regarded as indiscreet.

Exemption from the trammels was allowed for a few other causes. A perfectly virtuous young woman belonging to a somewhat lower class than Miss Yonge's own might be allowed far more freedom than 'a lady.' Edna Murrell, the schoolmistress, lives in a house by herself—a measure that could not have been contemplated by, for instance, the heiress Miss Charlecote, who would need the chaperonage of a maid, quite apart from her services.

Another reason for freedom from convention is found in *The Trial*. Charlotte draws with considerable admiration, the portrait of Cora, a young American:

A beautiful, motherless girl, under seventeen, left to all intents and purposes, alone in New York, attending a great educational establishment, far more independent and irresponsible than a young man at an English University, yet perfectly trustworthy—never subject to the *bevues* of the "unprotected female"; but self-reliant, modest and graceful in the heterogeneous society of the boarding-house, she was a constant marvel to Averil.

And finally there are signs in her latest book of all that Miss Yonge was beginning to adopt what the twentieth century would consider a more reasonable attitude to the question of allowing young people to go about together without inevitably assuming 'the worst.' Vera and Hubert (aged seventeen and twenty-three respectively) are swept out to sea in a boat, and picked up next day by Lord Rotherwood and his yacht. Here is his conversation about them with his daughter:

"Don't let that poor lad and the girl get together alone, Fly; the boy thinks he is bound to make her an offer."

"Oh, father! Surely not!"

"No more than if they had been two babies in a walnut shell. So I told him, but people don't see what infants they are themselves, and I want to hinder him from putting his foot in it before he has seen her aunt. . . ."

"You don't think him like Stephen in the *Mill on the Floss* who ought to have married Maggie Tulliver?"

"I believe that is his precedent—but it is sheer stuff."

Charlotte herself seems uncertain how far to trust her own judgment. There is more than one conversation on the theme. "It is difficult to know where old-fashioned distaste is the motive and where the real principle of modesty." Here are the two sides of herself, as it were, arguing the question of 'advanced' behaviour:

"It is worse and more changeable in this latter century than in any other. Does the world go round faster?"

"Of course it does," said Geraldine. "Think how many fashions, how many styles, how many ways of thinking, have passed away, even in our own time."

"And what have they left behind them?"

"Something good, I trust. Coral cells, stones for the next generation of zoophytes to stand upon to reach up higher."

"Is it higher?"

"In one sense, I hope. . . . But practically and unpoetically, perhaps—how the young folk mount upon all our little achievements in Church matters, and think them nearly as old-fashioned and despicable as we did pews and black gowns! Or how attempts like the schools that brought up Robina and Angela have shot out into High Schools, colleges, professions and I know not what besides."

There in both its point of view and its choice of metaphor, speaks the 'progressive' nineteenth century.

Convention was so all-embracing a law that it included the smallest details as well as the most important actions in life. You broke it, as we have seen, by 'going into trade' or, if you were a woman, by allowing yourself to be thought 'clever'—but you

broke it also by singing along the lane as you returned late from
an expedition, or by using a Christian name before you had
arrived at the right degree of familiarity with its owner. In fact,
this use of Christian names was a most delicate matter. The May
family were on very friendly terms with Meta Rivers before they
added her by name to their collection of Daisies, and even then
they agreed that it would have been most ill-bred to refer to her
in conversation with other people as anything but Miss Rivers.
Between men and women the convention was even more severe;
nomenclature was, in fact, a kind of barometer for gauging the
affections. When Norman and Ethel are discussing the possibility of a love-affair between Margaret May and Alan, Norman
brings up the point that the latter referred always to "your
sister" or used some other circumlocution instead of calling her
"Miss May." But he did not venture on "Margaret" till much
later. Robert Fulmort is deeply shocked to hear men at his club
making free with the names of his beloved, Lucilla, and her
cousin Horatia, as "Cilly Sandbrook and Rache Charteris."
Possibly Miss Yonge thought that the higher the circle the stiffer
the convention, for the Hon. Arthur refers to his wife as "Mrs
Martindale" even when speaking of her to his own sister.

As for the use of indecorous words in general, one must surmise
from her books that Charlotte would have felt like Cousin Hebe
in *H.M.S. Pinafore*:

> Did you hear him—did you hear him?
>   Oh, the monster overbearing!
> Don't go near him—don't go near him—
>   He is swearing—he is swearing.

Such an unprecedented breach of the *convenances* can never (or
'hardly ever') have taken place before her. Bad language is
referred to, but simply does not appear. Even slang is generally
commented on with some self-consciousness, and it is interesting
to note what words, at different periods, are regarded as unconventional or schoolboyish (and therefore not quite suitable for young
ladies). Here are two examples from *Henrietta's Wish* (1850):

"It is very——"
"Aggravating," said Henrietta, supplying one of the numerous
stock of family slang words.

.   .   .   .   .

S

"It would be absolute sneaking (to use an elegant word) I
suppose, to go down the back stairs?"

Countess Kate (1862) is reproved for using "jolly," and later
in the century Miss Yonge makes her younger characters offend
similarly:

"There is to be a sale of work, a concert and all sorts of jolly
larks."
"Larks! Oh Val!"
"You don't mean to ask him?"
"Catch me!"
"Slang! A forfeit."

She also makes use occasionally of dialect words, but arranges
that they should be explained, as if to a Londoner. 'Leasing,'
for 'gleaning,' has to be explained to Miss Fosbrook, and Mrs
Carbonel is told that a small girl is "*that* terrifying and contrary
that she would not go to school," and is made to realize that
'terrifying' is the local word for 'tiresome' or 'tormenting.'

Charlotte was sufficiently imbued with the spirit of her age to
make her selection of words 'nice' in every sense. Occasionally
this prevents her saying what she means in simple fashion—for
instance, "since the baby was weaned" becomes "since Flora's
many avocations had caused her to be set aside." But as a rule
her common sense and her facility of expression keep her from
being ponderous.

Victorian decorum and the matter of speech has become a byword, like the Victorian Sunday. Miss Yonge does not give the
impression of a lugubrious Sabbath, and, though a good deal of
churchgoing is mentioned, it is a delight rather than a duty to
those who indulge in it. The Brownlows, when in London
during the 'seventies, went to any church they chose in the morning. In the afternoon only the more pious members of the family
went. The rest spent the time in talking with friends who
dropped in. But even in her unregenerate period Carey was
shocked when Bobus spent a Sunday taking a German infidel
friend to see the flowers at Belforest, although they got out at a
country station to avoid "scandalizing the natives." One of
Arthur Martindale's more sympathetic remarks to Violet, when
she finds time hanging rather heavy on a wet Sunday is, "To be
sure, you can't smoke a cigar," from which we may gather how

the male spent *his* Sunday afternoon. By way of compensation, he takes his wife on an "acquatic excursion" to afternoon service.

As far as Miss Yonge was concerned, the two principles by which life should be guided (negative both) were, "It must not be unsuitable for a woman," and "It must not be too pleasant." Two final incidents may be taken to illustrate the dangers of not being bound by these rules. Mrs Duncombe has made a proposal at a public meeting.

"She should have got her husband to speak for her," said Mrs Poynsett.

"He was not there."

"Then she should have instructed some other gentleman," said Mrs Poynsett. "A woman spoils all the effects of her doings by putting herself out of her proper place."

Lady Temple, a widow of five-and-twenty, has received two proposals.

"Please will you tell me how I could have been more guarded? I can't talk about it and I would not have them know that Sir Stephen's wife cannot get his memory more respected."

"I don't think anyone could answer," he said.

"I did take my aunt's advice about the officers being here. I have not had them nearly as much as Bessie would have liked, not even Alick. I have been sorry it was so dull for her, but I thought it could not be wrong to be intimate with one's clergyman, and Rachel was always so hard on him."

"You did nothing but what was kind and right. The only possible thing that could have been wished otherwise was making a regular habit of his playing croquet here."

"Ah! but the boys and Bessie liked it so much. However, I dare say it was wrong!"

"*Out of her proper place*" and "*I dare say it was wrong.*" With these as keynotes let us turn for a moment to Charlotte's own views on life in general and on women in particular.

s*

BOOK SEVEN

MISS YONGE:
HER WORKS AND VIEWS

CHAPTER XVI

A VICTORIAN AUTHOR PASSES

CHARLOTTE YONGE'S work, though many of its characteristics provoke comparison with Jane Austen's, is neither so finished as her predecessor's nor, be it added, so limited in outlook. Yet limited it is, in so far as she is writing of her own day, both because of the small section of society from which she draws her material, and also, perhaps consequently, because certain types and situations are liable to recur quite recognizably. (This, however, is hardly surprising, considering the immense number of stories she wrote.) One such *motif*, for example, is the appearance of the child of a 'black sheep' brother; such a recurring character, as we have noticed, is the elderly, rather dry male—he can hardly be called a hero—who may have been drawn from Mr Bigg-Wither.

Just as the same section of society is worked on over and over again, so certain few principles strongly held tend to emerge constantly, and it is clear that Charlotte deliberately produces situations calculated to provoke discussion on, or opportunity for presenting, these principles.

One of the questions which constantly arises concerns the position of women. This is not surprising, for an outstanding phenomenon of the nineteenth century is the rise, during the latter half of it, in the status of the middle-class woman. (Equally important, of course, is the rise economically, educationally, and politically of the 'working-class man'—the two causes were often linked together and found the same champions—but from the nature of Miss Yonge's material the second phenomenon, though

277

not omitted, is not much in evidence.) Charlotte accepted—may be said to have swallowed in its entirety—the doctrine that woman is inferior to man, in mind, body, and will-power. It was not within her belief to allow that *differentiation* might exist between the sexes without *inequality*; with her the subjection of woman was a matter of faith, for it was directly due to the Fall, and was based on a literal interpretation of words in the book of Genesis. At the beginning of her career as an author, and again later, in her prime, she devoted, in effect, a whole book to this theme. *Henrietta's Wish* (of which the sub-title is *Domineering*) is a tale to prove that, as she puts it, "it is better for womankind to have leadable spirits than leading."

It is not only in the blame she accords to the heroine for her domineering spirit that Miss Yonge shows her views, but in accepting the standard shown in such a remark as "but then, boys are always so much more precious than girls." This is put into the mouth of Henrietta herself as a comment on her mother's extreme nervousness where her twin brother, Frederick, was concerned. Perhaps Charlotte was faintly aware of the unfairness of such a position, for she remarks that "the melancholy fact is that the devotion of womankind is usually taken as a matter of course . . ." No doubt the devotion of his womankind was entirely a matter of course to Mr Yonge, senior, and probably to Julian as well.

A far deeper study of the question is found in *The Clever Woman of the Family*, of which, perhaps, the following may be considered a fair summary:

> After all, unwilling as she would have been to own it, a woman's tone of thought is commonly moulded by the masculine intellect which, under one form or another, becomes the master of her soul. Those opinions once made her own, may be acted and improved upon, often carried to lengths never thought of by their inspirer, or held with noble constancy and perseverance even when he himself may have fallen from them, but from some living medium they are almost always adopted, and thus happily for herself, a woman's efforts at scepticism are but blind faith in her chosen leader, or, at the utmost, in the spirit of the age. And Rachel, having been more than usually removed from the immediate influence of superior man, had been affected by the more feeble and distant power, but it was not in the nature of things that, from

her husband and his uncle, her character should not receive that tincture for which it had so long waited, strong and thorough in proportion to her nature.

In two fields especially, education and what came to be called social work, or reform, Miss Yonge is most anxious to keep a woman in her proper place. We have seen how ill looked on was Mrs Duncombe for making a very sensible proposal about public hygiene at an open meeting. Far more disastrous is the downfall of Rachel Curtis when she attempts to do something out of her sphere to alleviate the condition of poor lacemaking girls. She might have been warned of her incapacity by the irony of her husband-to-be, who pointed out to her what the initials of the Female Union of Lacemakers Employment would spell—in Scots. But she continues with her plans, and arranges for some little girls to be put into the charge and employment of a couple who, it is later found, starve and ill-treat them, and from whom the children are only rescued by the efforts of the young woman whose femininity and gentleness Rachel has always despised. Moreover, Rachel has entrusted the funds collected for the girls to a plausible rascal who is finally had up for embezzling them, but cannot be convicted because of the foolishness of her dealings with him. Here is the account of the trial:

> She was examined upon her arrangement with the prisoner and on her monthly payment to him of the sums entered in the account book. In some cases she knew he had shown her the bills unreceipted; in others he had simply made the charge in the book and she had given him the amount that he estimated as requisite for the materials of wood-engraving. . . . The prisoner, acting as his own counsel, asked whether she could refer to any written agreement.
>
> "No, it was a viva voce agreement."
>
> Could she mention what passed at the time of making the arrangement that she had stated as existing between himself and her?
>
> "I described my plans and you consented."
>
> An answer at which some of her audience could have smiled, so well did it accord with her habits. . . . Pressed to define further . . .
>
> "I do not remember the exact words, but you acquiesced in the appearance of your name as Secretary and Treasurer. . . ."
>
> It of course came out that she had been her own treasurer, only entrusting the nominal one with the amount required for current expenses, and she was obliged to acknowledge that he had never in

so many words declared the sums entered to have been actually paid and not merely estimates for monthly expenditure to be paid to the tradesman at the usual seasons.

"I understood they were paid," said Rachel with some resentment.

"Will you oblige me by mentioning on what that understanding was founded?" said the prisoner, blandly.

There was a pause. Rachel knew she must say something but memory utterly failed to recall any definite assurance that those debts had been discharged. . . . And though perfectly conscious of the weakness and folly of her utterance, she could only falter forth: "I thought so."

As to education, the consequences of a woman's taking too much upon herself are quite as unfortunate for Rachel—or rather for her favourite schoolchild, whom she kills by trying to cure diphtheria by homœopathic methods derived from a book. In a lesser way her attempts at classical learning are made to appear as futile.

(After her marriage Rachel discovers that her husband, Captain Alick Keith, can read Hebrew, and characterizes her own knowledge of the subject as "enough to appreciate the disputed passages.") She asks:

"When did you study it?"

"I learnt enough, when I was laid up, to look out my uncle's texts for him."

She felt a little abashed by the tone, but a message called him away, and before his return, Mr Clare came back to ask for a reference in St Augustine. On her offer of her services, she was thanked, and directed with great precision to the right volume of the Library of the Fathers . . . (in translation) . . . but spying a real St Augustine, she could not be satisfied without a flight at the original. It was not, however, easy to find the place; she was forced to account for her delay by confessing her attempt and then to profit by Mr Clare's directions; and after all, her false quantities, though most tenderly and apologetically corrected, must have been dreadful to the scholarly ear, for she was obliged to get Alick to read the passage over to him before he arrived at the sense. . . . It was quite new to her to be living with people who knew more of and went deeper into, everything than she did.

We have already quoted the dreadful tale of Miss Fennimore, the governess whose attempt to force her pupils into learning beyond what was good for them had killed one and driven another to an elopement, brain-fever, and Rationalism. Perhaps, however, one has most sympathy with Ethel May—though not necessarily because she had to relegate her Hebrew grammar "to the shelf of the seldom-used." But, having worked neck and neck with the brother a year her senior who is now in the top form at school, she finds that, what with household and schoolroom tasks and her teaching at Cocksmoor, she is unable to keep up with him, and is informed, "We all know that men have more power than women." Girls, she is told, ought "to wait patiently . . . and not to be eager for self-imposed duties." The phrase about waiting sounds dangerously related to the complaint of one pioneer in the educational movement: "Girls . . . are not educated to be wives, but to get husbands," though Miss Yonge would have been the first to disclaim any such intention. A certain type of education was desirable; the husband would come in God's (or the novelist's) good time. For, though they may not pursue any branch of solid learning too far, her heroines, as we have seen, are expected to (and do) attain a high standard of general culture. And even on moral questions, where their decisions are least to be trusted, there is a great deal of argument and introspection, of which Miss Yonge highly approves. She entirely condemns the attitude of "it saves one the trouble and perplexity of thinking for oneself," which might have been regarded as the compensation for having eventually to acquiesce in the views of the nearest, or most oppressive, male relative. One had to think for oneself, and then (like Rachel) learn how much better and deeper were one's husband's ideas. On Miss Yonge's theory, evidently, women were entitled to all the kicks and none of the ha'pence.

Charlotte's second principle, briefly stated, was, "if it is too nice, it is wrong." She would have disliked to be called Puritanical, and would hardly have appreciated 'ascetic'—indeed, we have seen how, in later life, she condemned mortification for mortification's sake. But the principle of self-discipline, inculcated by her upbringing, ran through her whole existence, as it did through the lives of thousands of her generation. It was no mere lip-service that was paid to this principle, and Ruskin had hard work to persuade the schoolgirls in *Ethics of the Dust* that suffering and sacrifice are not *in themselves* good things. We can be sure that Charlotte herself would have acted like her heroine, when Marian (*The Two Guardians*), told that she may decide for herself whether to have a tooth out or not, determines to suffer at the dentist's hands without, as far as one can see, any real necessity. Her motive is explained—probably more crudely than it would have been in a later book:

"Do you mean to say that not liking a thing makes it right?"
"Very often . . . self-denial is always best, and in a doubtful case the most disagreeable is always the safest."

Miss Yonge's stories are crowded with instances, great and small, of such self-sacrifice, and in raising this motive to the dignity of a principle she was thoroughly in tune with her surroundings.

For both these principles, the subjection of women and the virtue of self-discipline, were rooted in her religious beliefs. Such beliefs, as we have seen, were fundamentally those of the Oxford Movement in its earlier days. They were coloured by her own characteristics—her strong instinct for submission, and her very keen sense of the spiritual. The former led her to cling to what was 'safe'; outside that which was prescribed or definitely approved by her Church she would not go. We have quoted her attitude towards 'dangerous books'—and the illustration of their dire effects on Miss Fennimore and her kind. The same attitude is held, in almost her last book, where "interpretation of hand-writing" is pressed into the service of a Church *fête*, but palmistry is condemned as "not a safe study." 'Safety first'—the instincts of self-preservation and of submission were easily linked. Charlotte was no rebel.

But besides the longing to be 'safe' there was the conviction that all virtue, all sacrifice, all behaviour of any worth, must be inspired by a genuine religious feeling. Her shrewd definition of altruism—"love of the neighbour without love of God"—shows how completely she distinguished between humanitarian feeling and Christian principles. Perhaps the experience of the last twenty years has brought us more understanding of the views of Charlotte and of Keble, her 'master,' than would have seemed possible to the generation which immediately succeeded her.

What of the character which emerges—of this woman so typical of her times, yet so individual as an author? Docile, yet

unmoving; prejudiced, yet honest; introspective, yet observant—
was it by pure intuition that she could pierce so truly, and often
so ironically, to the heart of a situation and delve into the motives
of a character, or was it merely that her sharp eyes and sensitive
ears, always recording impressions of what was going on about
her, enabled her to produce the really convincing studies and
stories, so captivating to her public? In addition to observation
there must have been 'flair'—that faculty for going to the heart
of a situation and laying it bare. Here, for instance, is a state of
things such as we ourselves constantly come across:

> When her daughter-in-law was at a distance, she (old Mrs
> Langford) secretly regarded with a kind of respectful aversion both
> her talents and her leaning to the fashionable life to which she had
> been accustomed, but in her presence, the winning, lively simplicity
> of her manners completely dispelled all these prejudices in an
> instant, and she loved her most cordially. . . . On the contrary, the
> younger Beatrice, while absent, was the dear little granddaughter
> —the Queen of Bees, the cleverest of creatures, and while present,
> it has been shown how constantly the two tempers fretted each
> other.

Few modern authors could put a familiar situation like this so
clearly and in so few words.

Charlotte can also create a character which illustrates a principle
without allowing it to develop into a mere example of a quality
of a theory. Ethel, for instance, asking what is the difference
between self-contemplation and self-examination, is told:

> The difference between your brother and yourself; . . . self-
> examination notes the symptoms and combats them; self-contempla-
> tion does as I did when I was unstrung by illness and was always
> feeling my own pulse. It dwells on them and perpetually deplores
> itself.

An answer, in effect, commonplace enough—but few authors
would succeed in drawing the Ethel and Norman whom it
describes, so completely, so much 'in the round.'

Enough extracts have been quoted to enable the reader to
judge of Charlotte Yonge's style. It is not an aspect of her work
that strikes one, for the reason that it does not seem to have
been of primary interest to Miss Yonge herself. She does not
appear to have thought of 'good writing'—still less 'fine writing'
—as an object to be aimed at; not, at least, in her own case.

For her purpose, a photographic description of the places she had seen or imagined, a dictaphone-like recording of people's conversation, a detached interpretation of motive, or a clear account of action—these were the methods by which a story was to be told and a truth brought out. There are very few purple patches, and even her moralizing is conversational—it lacks the irony of Thackeray, the power of Kingsley, the wit of Jane Austen—if Miss Austen can be said ever to have pointed a moral.

If her ordinary writing is in a quiet strain, this at least shows up the passages where she reaches to a higher pitch. She is always restrained, but there is an imaginative touch, for instance, in the following which has its own quiet beauty:

(Margaret May lies waiting for news of her betrothed; her brother Harry, who has sailed with him, returns alone.)

> Hand in hand [Ethel and Harry] silently ascended the stairs, and Ethel pushed open the door. Margaret was on her couch, her whole form and face in one throb of expectation.
>
> She looked into Harry's face—the eagerness flitted like sunshine on the hill-side before a cloud, and, without a word, she held out her arms.

Thus there is a restrained dignity in the closing passage of the chapter in *The Long Vacation*, where Dolores sees her lover, with the sister he has undertaken to support, drive away from her, for the last time:

> Dolores came to the gate with them. There was only space for a fervent embrace and "God bless you!" and then she stood watching as they went away into the night.

And here is Charlotte's rather sad little comment on her own position as she watched the new generation itself fleeting away and leaving her behind:

> But is not each generation a *terra incognita* to the last? A question which those feel most decidedly who stand on the borderline of both with love and sympathy divided between the old and the new, clinging to the one and fearing to alienate the other.

Yet, in spite of this feeling, Miss Yonge was writing up to the end of her life, and she rounded off the histories of the old friends who were so dear both to herself and to her public in *Modern Broods*, which, with a last historical tale and a collection of essays, came out in the first year of this century.

No cloud marred the calm brightness of the last years of Charlotte Yonge's life. Her sight and hearing remained unimpaired until the end, and she kept her lively interest in the small doings round her. In the spring of 1900 she had a severe illness resulting from a chill. In spite of this, however, no one could make her slow down her life to the *tempo* of old age. She still taught in the schools twice on a Sunday and every weekday morning, when she gave a Scripture lesson to boys and girls alternately. She could enter also with zest into the preparation of her kitchen-maid for the tests of the G.F.S. Reading Union. These habits she kept up until within a fortnight of her death. Miss Coleridge, who was much at Elderfield during the last year of Charlotte's life, tells us that

> she still wrote and talked eagerly of her writings, still noticed every bird, insect or flower that came in her way, and though her walks were curtailed in length and she moved about with some difficulty, it was still a yearly joy to visit all her favourite places and see them in spring, summer, or autumn beauty.

In March 1901 Charlotte was, as usual, filled with joy at the coming of the first daffodils, but no sooner had she greeted her favourite flowers than she was suddenly taken ill with bronchitis and pneumonia. Death came, as she had always hoped it would, with no painful lingering. The day before she died, Charlotte Yonge received the last rites of the Church, and on a Sunday evening, after twenty-four hours of merciful unconsciousness, she slept peacefully away.

Funeral honours were showered on Miss Yonge as thickly as she herself had showered them on so many of the characters of her tales, to the delight of a generation that loved to dwell on the trappings of woe. The villagers of Otterbourne showed their sorrow by bringing handfuls of daffodils and primroses, so that Miss Yonge might be surrounded with the homely flowers, whose haunts she knew so well. On the day before the funeral she was carried to the parish church, now fragrant with the wreaths of countless admirers, where crowds of relations and friends sang the vespers for the dead. Charlotte Yonge lay in state before the chancel screen, with six tall tapers lighted round her coffin. All through the night friends watched in turn beside her. The next day there was a very early celebration of the Holy

Communion, and later a Requiem Mass, which was celebrated
by a Chaplain to the Forces. (This would have pleased Charlotte,
who was always proud of being the daughter of a Waterloo man.)
No rite was omitted that might do honour to Miss Yonge as one
of the pillars of the High Church party, which had now moved
far from the simplicity of the 'Puseyite' days.

Charlotte Yonge was buried on the afternoon of Friday,
March 29, 1901, the thirty-fifth anniversary of the death of
John Keble. Nature was determined to afford an impressive setting
for the last farewell to one who had noted her aspects with such
fidelity. The churchyard had a shining covering of light snow,
which threw up the deep black of the mourners and the long
lines of black-clad schoolchildren. They buried her near Keble's
memorial cross, which she had long ago put up:

TO THE MASTER AND INSPIRER

OF

CHARLOTTE MARY YONGE

There were some among the throng in Otterbourne churchyard that day whose thoughts went back irresistibly to the
funeral of a much greater personage that had taken place in
London only two months before. Charlotte Yonge had mirrored
the years of Victoria's reign, and remained stubbornly true to its
code. It was fitting that she should not long survive the great
Queen.

INDEX

References to characters will be found under the books in which they appear.